Rehearsing God's Just Kingdom

Stephen S. Wilbricht, CSC

Foreword by
Rev Msgr. Kevin W. Irwin

Rehearsing God's Just Kingdom

The Eucharistic Vision of Mark Searle

A PUEBLO BOOK

Liturgical Press   Collegeville, Minnesota
www.litpress.org

A Pueblo Book published by Liturgical Press

Cover design by Jodi Hendrickson. Illustration: *The Attainment: The Vision of the Holy Grail to Sir Galahad, Sir Bors, and Sir Perceval*; tapestry designed by Edward Burne-Jones, woven by Morris & Co., 1895–96.

1   2   3   4   5   6   7   8   9

Library of Congress Cataloging-in-Publication Data

Wilbricht, Stephen S.
    Rehearsing God's just kingdom : the eucharistic vision of Mark Searle / Stephen S. Wilbricht.
        pages   cm
    "A Pueblo book."
    Includes bibliographical references and index.
    ISBN 978-0-8146-6272-4 — ISBN 978-0-8146-6297-7 (e-book)
    1. Catholic Church—Liturgy.   2. Church renewal—Catholic Church. 3. Searle, Mark, 1941–1992.   I. Title.
BX1970.W54   2013
264'.02—dc23   2013026109

To my parents, David and Sue,

who provided for their only child a household of faith

Contents

Foreword

Rev. Msgr. Kevin W. Irwin

If the realtor's mantra is "location, location, location" about prized properties to be sold, the publisher's mantra is certainly "timing, timing, timing" about the publication of an important book. This is an important book. Its publication is timely.

As the church observes the fiftieth anniversary of the promulgation of *Sacrosanctum Concilium* at Vatican II, many of us find ourselves in the position of assessing the effects of implementing the reformed liturgy. For a variety of reasons this book is an excellent tool to do just that now as we assess what we have done well and what we have failed to do. But in a way that is typical of Mark Searle, what is collected here will serve for ongoing reflection and meditation on the liturgy for years to come. We have missed Mark Searle's voice in American liturgical circles since his untimely death over a decade ago. Fr. Wilbricht does us a great service in collecting in one volume many of Mark Searle's disparate writings as well as updating and adding to them with other more recent and current voices from largely American authors in the liturgical field. This is indeed a timely book. But in addition to the triad "timing, timing, timing," allow me to offer the flowing three ideas which, I judge, characterize Searle's writings so admirably summarized here.

Prophet

Mark Searle was a true prophet, not in the sense of foretelling the future, but in the traditional sense of prophecy—assessing where the pilgrim church is here and now based on God's revelation and salvation as enacted in the liturgy and how faithful we have been to this divine revelation and salvation. Searle's insights about the challenges of American culture's emphasis on the individual and of privatization over the communal nature of the liturgy are as pertinent and poignant today as they were when he first wrote them. (Perhaps even more so.) His insights about the value of liturgical forms and the priority of ritual over accommodating rites in order to make them more relevant offer an important caution to any who wish to refashion what are meant to be stable rites and the staples of the Christian life. His insights about the familiarity of the music sung at the liturgy offers pause to the way music and liturgy interface (or do not) today and how. But like any prophet, Searle remained hopeful and faith-filled to the end. Fr. Wilbricht's careful and gentle prose reflects perfectly the man whose corpus he synthesizes here.

Poet

Mark Searle's *oeuvre* is hard to characterize simply because he wrote for a variety of publics and in a variety of genres. A distinct and lasting contribution of this book is the way Fr. Wilbricht has collected these varied pieces into one narrative. In particular, his careful selection from Searle's many editorials in the journal *Assembly* remind us of Searle's reverence for words and his poignant use of them—especially in poetry. This is a subtle reminder that what underlies the liturgy is more poetry than prose, more ritual gesture than rubric, more aesthetics than practicality, more music than text. These are especially important building blocks for any assessment of the present reformed liturgy. More to the point is the way Searle's insights always lift us from the day-to-day to the vision of what can and should characterize the liturgy in all its forms and manifestations. While the implementation of the liturgical reforms required attention to externals in rites and texts, Searle never failed to offer keen insight into the depth of meaning conveyed by them. Fr. Wilbricht serves Searle well when he does precisely this when commenting on the revised General Instruction on the Roman Missal. Welcome indeed is his theological approach to it based on Searle's unfailing recourse to a poet's vision about the liturgy. (A prime example is the way Searle approaches and describes the gathered assembly's posture of kneeling during the eucharistic prayer, which was not his preference but which he interprets with keen insight and vision.)

Pastor

In the end, I would regard Mark Searle as a pastoral liturgical theologian. His regular participation in the liturgy and commitment to it was always obvious to those of us who knew and loved him. But it was also his commitment to others in the liturgical assembly and to serving the Lord outside that gathered assembly that marked this true Christian gentleman. With typical, keen insight Searle reflects repeatedly about the way God's justice is celebrated and revealed through Christ, the Just One, whose justice challenges (dare I say confounds) the usual definitions of "justice" used in American culture today. The experience of justice in the liturgy is not an idea. It is the experience of the way God would have us live, both inside and outside the liturgy. This is but one example of the kind of liturgically astute pastor that Mark Searle was to so many. In my opinion, this is what makes Fr. Wilbricht's study of Mark Searle a perfect "fit." Before coming to graduate studies in liturgy at The Catholic University of America, Fr. Wilbricht served in pastoral ministry for several years in the Diocese of Phoenix. As I witnessed his growing in knowledge of the liturgy at the university, I also saw the mind and heart of a pastor at work. In the end, Fr. Wilbricht never lost his pastor's heart. My sense is that his study of the liturgy in general and Mark Searle in particular only served to deepen and broaden what it means to be a true pastor.

This highly engaging book can be read on many levels and can be very useful in a number of ways. I would recommend that the reader read the conclusion first. Here, Fr. Wilbricht summarizes his project admirably and modestly. The central four chapters on the structure and rich theological meaning of the liturgy of the Eucharist can be used in courses and discussion groups about the Eucharist. People committed to preparing and executing the liturgy of the Eucharist will be enriched here beyond measure, but again through a modest style and moderate prose. The other chapters taken together reflect Searle's evolution in thought and in assessing the reformed liturgy in the United States. The way Fr. Wilbricht incorporates the findings of the Notre Dame Study on Parish Life through Searle's summaries is masterful. This is another example of the way Fr. Wilbricht has been able to synthesize and respect the breadth and depth of Searle's various writings.

The second appendix, on liturgy and social justice, should be required reading for all who serve the Lord in justice and liturgical ministry. It may well serve to bridge a gap between the two that many have diagnosed as one of the less helpful results of the liturgical reform—the separation of what we should be intrinsically intertwined. This appendix should also be required reading for any course in liturgy and for anyone who wishes to enter the season of Advent more deeply.

More often than not, Fr. Wilbricht reflects Searle's emphasis on obedience and humility, virtues not always found in abundance in some politicized liturgical circles today (much to our collective shame). What should always unite, the liturgy, sometimes today regrettably divides. Is there anything worse than that?

In the end, Mark Searle wanted to help change hearts, not rites; he wanted to change minds, not words; he wanted to foster conversion to the Lord in worship, both his own and that of his readers. We need to thank Fr. Wilbricht for offering us this skillful and important insight into the life and work of one who left us too early in life but whose legacy will lead all of us to appreciating that what matters is life eternal and the celebration of the eternal in time.

In the meantime, the words of T. S. Eliot, which nurtured Mark Searle's approach to liturgy, should shape our own, especially as we assess the strengths and weakness of the liturgical reform, which is more about discovering and being discovered by God again and again through word, gesture, song, and rite than it is about deciding what to say, sing, or do in the liturgy:

> We shall not cease from exploration
> and the end of all our exploring
> will be to arrive where we started
> and to know the place for the first time.
> ("Little Gidding," *The Four Quartets*)

Acknowledgments

As will become abundantly clear in the pages ahead, liturgical theologian Mark Searle believed that attitude is everything in celebrating the Eucharist, a rehearsal of Christ's worldview of constant hope and unfailing trust in God's Just Kingdom. Gratitude for Christ's obedience must be the fundamental attitude of the Christian, and, indeed, it is my outlook as I attempt to bring Mark Searle's vision to the fore once more. For this reason, I offer my thanks.

Since some of the material presented here first saw the light of day in the form of a doctoral dissertation at The Catholic University of America, I owe a world of gratitude to my director, Monsignor Kevin W. Irwin, professor in the School of Theology and Religious Studies and holder of the Walter J. Schmitz Chair in Liturgical Studies. Under his keen tutelage, I came to understand well the relationship of mentor to apprentice. I am also indebted to Catherine Dooley, OP, Margaret Mary Kelleher, OSU, and Dominic Serra for their participation in the dissertation-writing phase of this project.

I would like to thank, in a very special way, Dr. Barbara Searle. She opened Mark's files for me, read my writing along the way, and allowed me to put into print for the first time the talk, "Grant Us Peace . . . Do We Hear What We Are Saying?" I will forever be grateful for her kindness and support.

I am appreciative for all the people who have been a part of the parish communities in which I have been able to participate, on the altar and in the pews—in Goodyear and Phoenix, Arizona; in Washington, DC; and in Massachusetts, as well as in my childhood parish of St. John the Evangelist in Hanover, Illinois. I am particularly grateful to Dixie Miller, Karen Baroni, Kathryn Dowell, Mary Durand, Anna Maie Murphy, and the late Dr. Frances Amabisca for their excitement for this project.

To my confreres in the Congregation of Holy Cross, who have helped me to experience the bond between liturgy and life; to my colleagues at Stonehill College, who lightened my workload during the preparation of this manuscript; to Christine Taylor, who assisted in the cataloging of the Searle files; to Patricia Stenke, whose photograph of Mark Searle's headstone appears in the conclusion; to my friends, Daniel Cebrick, James Sabak, OFM, Michael Woods, SJ, Margaret Schreiber, OP, Nicholas Denysenko, Gary Stenke, Tony Tomelden, and Stephanie Coleman, who all journeyed with me throughout this process—please know of my deep gratitude for your presence in my life. To Hans Christoffersen, publisher, who provided steady collaboration, and to all at Liturgical Press, who labored diligently to put this text into a readable form, I offer you my sincerest thanks.

Finally, I wish to give thanks to the Author of all life and for the gift of his servant Mark Searle, whose wisdom has given me the courage and insight to dream for new possibilities in liturgical reform and in whose spirit I have often implored a word of confidence or an assurance of hope. I am quite certain that he has given the hosts of angels a lesson or two on how to participate more fully and actively in the heavenly liturgy.

Introduction

In the course of a much-abbreviated teaching and writing career spanning fewer than twenty-five years, Mark Searle (1941–92) provided a worthy contribution to the study of liturgy. When his life was cut short in the summer of 1992, ending a fifteen-month battle with cancer, Searle had published nearly a dozen books and more than eighty articles, in addition to numerous book reviews and videotaped lectures.[1] The breadth of Searle's liturgical interests and his desire to integrate a wide range of academic areas (anthropology, sociology, and semiotics to name just a few) with the study of liturgy mark this scholar as a gifted thinker and author—arguably a *pioneer*. This book explores two intrinsically related themes of Searle's thought: first, liturgy as the "rehearsal of Christian attitudes," in which participants are trained to embody the interconnectedness between worship and worldview, and second, liturgy as the enactment of "God's Just Kingdom," meaning that the construction of right relationships lies at the foundation of celebration itself rather than as a moral follow-up to worship. "When we begin to rehearse the Kingdom in our liturgy," Searle writes, "hearing the words of the Kingdom, practicing the gestures of the Kingdom, experimenting with the lifestyle of the Kingdom, then we Christians will once again be in a position to take up our vocation to be priests and prophets and peacemakers in the society in which God has placed us."[2]

SEARLE'S EARLY YEARS

Mark Searle was born on September 19, 1941, to Paul and Eileen Searle of Bristol, England.[3] The firstborn of eleven children, he was

---

[1] See appendix 1 for Mark Searle's complete chronological bibliography.

[2] See Mark Searle, "Grant Us Peace . . . Do We Hear What We Are Saying?" in Mark Searle Papers (hereafter MSP), Private Collection, Notre Dame, Indiana, Folder B16. This unpublished manuscript has been reproduced as appendix 2 of this volume.

[3] Most of the details of Searle's biography are taken from the *Searle Family History* compiled by his father, Paul Searle. This information has been supplemented by an interview with Barbara Searle, Mark's wife, on April 19, 2006. See also the "Chronology" in Anne Y. Koester and Barbara Searle, eds., *Vision:*

baptized several weeks later (October 12, 1941) at the neighborhood church, St. Bonaventure, where his parents had been married a year earlier. This parish would prove to be an influential locus of Searle's education and Christian formation. Because his father served as a medic in the Second World War, Searle's initial nurturing was provided largely by his mother as well as by both sets of his grandparents.

As a young boy Searle attended St. Bonaventure's parish school, where he proved himself to be an avid reader and a budding artist. At age eleven, Searle enrolled at St. Brendan's College in Clifton, where he developed an interest in the study of foreign languages, specifically Latin and French.[4] Clearly influenced by the Franciscans at St. Bonaventure's,[5] Searle completed his education at St. Brendan's by announcing his wish to pursue a vocation in religious life. Regarding this decision, Paul Searle writes, "He had for a long time cherished the thought of becoming a priest, and after he had successfully completed

---

The Scholarly Contributions of Mark Searle to Liturgical Renewal (Collegeville, MN: Liturgical Press, 2004), 255–257.

[4] See Barbara Searle, "Acceptance Speech Given in Response to the Presentation of the Michael Mathis Award to Mark Searle, Posthumously, June 17, 1993." Ruminating on her husband's early childhood, Barbara writes, "There was a man who came to us from another land. He grew up amid castles and cathedrals, many of which were built before this country was discovered. From his mother he inherited a heart of gold and a love for things ordinary; from his father a keen intellect and a love of travel. As the eldest of eleven children he assumed a natural leadership and learned at a young age the lessons of give and take. He received a classical English education and began to specialize in languages and literature."

[5] See Mark Searle, "Grant Proposals: Lilly Endowment Faculty Open Fellowships 1988-89 Application," 4–5 in MSP: "Matthew." Here, Searle comments on the role of tradition and "historical memory" in his own religious upbringing: "I grew up in a country where Roman Catholics were not only a minority but were in a minority which laid particular claim to historical memory. English cathedrals and village churches, all 'once ours' we believed, bore silent testimony to our tradition. A mere thirty miles away from my home was Glastonbury where, according to legend, Christianity in Britain had all begun. My own parish was staffed by a community of Franciscans, with their medieval dress and rule and their rich liturgical celebrations. My teachers, too, for the most part, played into this sense of continuity, this sense of more-than-nostalgic reverence for the past, this sense of a tradition that, despite everything, still lived."

his final exams, he stated his desire to become a Franciscan."[6] Thus, in 1958, before his seventeenth birthday, Searle entered the Franciscan Novitiate at Chilworth, where he was formed in the history and the manner of prayer particular to the Franciscans. After his simple profession in 1959, Searle spent the next six years at St. Mary's Friary in East Bergholt, the theologate for the English Province of Franciscans, where he received the requisite philosophical and theological training for ordination to the priesthood.[7]

GRADUATE STUDIES AND SEMINARY FORMATION

Searle was ordained in 1965 and celebrated his first Mass at his beloved St. Bonaventure. Immediately after his ordination, he was assigned to begin graduate studies in Rome, where he chose to pursue an education in liturgical studies rather than canon law.[8] During his time in Rome, Searle was clearly influenced by the intellectual environment of the city, which was enlivened by the closing of the Second Vatican Council. Concerning this, he once wrote:

> But the teacher that had the greatest influence on me in my formative years was undoubtedly the Second Vatican Council, whose closing session coincided with my first year of graduate studies in Rome. It was, to me, a massively impressive demonstration of the catholicity of the Church and of the vitality of the Christian tradition, gearing for the future by returning to its sources.[9]

With his thesis titled "The Sacraments of Initiation in the Catechesis of St. Cyril of Jerusalem," Searle was awarded a Licentiate in Sacred

---

[6] Paul Searle, *Searle Family History*, 57.

[7] In reference to these six years of academic training, Barbara Searle states: "He often referred to those as great years. . . . That is where he really grew up. It was an important time in his life" (Interview with Barbara Searle, April 19, 2006). In a conversation with Barbara Searle on September 22, 2008, she clarified this observation, stating that his entrance into the Franciscans marked a time of overall development in Searle's life: "Physically he matured, emotionally he matured, and intellectually he matured."

[8] See Barbara Searle, "Acceptance Speech Given in Response to the Presentation of the Michael Mathis Award to Mark Searle, Posthumously, June 17, 1993." See also Mark Searle, *Eight Talks on Liturgy* (Private circulation, 1974), 9.

[9] Searle, "Grant Proposal: Lilly Endowment Faculty Open Fellowships 1988–89 Application," 5.

Theology (STL) from the Pontificio Ateneo di S. Antonio in 1966. During his short time of study in Rome, Searle became well grounded in both systematic theology and historical liturgical studies.

Continuing doctoral studies under the guidance of Balthasar Fischer, Searle spent the next three years in Trier, Germany, where he wrote a dissertation titled "The Communion Service of the Church of England, with Particular Reference to the Experimental Order for Holy Communion, 1967: A Study in 'Comprehensive Liturgy.'" However, before completing this degree, Searle decided to spend several months in late 1968 studying at the Institut Supérieur de Liturgie in Paris, France. Albeit extremely brief in duration, this period would play a major role in his future work in liturgical studies. Searle writes:

> In response both to the academic ferment in France and to the new situation in the Catholic Church, the Paris Institute was looking to supplement its established programs in history and theology with courses in anthropology, religious psychology, semiotics and other aspects of the "human sciences." These were intended to provide ways of taking into account, as the initial phases of reform had not, the cultural conditions governing liturgical celebrations and the possibilities of liturgical change.[10]

He continues by describing the role this time in France played in forming his own understanding of the need to apply the "human sciences" to the study of liturgy, namely, that "it sufficed to lodge firmly in my mind the importance of attending not only to the texts of the rites, but to the ritual performance as a whole, and of paying attention to the rooting of ritual in the human condition."[11]

After earning both a doctorate of theology and a diploma in liturgical studies from the Liturgisches Institut in Trier in 1969, Searle returned to England where he lectured at the Franciscan Studies Center in Canterbury until 1977. During this period, from 1969 until 1975, he also served his religious community as the director of postnovitiate formation. While working in a seminary did not allow him the freedom to pursue academic research intensely, the experience taught Searle the need for finding new ways of teaching liturgy, ways that challenged the traditional historical and theological approaches. As he himself wrote: "Teaching in a seminary, as I did for the next eight

---

[10] Ibid., 5–6.
[11] Ibid., 6.

4

years, only heightened my sense of the need to develop new approaches to the teaching of liturgy, but offered little or no opportunity for research or experimentation."[12]

CAREER AT NOTRE DAME

Seeking a respite from the rigors of teaching, formation, and provincial leadership, Searle came to the heartland of the United States in the fall of 1975 to begin a sabbatical year as a visiting instructor at the University of Notre Dame in South Bend, Indiana, and as a consultant to the Notre Dame Center for Pastoral Liturgy (then the Murphy Center for Liturgical Research). He returned to England the following year and there began questioning the direction of his life. Searle's brief exposure to the United States had excited him about the possibilities for liturgical renewal—something that he had not experienced in his homeland. In the words of Barbara Searle, "He had been deeply moved by the American Church's response to the Council's mandate for liturgical renewal; he sensed there was great promise here."[13] Thus, in 1977, he returned to Notre Dame to test the desire to live and work in new ways. After a great deal of soul-searching, he parted ways with the Franciscans and resigned from active ministry as a priest. Also, he accepted a job to teach at Notre Dame and to serve as the associate director of the Notre Dame Center for Pastoral Liturgy, a position he held from 1978 until 1983. Through his work at the center, especially in his role as editor of its publication *Assembly*,[14] Searle began to pave what would be a lasting contribution to the work of liturgical renewal.

Stepping aside for a brief moment from Searle's academic biography, it is important to note the life-changing decision to marry Barbara Schmich, which he did on May 18, 1980. Also significant was the role he would take on as father, as he participated in the birth of three children: Anna Clare in 1981, Matthew Thomas in 1983, and Justin

[12] Ibid. It is worth noting that, during his time as lecturer at Canterbury, Searle was invited to teach a course on liturgy to native Franciscan catechists in South Africa. This experience was informative because it allowed him to observe the implementation of liturgical renewal in a part of the world where the Church was still taking root.

[13] Interview with Barbara Searle, November 2, 2006.

[14] This journal was formerly published under the title *Hucusque*. Under its new name, *Assembly*, the journal identified its mission as fostering liturgical renewal; its subtitle read: "for those who want to enter into the spirit of the liturgy."

5

Francis in 1985. Undoubtedly, Searle's intellectual pursuits were now combined with his duties as husband and father, a reality that served only to enhance his writing and perspective on liturgy. Interestingly enough, Searle's bibliography bears testimony to the fact that, rather than pull him away from his writing and academic research, his family would actually help to increase his energy for his research and writing.

Recognized both within and outside the confines of Notre Dame, Searle quickly became popular as a lecturer and as a professor. For instance, from 1982 to 1983, Searle served as the vice president and, subsequently, president of the North American Academy of Liturgy. In the summer of 1983, he was invited to teach at Saint John's University in Collegeville, Minnesota. That fall semester, he was granted tenure as an associate professor in Notre Dame's Department of Theology, while also being appointed director of the MA program in theology and the coordinator of the graduate program in liturgical studies. Finally, that same year (1983) Searle began his association with the Notre Dame Study of Catholic Parish Life, serving as the associate director for the liturgical component. The wide range of positions he held at Notre Dame during his early years at the university provided the opportunity to broaden his pedagogical lens, as he began experimenting with the application of the human sciences to liturgical studies.[15] Barbara Searle writes: "Mark's intellectual history of these years can be seen in his bibliography, how he easily moved between the rigors of the academy with its need to define a scope and methodology for this new science of pastoral liturgy, and the demands of an authentic contemporary mystagogia."[16]

Searle's desire to incorporate the human sciences into the intellectual study of liturgy clearly came to the forefront in two articles published in 1983. In the first, "Liturgy as a Pastoral Hermeneutic,"

[15] Searle, "Grant Proposal: Lilly Endowment Faculty Open Fellowships 1988–89 Application," 6. Searle writes: "It was only after I had come to Notre Dame, and particularly in working with graduate students, that I had the opportunity to take up the matter (role of the 'human sciences' in the study of liturgy) again and to try to develop for myself a satisfactory way of posing the problem. I did so by reading widely and by introducing in my courses, on the experimental basis, models from the social sciences which would help students to see that the theological meaning of the rites could not be viewed in isolation from their broader human significance."

[16] Barbara Searle, "Acceptance Speech Given in Response to the Presentation of the Michael Mathis Award to Mark Searle, Posthumously, June 17, 1993."

Searle asserted that "pastoral" liturgy requires studying the liturgical event on the basis of the social (psychological, economic, etc.) reality of those who enact it.[17] For Searle, this task requires asking the following question: "In what sense, and under what conditions are the liturgical event and the human situation mutually illuminated to the point where a new avenue of praxis is opened up for the participants?"[18] Later in 1983, in an article titled "New Tasks, New Methods: The Emergence of Pastoral Liturgical Studies," Searle continued to posit his belief that a method must be developed that takes into account the "multidimensionality" of the liturgical event, which he contended stems from the mystery of the Incarnation itself.[19] In other words, the study of liturgy must be solidly rooted in an appreciation and the contemplation of the "fleshly" reality of all those taking part in a specific liturgical celebration.

SEMIOTICS AND A NEW LITURGICAL MOVEMENT

Beginning in the latter half of the 1980s, Searle's academic career was marked by two passionate interests. First, he articulated the need to develop and hone an academic expertise in an area outside the realm of liturgy that could be used as a starting point for "pastoral"

[17] See Mark Searle, "Liturgy as a Pastoral Hermeneutic," in *Theological Field Education: A Collection of Key Resources*, vol. 4, *Pastoral Theology and Ministry*, ed. D. F. Beisswenger and D. C. McCarthy (Association for Theological Field Education, 1983), 141. Searle's vision for the study of liturgy through a "pastoral" lens is as follows: "*pastoral* hermeneutics I assume to be the project of relating the liturgical event and the situation of the participants in such a way that they mutually interpret one another and thereby open up new horizons for Christian living. In other words, the import of the adjective 'pastoral' is such as to relate the hermeneutics to Christian praxis rather than simply to the enlargement of Christian understanding, such as would be the case with fundamental or systematic or historical theology."

[18] Ibid.

[19] See Mark Searle, "New Tasks, New Methods: The Emergence of Pastoral Liturgical Studies," *Worship* 57 (1983): 307. With regard to the relationship between the mystery of the Incarnation and liturgical studies, Searle writes: "As pastoral liturgical studies develops, then, more and more data concerning the actual worship of the church should become available for reflection, as well as a whole range of theological problems relating to the anthropological, sociological and psychological structures and preconditions which constitutes the 'flesh' in which the mystery of grace is incarnated in the worship life of contemporary communities."

liturgical studies. Thus, before the close of the fall semester of 1987, Searle pursued funding for a sabbatical the following year that would allow him to move his entire family to The Netherlands, where he would concentrate on the study of semiotics with Gerard Lukken and members of a study group called "Semanet." Semiotics (most basically defined as "the study of signs") had long captured Searle's imagination, as he believed this science could effect liturgical renewal, in the sense of turning the examination of meaning from a question of "what" to "how" with regard to liturgical texts and celebration. Searle writes:

> Semiotics has been an intermittent interest of mine ever since I read Ferdinand de Saussure, Roland Barthes and Pierre Guiraud in the late sixties. In attempting to account not so much for *what* texts mean as for *how* they mean, semiotics offers the possibility of studying how ritual works without singling out any one aspect of it—be it sociological, psychological or theological—for privileged status. This is precisely the direction I see the need to take as I enter the second half of my career as a teacher.[20]

In his attempt to supplement liturgical studies, Searle saw semiotics as providing a route by which the study of liturgy could move beyond the text to a level of describing and analyzing liturgical events themselves. Admitting that semiotics is a "field notorious for its jargon and the opacity of its concepts," Searle nonetheless proposed to develop a "simplified and less technical methodology" that would be accessible to students of liturgy.[21] Personally and professionally renewed from his time spent in The Netherlands, Searle returned to full-time teaching in the Department of Theology at Notre Dame in the fall of 1989, with the plan to incorporate the fruits of his sabbatical into his graduate seminars.[22]

---

[20] Searle, "Grant Proposal: Lilly Endowment Faculty Open Fellowships 1988–89 Application," 7.

[21] Ibid., 8.

[22] See Mark Searle, "Semiotic Study of Liturgical Celebration: A Report Submitted to Lilly Endowment, Inc.," 1989 in MSP "Matthew." Commenting on the effect of the sabbatical on his teaching, Searle writes: "Here perhaps the first thing to be remarked is that, after a year's break, I am rediscovering the joy of teaching, the joy I had once known but had gradually forgotten over the long years since I first began. This is all the more remarkable because I so

However, Searle's passion for studying semiotics and his desire to make the field available to students of liturgy was accompanied by his pursuit of another interest in the latter part of the 1980s. Searle's work with the Notre Dame Study of Catholic Parish Life (1983–85) had left him with the burning need to critique the direction of liturgical renewal in the United States and to call for a "new liturgical movement." Searle's major concern was the issue of liturgical participation, as he believed what was being lost in the implementation of the principles of Vatican II reform was basic training geared to lead people into the depths of the mystery of liturgy. From his perspective, too much emphasis was being placed on creativity rather than on internalizing the established rhythm of liturgical prayer. And so, in a 1988 article that appeared in *Commonweal*, titled "Renewing the Liturgy—Again. 'A' for the Council, 'C' for the Church," Searle wrote:

> Clearly, we are far from realizing the hopes which the council placed in the liturgical renewal. . . . [I]f it was a major weakness in the reform that it was not adequately prepared from below, then it must be at the grassroots level that the renewal of the liturgy must begin again. *The time has come, surely, to relaunch the liturgical movement.*[23]

Searle's enthusiasm for the topic of inaugurating a new liturgical movement was apparent in several other publications during this time and was the focus of a six-week lecture tour of Australia and New Zealand in the summer of 1990.[24] Also, by this time, Searle was hard at work on a manuscript on liturgical participation. Although unpublished upon his death in 1992, Searle's "manifesto,"[25] *Called to Participate: Theological, Ritual, and Social Perspectives* (published posthumously in 2006 by Barbara Searle), represents his primary conviction that surrendering to

---

enjoyed the sabbatical that I was afraid I would resent having to return to the classroom!" (3).

[23] Mark Searle, "Renewing the Liturgy—Again. 'A' for the Council, 'C' for the Church," *Commonweal* (November 18, 1988): 621. Emphasis mine.

[24] For example, see Mark Searle, "Ritual and Music: A Theory of Liturgy and Implications for Music," *Assembly* 12:3, 314–317 (Reprinted in *Church* 2:3 [1986]: 48–52; Reprinted in *Pastoral Music* 11:3 [1987]: 13–18). See also, Mark Searle, "Trust the Ritual or Face 'The Triumph of Bad Taste,'" *Pastoral Music* 15:6, 19–21.

[25] This description comes from Barbara Searle in an interview on November 2, 2006.

the demands of the liturgy is a forgotten attitude that must be relearned for the liturgy to truly be renewed.[26]

CONFRONTING CANCER

Less than two years after Searle and his family returned from The Netherlands, he was diagnosed with cancer in June of 1991. In addition to professional medical treatment, he and Barbara quickly educated themselves about the disease and attempted to confront it through a radical change in diet and exercise. Searle was granted a medical leave for the fall semester but returned to teaching in January of 1992. After a year of promising results, he was able to journey to England to visit relatives and friends. Upon his return to the United States, Searle's health rapidly deteriorated. Yet despite increased levels of pain and decreased levels of energy, he taught his final class in the summer school program of 1992, immediately prior to his last few days of life. Barbara Searle describes these final days as ones of surrender:

> He must have made many surrenders along the way, but it was in the last week of his life that they were most dramatic. On the Sunday before his death, he could no longer drive the car. On Monday, he could no longer work at the computer. On Tuesday, he could no longer bathe and dress himself. On Wednesday, he could no longer eat by himself. On Thursday, he could no longer sign his name. On Friday, he could hardly walk. On Saturday, he was completely silent. But through all these surrenders, there was a tangible peace and joy in him, so much so that we felt God had come very close to us in him.[27]

Surrounded by his wife, two sisters, and his mother and father, Searle died in the early hours of the morning on August 16, 1992. Just two days earlier, this same group was joined by Searle's children, col-

---

[26] See Mark Searle, *Called to Participate: Theological, Ritual, and Social Perspectives*, ed. Barbara Searle and Anne Y. Koester (Collegeville, MN: Liturgical Press, 2006). See especially page 13: "Perhaps instead of asking what will engage the assembly, we could begin to ask what the liturgy demands. Instead of asserting our ownership of the liturgy, we might ask how we can surrender to Christ's prayer and work. Instead of asking what we should choose to sing, perhaps we could start imaging how we might sing in such a way that it is no longer we who sing, but Christ who sings in us."

[27] Barbara Searle, "Acceptance Speech Given in Response to the Presentation of the Michael Mathis Award to Mark Searle, Posthumously, June 17, 1993," 3.

leagues, and family friends for the celebration of Viaticum, after which he repeated aloud the Lord's words: "I shall not drink wine again until I drink it in the Kingdom."[28]

In the end, Searle's struggle with cancer became a testament to what he had studied and taught so well—namely, that to celebrate the liturgy is to rehearse for that life which triumphs over death, to learn the Christian attitude of surrender. As Searle wrote shortly before his death: "Liturgy would deliver us from this futile and self-defeating campaign of self-justification by offering us an alternative: that of dropping the illusion we cling to, rehearsing the trust that will enable us to let go in the end to life itself and surrender ourselves one last time into the hands of the living God."[29]

SCOPE AND STRUCTURE OF THE BOOK

The objective of this book is to continue Mark Searle's praiseworthy contribution to liturgical renewal through the elaboration and application of two important concepts in his writings. Chapter 1 examines Searle's guiding principle of liturgy as the "rehearsal of Christian attitudes." Adapting this term from the writing of philosopher Suzanne Langer, he wanted to underscore the important value of the regular and repeated ritual activity of the Body of Christ. Chapter 2 investigates a second significant theme in Searle's writings, namely, that the liturgy does not simply provide a platform upon which to preach and instruct about matters of justice; rather, it *is* the Church's privileged means of enacting here and now the "justice of God." For this very reason, participants in the liturgy bear a great responsibility to master the ritual in all its various dynamics.

Thus, after exploring these two interrelated concepts as fundamental for Searle, we then turn to the four principal parts of the Roman Catholic Mass to employ his theology in an attempt to understand what it means to call our participation in liturgy a "rehearsal" of God's Just Kingdom. Chapter 3 outlines the rehearsal of *gathering* as Christ's Body; chapter 4 reveals necessary participatory skills involved in *listening* to God's Word; chapter 5 examines how the lived attitude of *sacrificing* is fundamental to true participation at the altar; and chapter 6 suggests that the ultimate goal of *communing* in divine life demands a oneness with God, others, and all created things.

---

[28] See *Searle Family History*, 63.
[29] Searle, *Called to Participate*, 40.

Finally, prior to the two appendices, which provide Mark Searle's chronological bibliography and an unpublished talked titled "Grant Us Peace . . . Do We Hear What We Are Saying?," as well as the book's overall conclusion, chapter 7 reveals Searle's bold critique of American society and culture and his call for the Church to respond by relaunching the liturgical movement. It was Searle's basic conviction that liturgy is composed of basic Christian attitudes in which its participants are to be formed. So much more than an expression of subjective feeling and emotion, liturgy represents the essential commitments of the Christian community. As he states: "Liturgy will not leave us on an emotional high because that is not its purpose. But regular, persevering participation and growing familiarity with liturgy's images and gestures will eventually shape our attitudes, our thoughts, and even our feelings."[30] A favorite quote of Searle's came from Romano Guardini's 1964 letter to a gathering of German bishops in preparation for the implementation of Vatican II liturgical reforms and which reads:

> The question is whether the wonderful opportunities now open to the liturgy will achieve their full realization; whether we shall be satisfied with just removing anomalies, taking new situations into account, giving better instruction on the meaning of ceremonies and liturgical vessels or whether we shall relearn a forgotten way of doing things and recapture lost attitudes.[31]

Thus, true liturgical reform and the implementation of active participation on the part of the entire assembly depend on the reawakening of attitudes, or worldviews, that comprise the structure and celebration of the liturgy itself. Commenting on Guardini's thought, Searle writes, "By 'lost attitudes' and 'a forgotten way of doing things' he seems to suggest a way of approaching the liturgy and engaging in its sights and sounds, its words and gestures, that had been eclipsed by the rise of individualism and the split between inner and outer dimensions of the self."[32] Thus, Searle demonstrated consistently in his writing that, through the rehearsal of "lost attitudes," the Christian

---

[30] Ibid., 62.

[31] See Romano Guardini, "A Letter from Romano Guardini," in *Herder Correspondence* (August 1964), 237. Two of the places in Searle's corpus where this quote by Guardini appears are: "Liturgy as Metaphor," *Worship* 55 (1981): 99; "Renewing the Liturgy—Again: 'A' for the Council, 'C' for the Church," 47.

[32] Searle, *Called to Participate*, 47.

community would recognize anew the meaning of liturgical participation as the Body of Christ.

In an age when so much depends on instant gratification and in which institutional commitment is often held in contempt, Searle's thinking provides an avenue for liturgical renewal that hinges upon a respect for and trust in ritual forms and behavior. For him, locating the source of this renewal in the worshiping assembly (rather than the officiating presider) is critical. This means that attention must be paid to the matter of *how* the Body of Christ lifts up its heart in prayer, which necessitates facilitating the formation of the corporate body in the first place. Paul Janowiak mirrors Searle's theological outlook when he writes: "The truth of the Spirit unfolds within the rubric of our being guided, led, and nudged forward—dynamic acts of trust and surrender. It eschews dispirited passivity and demands engagement, willingness, discernment, and courage."[33] These are the kind of spirited Christian attitudes that Searle envisioned when he called for the Church's liturgy to be embraced as a rehearsal that it is performed over and over, again and again, until it is practiced perfectly in the Kingdom of Heaven. Such is, I believe, an appropriate vision for liturgical prayer in our day.

[33] Paul A. Janowiak, *Standing Together in the Community of God: Liturgical Spirituality and the Presence of Christ* (Collegeville, MN: Liturgical Press, 2011), 30.

Chapter 1

Liturgy as "Rehearsal of Christian Attitudes"

The Fathers at the Second Vatican Council decreed in *Sacrosanctum Concilium* that the Church desires "to undertake a careful general reform of the liturgy in order that the Christian people may be more certain to derive an abundance of graces from it."[1] The same document suggests repeatedly that reform of the rites is inseparable from a renewed understanding of the general nature of liturgy. For example, paragraph 5 states that liturgy is the sacrament of Christ's "work of human redemption and perfect glorification of God." This is reiterated in paragraph 7, which asserts that liturgy is "an exercise of the priestly office of Jesus Christ." Perhaps most well-known is the description of liturgy found in paragraph 10—namely, that it is the "summit toward which the activity of the church is directed" and the "source from which all its power flows." Such theological assertions as these reveal the constitution's aim to promote the understanding that "exterior" changes in prayer texts and rubrics must always be accompanied by an "interior" spiritualization of the liturgy.[2]

---

[1] *Sacrosanctum Concilium* 21 in Austin Flannery, ed., *The Basic Sixteen Documents: Vatican Council II Constitutions, Decrees, Declarations* (Northport, NY: Costello Publishing Company, Inc., 1996).

[2] See, for example, the address by Paul VI to a group of Italian bishops on April 14, 1964, in *Documents on the Liturgy, 1963–1979, Conciliar, Papal, and Curial Texts*, International Commission on English in the Liturgy (Collegeville, MN: Liturgical Press, 1982), 87. In advocating liturgical reform, Paul VI states: "The liturgical reform provides us with an excellent opportunity in this regard (the place of religion in life): it calls us back to the theological view of human destiny that the action of grace, and thus of the life of the sacraments and prayer, has primacy. The liturgical reform opens up to us a way to reeducate our people in their religion, to purify and revitalize their forms of worship and devotion, to restore dignity, beauty, simplicity, and good taste to our religious ceremonies. *Without such inward and outward renewal there can be little hope for any widespread survival of religious living in today's changed conditions.*" Emphasis mine. Therefore, it may be understood that inward renewal involves deciphering the nature

At the time of the Council, various "methods" of studying the nature of liturgy were popularized that served to enhance the Church's almost exclusive reliance upon theological and historical perspectives alone.[3] One particular method that became widely recognized was what may be called a "ritual studies" approach to liturgy.[4] Acknowledging that "ritual studies" began to be taken seriously as an academic discipline in the mid-1970s, American sociologist Ronald Grimes writes:

> The study of ritual is not new. Theologians and anthropologists, as well as phenomenologists and historians of religion, have included it as one of their concerns. What is new about ritual studies is the deliberate attempt to consolidate a field of inquiry reaching across disciplinary boundaries and coordinating the normative interests of theology and liturgics, the descriptive ones of the history and phenomenology of religions, and the analytical ones of anthropology. As a result of this goal, the discipline of ritual studies is less a method one applies than a field one cultivates.[5]

While ritual studies certainly takes into account written texts and rubrics, its starting point lies in the observation of human behavior and communication.[6] Applied to the study of the liturgy, this means that basic components of "ritualization"[7]—such as the expression of

---

of liturgy, while outward renewal involves the work of promulgating liturgical texts and rites.

[3] For example, one widespread entry point into liturgical study was to focus on the etymology of the word "liturgy." In this approach, the Greek word *leitouría* is broken apart into its constituent parts: *érgon* ("work") and *laós* ("people"). In what could be interpreted as a reaction against worship as the exclusive action of the priest, liturgy was thereby defined as the "work of the people." See James White, *Introduction to Christian Worship* (Nashville: Abingdon, 1980), 23–24.

[4] See Jack Goody, "Religion and Ritual: The Definitional Problem," *British Journal of Sociology* 12 (1961): 142–64.

[5] Ronald Grimes, "Ritual Studies," in *The Encyclopedia of Religion*, vol. 12, ed. Mircea Eliade (New York: Macmillan, 1987), 422.

[6] See Ronald Grimes, *Ritual Criticism: Case Studies in Its Practice, Essays on Its Theory* (Columbia: University of South Carolina Press, 1990), 9. Grimes states: "Although ritual studies may include textual analysis, it pays primary attention to performance, enactment, and other forms of gestural activity."

[7] "Ritualization" is a technical term that refers to the way in which ordinary human behavior is elevated gradually to the more stylized behavior of formal

movement and gestures in the liturgy, the interaction between priest and people, and the social cohesion achieved (or lack thereof)—are examined in order to arrive at meaning. In other words, a "ritual studies" approach strives to find significant data for interpretation in the liturgical act as a whole.[8]

Although ritual studies gained both momentum and credence in the years immediately following the Second Vatican Council, such a shift away from an exclusively "classical" approach to the study of liturgy would not happen overnight. The Scholastic method of studying sacraments according to "matter" and "form" and liturgy according to ceremonial rubrics would prove to be a venerable tradition resistant to change. As Kevin Irwin writes:

> It was especially after the Council of Trent that a clear separation developed between the liturgy and sacramental theology. In the wake of the Tridentine concern for rubrical precision in the doing of the liturgy, demonstrated by the printing of rubrics in the Roman Missal and Ritual, liturgy became equated with the external performances of the Church's rites. . . . The divorce between the *lex orandi* [what the

---

ritual. See, for example, Catherine Bell, *Ritual Theory, Ritual Practice* (New York: Oxford University Press, 1992), 74. Bell states that ritualization "is a way of acting that is designed and orchestrated to distinguish and privilege what is being done in comparison to other, usually more quotidian, activities." See also Bell's description of "ritualization" in *Ritual: Perspectives and Dimensions* (New York: Oxford University Press, 1997), 81–82. She writes: "A practice approach to ritual will first address how a particular community or cultural ritualizes (what characteristics of acting make strategic distinctions between these acts and others) and then address when and why ritualization is deemed to be the effective thing to do." See also Ronald Grimes, *Beginnings in Ritual Studies*, rev. ed. (Columbia: University of South Carolina Press, 1995), 43: "Ritualization includes the patterned and the random (the repeated and the idiosyncratic, the routine and the nonpragmatic, the habitual and useless) elements of action and interaction."

[8] See, for example, Aidan Kavanagh, *On Liturgical Theology* (Collegeville, MN: Liturgical Press, 1992), 100–101. He writes: "*A liturgy of Christians is thus nothing less than the way a redeemed world is, so to speak, done.* The liturgical act of rite and the assembly which does it are coterminous, one thing: the incorporation under grace of Christ dying and rising still, restoring the communion all things and persons have been gifted with in Spirit and in truth. A liturgy is more than an act of faith, prayer, or worship. It is an act of rite." Emphasis mine.

Church prays] and *lex credendi* [what the Church believes] was exemplified in the division of what had been a single area of study into two: liturgy and sacramental theology. Thus what resulted was a rather legalistic understanding of liturgy with sacramental theology assigned to dogmatic tracts.[9]

The study of liturgy prior to the Second Vatican Council, a pursuit almost exclusively undertaken by men preparing for ordination, could be considered the learning of rubrics and the mastering of ritual gestures. All of this was seen as secondary to the primary theological and historical study of sacraments.

MARK SEARLE'S "RITUAL" APPROACH TO LITURGY

It was this form of "classical" training that Mark Searle received in preparation for priestly ministry in the years immediately prior to the Second Vatican Council.[10] However, it would not be the approach he would adopt in his career as a professor of liturgy; rather, he believed that a more complete study of liturgy—one which would help to reunite the execution of liturgical rubrics with theological and historical study—is best rooted in a "ritual" approach. "To study liturgy as ritual," Searle writes, "is to study liturgy, whether in history or in the present, in its empirical reality as a species of significant human

[9] Kevin W. Irwin, *Context and Text: Method in Liturgical Theology* (Collegeville, MN: Liturgical Press, 1994), 17–18.

[10] See Mark Searle, "Description of Proposed Study" in MSP, C19, Folder "Ritual, Definitions of." Searle argues the point that liturgy needs to be studied from a ritual perspective and states the following about his seminary training in liturgy: "My own interest in the study of ritual is longstanding, but the methods in which I was trained—the methods which have almost exclusively dominated the study of ritual in theology and religious studies—were historical and theological. Over the years, however, I have become increasingly aware of the limitations of these approaches, namely: a) they are almost exclusively text-based and thus overlook the most characteristic feature of ritual, viz. that it only really exists when it is performed; b) they have tended to 'explain' rites by studying their origins and historical development; c) they give privileged status to 'normative' meanings (those proposed by leaders and commentators) at the expense of the actual meanings conveyed to participants in the performance of the rites; d) they generally study rites in their ideal form (as they are meant to be celebrated) instead of studying the form they take in actual practice."

behavior."[11] While such an approach may not have been the intention of the reformers at the Second Vatican Council, retrieving the requirement for the active participation of all worshipers would necessarily introduce the issue of "human dynamics" in the examination of liturgical celebration. Thus, Searle states:

> Since the 1960s, however, there has been a new interest in ritual both among liturgists and in the human sciences. For liturgists, the mixed results of the reforms introduced by the Second Vatican Council prompted new attention to the human dynamics of the liturgy. By 1968, it was becoming apparent that the implementation of the reform was raising problems to which historical and theological studies alone could give no answer: problems raised by negative reaction to the reforms and even more by the rash of radical "experiments" which they unwittingly unleashed. *What was needed, it seemed, was a more profound understanding of the human dynamics of liturgy as ritual behavior.*[12]

However, Searle recognized that, like the realm of liturgy, the meaning of and methodology involved in understanding the nature of ritual itself was still a field in its infancy stage. Therefore, he was convinced that greater attention must be devoted to probing and identifying the various dimensions of ritual behavior.

For Searle, the greatest challenge offered by a "ritual" approach to the study of liturgy could be found in the fundamental shift away from an almost singular interest in liturgical books and rubrics contained therein to the observation of liturgy as it is actually performed. "Liturgy," Searle contends, "is uniquely a matter of the body: both the individual body and the collective body."[13] He continues:

> In liturgy, the world is encountered *in sensu*, and reveals itself as sacrament through an almost experimental acting out of the ritual, through an exploratory assumption of the prescribed words and gestures, whose meaning is revealed in the doing. This is perhaps why liturgy

[11] Mark Searle, "Ritual," in *The Study of the Liturgy*, rev. ed., ed. Cheslyn Jones et al. (London: SPCK, 1992), 52. Regarding the popularity, or lack thereof, of a "ritual" approach to the study of liturgy, Searle writes: "This is an approach to liturgical studies which has remained largely unexplored until very recent times, perhaps because the very idea of ritual was somewhat suspect."

[12] Ibid., 53. Emphasis mine.

[13] Ibid., 56.

has survived—in the case of the Roman liturgy, for centuries—in a hieratic language unintelligible to most participants, and why neither in the 16th nor in the 20th century did translation into the vernacular have the immediate hoped-for effect. *While ritual is subject to discursive analysis and theological evaluation, it is always more than words can tell.*[14]

Breaking through the barrier of a predominantly theological and historical study of liturgy demands a reawakening of symbolic imagination. In other words, a community's belief is not simply contained in the verbal expressions of vocalized prayer; belief is also expressed in "ritual doing." However, even the "doing" of ritual will more likely yield a greater sense of contemplation than it will produce meaning. "Ritual will always be more than doctrine-in-action," he writes, "as encounter will always be more than its description."[15]

Although the meaning of ritual will always be polyvalent, meaning is nevertheless conveyed in the act of performance. Searle suggests that ritual meaning is found in the expression of "attitudes, emotions, and relationships."[16] Ritual develops and takes on an established form when "what previously was a spontaneous *expression* of attitudes, emotions and relationships now becomes an activity aimed at *eliciting* such attitudes etc."[17] Furthermore, in the sphere of established Christian ritual, the "eliciting" of attitudes is aimed at realizing and expressing God's "attitude" for creation.[18] As Searle writes:

[14] Ibid., 57. Emphasis mine.

[15] Ibid., 58.

[16] See Mark Searle, "Christian Initiation" in MSP, C38, Folder "Ritual: Experience, Feelings, Emotion." Searle writes: "Ritual fulfills a basic human need to express and give an added meaning to man's attitudes, emotions and relationships. Man meets this need by symbolizing his attitudes, emotions and relationships either in word or gesture or in a combination of both."

[17] Ibid., 2.

[18] Ibid., 4. To suggest the objective of ritual is to realize God's attitude toward the world is to say that ritual is an act of divine revelation. Searle writes: "Since the Church is a human community, however, her most expressive and significant activity is, as is the case for all communities, her ritual actions. These point to what is truly sacred in human experience. They express and reveal the deepest meaning of human existence itself, insofar as they 'reveal the deepest truth about God and the salvation of men [which] is made known to us in Christ' (*Dei Verbum* 2)." Similarly, Kevin Irwin writes: "From the outset it is important to set a proper perspective on liturgy, prayer and spirituality (in fact on all aspects of the Christian life) by exploring the

It [Christian ritual] expresses the attitudes which are those of God himself towards his creation and serves to arouse an echo of acceptance and response in the hearts of the participants. The relationships which it mediates are those between God and men and between men themselves in the light of their relationship to God, inaugurating, deepening, changing, renewing them. These rituals demand and express a commitment which goes beyond what is merely intellectual and which claims the whole man. Since what a man is, even to himself, is more than he can put into words, we can speak of Christian liturgy as having a role in eliciting and expressing appropriate emotion: but this is far more than is suggested by the term "emotionalism" which, in current usage, seems to suggest a merely partial and even superficial involvement.[19]

It is important to underscore the wisdom of Searle's thought here— namely, that the ritual activity we call liturgy is an expression of God's "attitude" toward all of creation. The worldview that is mediated in the celebration of liturgy is nothing less than the perfection of all things dwelling within the Kingdom of God. More will be said of this in the next chapter.

Perhaps it should be no surprise that a man trained as a Franciscan would come to the study of liturgy from a perspective of divine love for all creation. From his earliest published work, Searle held to the belief that liturgy can be defined only in terms of God's action upon the world. For example, in a 1972 piece titled "The Word and the World," Searle defines liturgy as a "happening," an event that, in its entirety, is nothing less than the Word of God. He writes:

In this assembly, in its words and actions, the Word of God finds its most explicit utterance in the world of men, calling them to faith, deepening their faith, revealing their true identity and purpose, inviting them to work for the fulfillment of the destiny of man, for the completion of that future which was both revealed and inaugurated in Christ.

---

dynamic of our search for God and God's prior and unceasing search for us in the gifted relationship of faith. . . . The priority of God's initiative will serve to illustrate that the foundation of all that we do at worship and of all that comprises spirituality for us is God's prior and constant search for us. The place of the liturgy as the means of experiencing the mystery of God until we come to know him in the kingdom will be emphasized." See Kevin Irwin, *Liturgy, Prayer and Spirituality* (New York: Paulist Press, 1984), 25.

[19] Searle, "Christian Initiation," 4.

Consequently, the liturgy as such, and in its entirety, is the Word of God in the World.[20]

Here, Searle's definition suggests that liturgical celebration, from beginning to end, is God's self-revelation to the world. Every aspect of this celebration—from the proclamation of scripture to the performance of gestures to all that comprises the liturgical environment—is the means by which God confronts the Church, and thus the world, with the truth of his Word. Furthermore, Searle's notion of liturgy demands that the liturgical assembly must not only receive God's Word, but must also be challenged to *be* God's Word—there can be no separation between liturgy and life. "The holiness of the Christian people," Searle contends, "is demanded not because the liturgy is apart from the world and *thus* holy, but because it declares the world to be holy, the place of God's presence among men."[21]

Therefore, the very project of liturgy may be defined in terms of the Church becoming the Word for the world; this is the purpose of liturgical prayer, a task which is pursued by the Christian community together. Because liturgy is an act of divine revelation, Searle's "ritual studies" approach seeks to ask questions regarding effective communication in every aspect of the liturgical celebration. He writes:

> We need to appreciate how much the sacramental celebration depends, at least for its subjective effectiveness, or fruitfulness, on far more than valid matter and integral recitation of the words of the form. Everything which happens in a liturgical assembly contributes to the effectiveness of the communication of God's Word to men—or distorts it. It is as well, therefore, when planning a liturgy, to be aware of the need to ensure that everything in the liturgical assembly contributes to the effective proclamation and hearing of the Word. Here again, the Word is not simply the spoken word, but the total celebration as such: so that everything which belongs to that celebration or affects it in any way—

[20] Mark Searle, "The Word and the World," *Life and Worship* 41 (1972): 5. Emphasis mine.

[21] Ibid., 8. Searle also writes: "If the liturgy really is the celebration of the ultimate meaning of our life in the world of men, the divorce between that life and the liturgy will be healed when our lives as individuals and as a community are themselves manifestations of that same meaning. As members of the Church and active participants in her liturgical celebrations, we have the responsibility not merely to hear the Word, but to *become* the Word."

atmosphere, order, sounds, light, movement, vesture—all form part of the whole and affect the process of God's self-communication.[22]

Searle argues that what is crucial to the study of liturgy is a twofold inquiry regarding communication: what makes God's Word evident and available to the world, and what contributes to its being muted? He will go so far as to say that "relevance" in liturgy is a factor only insofar as attention is devoted to the accessibility of "hearing" God's Word.[23]

Such is the central theme of a short piece by Searle titled "What Is the Point of Liturgy?" that appeared the following year (1973) in *Christian Celebration*. It is the opening words of *Gaudium et Spes* that reinforce for Searle the meaning of relevance in liturgical celebration:

> The joys and hopes, the grief and anguish of the people of our time, especially of those who are poor or afflicted, are the joys and hopes, the grief and anguish of the followers of Christ as well. Nothing that is genuinely human fails to find an echo in their hearts. For theirs is a community composed of people united in Christ and guided by the holy Spirit in their pilgrimage toward the Father's kingdom, bearers of a message of salvation for all of humanity. That is why they cherish a feeling of deep solidarity with the human race and its history.[24]

Searle believes that this vision of the Second Vatican Council will go unrealized as long as Christians fail to understand liturgy as the place where the Word and the world are intimately joined, as long as liturgy is seen as a brief escape from the affairs of the world. "When we celebrate the Eucharist," Searle writes, "we celebrate the intervention of God in a human, historical way in the life of our community."[25] Once again, the dynamic of effective communication—i.e. the care given to the revelation of God's Word in every dimension of liturgy—attends to

[22] Ibid., 6.

[23] Ibid., 8. Searle writes: "The quest for relevance in the liturgy is thus of paramount importance, for it is a matter of facing our responsibility to the Word of God in the world and ensuring that everything is done to allow the Word to reverberate in our world with all possible clarity and vigour."

[24] *Gaudium et Spes* 1, p. 163. See also Mark Searle, "What Is the Point of Liturgy?," *Christian Celebration* (Summer 1973): 26.

[25] Searle, "What Is the Point of Liturgy?," 27.

the theological vision that liturgical prayer expresses God's "attitude" toward creation.

THE INCORPORATION OF SUSANNE LANGER'S RITUAL THEORY

While it is clear that Searle wanted to ground the study of liturgy in the examination of ritual behavior in general, it is apparent that he did not develop his understanding of ritual action as the expression of "attitudes, emotions and relationships" without prior influence. In fact, it was the writing of philosopher Susanne Langer that captured his imagination with regard to the meaning of ritual. More specifically, it was Langer's definition of ritual as "rehearsal of right attitudes" that became vital to Searle's own understanding of Christian liturgy. Therefore, in order to better understand Langer's impact on Searle's thought, it will be helpful to briefly introduce her contribution to the field of ritual studies.

Susanne Knauth Langer (1896–1985) studied under the guidance of Alfred North Whitehead at Harvard University and was considered a leading thinker in the area of aesthetics in the 1940s and 1950s.[26] Her major work, *Philosophy in a New Key: A Study in the Symbolism of Reason, Rite, and Art*, was published in 1942 and had sold more than five hundred thousand copies at the time of her death in 1985.[27] The primary contribution of this work is Langer's thesis that humans have a fundamental need for symbolization.[28] Langer contends that with the

[26] See William R. Greer, "Susanne K. Langer, Philosopher, Is Dead at 89," *New York Times* (July 19, 1985): A12. An interesting fact about Langer's life is that she was proficient at playing the cello, which "gave her the expertise lacked by many other philosophers in studying the philosophy of aesthetics."

[27] Ibid. See also Max Hall, *Harvard University Press: A History* (Cambridge, MA: Harvard University Press, 1986), 79. Hall details the publishing success of *Philosophy in a New Key*: "By 1984, *Philosophy in a New Key* had sold at least 545,000 copies. This figure included about 12,000 in the Press's hardcover; 447,000 as a low-priced commercial paperback; 43,000 as a Harvard Paperback beginning in 1971; at least 32,000 in a Japanese translation; and about 11,000 in nine other translations. The book became required or recommended reading for students of semantics, general philosophy, English, aesthetics, music, and the dance."

[28] See Susanne K. Langer, *Philosophy in a New Key: A Study in the Symbolism of Reason, Rite, and Art* (Cambridge, MA: Harvard University Press, 1942), esp. 40–41. She writes: "This basic need, which certainly is obvious only in man, is

scientific revolution came the end of an "exhausted philosophical vision," in which the "rational" dominated the "empirical."[29] However, with the rise of scientific observation came the flourishing of the symbol, for what is observed must be put into language, which is itself a symbol. Langer writes: "Not simply seeing is believing, but *seeing and calculating, seeing and translating*."[30] Thus, for Langer, the "new key" to philosophy and to the search for meaning in this world is "symbolic transformation."[31] "Symbolism," Langer maintains, "is the recognized key to that mental life which is characteristically human and above the level of sheer animality."[32] Human beings do not simply respond to their senses; they *translate* what they sense into symbols.

Thus, according to Langer, while animals are capable only of performing "practical" acts such as gathering food and procreating, humans perform many different types of "impractical" acts that serve to express feeling, which she associates with such words as "intuition," "deeper meaning," "artistic truth," and "insight."[33] For Langer, speech is the primary example of an "impractical" act that serves as the "symbolic transformation of experiences."[34] Similarly, ritual behavior may also be called an "impractical" activity:

---

the *need of symbolization*. The symbol-making function is one of man's primary activities, like eating, looking, or moving about. It is the fundamental process of his mind and goes on all the time. Sometimes we are aware of it, sometimes we merely find its results, and realize that certain experiences have passed through our brains and have been digested there."

[29] Ibid., 15–16.

[30] Ibid., 20.

[31] See Arabella Lyon, "Susanne K. Langer: Mother and Midwife at the Rebirth of Rhetoric," in *Reclaiming Rhetorica: Women in the Rhetorical Tradition*, ed. Andrea A. Lunsford (Pittsburgh, PA: University of Pittsburgh Press, 1995), 270. Maintaining that Langer's primary contribution is the grounding of philosophy in symbolic transformation rather than logic, Lyon writes: "She proclaimed as intrinsically human the constant and necessary transformation of sensual experience into personal symbols. From the flux of sensations felt by our bodies, our eyes, our ears, our mouths, and our noses, our minds abstract what is significant—the forms that affect us. Every act of thinking is an act that expresses these feelings by transforming them into symbols, insists Langer. In privileging feeling over logic in meaning making, Langer defied the mainstream of her discipline."

[32] Langer, *Philosophy in a New Key*, 28.

[33] Ibid., 92.

[34] Ibid., 44–45.

Ritual "expresses feelings" in the logical rather than the physiological sense. . . . The ultimate product of such articulation is not a simple emotion, but a complex, permanent *attitude*. This attitude, which is the worshipers' response to the insight given by the sacred symbols, is an emotional pattern, which governs all individual lives. . . . A rite regularly performed is the constant reiteration of sentiments towards "first and last things"; it is not a free expression of emotions, but a *disciplined rehearsal of "right attitudes."*[35]

Ritual serves as a vehicle of symbolic transformation in which the "disciplined rehearsal of right attitudes" aims at expressing "deeper meaning" and "insight." "Human attitudes," writes Langer, "vaguely recognized as reasonable and right, are expressed by actions which are not spontaneous emotional outlets but prescribed modes of participation and assent."[36]

All of this leads Langer in the direction toward aesthetics and her belief that art and music, like ritual, have an objective reality—they are not means of "self-expression" but rather serve as symbolic transformations of life "attitudes." In other words, they transcend immediate emotions and are "the reflection of inner life in physical attitudes and gestures" and of tensions created therein.[37] In other words, art and music fall into the realm of symbolic translation; they are not meant to evoke a particular emotion as they are meant to provide insight. Langer writes:

The fact is, that we can *use* music to work off our subjective experiences and restore our personal balance, but this is not its primary function.

[35] Ibid., 153. Emphasis mine.

[36] Ibid., 162. Langer states this in another way on page 171: "Ritual begins in motor attitudes, which, however personal, are at once externalized and so made public."

[37] Ibid., 226. See also Susanne K. Langer, *Feeling and Form: A Theory of Art Developed from Philosophy in a New Key* (New York: Charles Scribner's Sons, 1953), 372. Here Langer writes: "But the fact that music is a temporal, progressive phenomenon easily misleads one into thinking of its passage as a *duplication* of psychophysical events, a *string of events* which parallels the passage of emotive life, rather than as a symbolic projection which need not share the conditions of what it symbolizes (i.e. need not present its import in temporal order because that import is something temporal). The symbolic power of music lies in the fact that it creates a pattern of tensions and resolutions. . . . Painting, sculpture, architecture, and all kindred arts do the same thing as music."

25

Were it so, it would be utterly impossible for an artist to announce a program in advance, and expect to play it well; or even, having announced it on the spot, to *express himself* successively in *allegro, adagio, presto,* and *allegretto,* as the changing moods of a single sonata are apt to dictate. Such mercurial passions would be abnormal even in the notoriously capricious race of musicians![38]

What is said here about music can be applied to ritual behavior as well, namely that participation in ritual is not meant to serve the goal of evoking subjective, personal feelings but is meant to practice the fundamental attitudes it seeks to express. Thus, ritual is not about *self*-expression but rather *life*-expression, which depends on the communal transformation of symbols for meaning to take place. As Langer contends, "A life that does not incorporate some degree of ritual, of gesture and attitude, has no mental anchorage."[39]

A further dimension of Langer's philosophy that is important in terms of ritual theory is that all means of symbolic transformation must be examined in terms of an overall experience that creates what she calls "semblance of life." When a piece of music is played, a painting unveiled, or a ritual performed, meaning is to be found in the overall experience, in the entire complex comprised of artists, art, and art admirers. Langer writes:

> This total semblance is, I think, what critics often refer to as the poet's "vision." I can find no other justification for that word. In the framework of the present theory, however, it is perfectly justified. A poem is essentially and entirely a creation; the words beget virtual elements, that exhibit forms of sensibility and emotion and thus carry a meaning beyond the discursive statements involved in their construction. But the meaning is not something to be read "between the lines"; it is *in* the lines, in every word and every punctuation mark as well as in the literal content of every sentence. The whole fabric is a work of art.[40]

[38] Langer, *Philosophy in a New Key,* 217.

[39] Ibid., 290.

[40] Susanne K. Langer, "The Primary Illusions and the Great Orders of Art," *Hudson Review* 3 (1950): 230. Langer opens this article with the following sentence: "All art is the creation of forms expressive of human feeling, from the primitive sense of vitality that goes with breathing and moving one's limbs, or even suddenly resting, to the poignant emotions of love and grief and ecstasy."

The idea of the "total semblance," when approaching aesthetics or ritual performance, is important as it rejects the notion of trying to examine distinct parts in order to determine meaning. For example, music is created when individual notes are in relationship with one another; therefore, to examine one note by itself or even a series of notes and rests apart from the entire piece is futile.[41] Thus, in the composition of an overall art form, all constituent elements "are illusions achieved by abstracting semblances *from* the actual world" that then create "these sheer appearance into new forms that mirror the logic of feeling."[42]

To summarize Langer's contribution to the body of knowledge of ritual theory, she first and foremost claimed symbols as fundamental to the human condition. Furthermore, Langer believed that symbols do not arise from the level of cognition but rather out of the need to express feeling. In the realm of ritual, symbols are employed to articulate the "deeper meaning" of attitudes. She propositioned, therefore, that ritual is in fact the "rehearsal of right attitudes," expressing a corporate worldview. To "rehearse" attitudes is not to express one's emotional state but to surrender the self to the symbols of the rehearsal. For this reason, Langer subscribed to the notion that there is an objective meaning to be found in the "total semblance" of ritual (as well as in music and art) since ritual behavior is not about "a simple emotion, but a complex, permanent *attitude*."[43] Therefore, identifying the underlying attitudes of ritual is a necessary project of those interested in understanding what it intends to perform and accomplish.

SEARLE'S DEFINITION OF LITURGY AS "REHEARSAL OF CHRISTIAN ATTITUDES"

As previously stated, while it is clear that Searle was familiar with the overall content and breadth of Langer's work, it is most certain that his imagination was captivated specifically by her definition of ritual as "rehearsal of right attitudes." An adapted form of this definition began to appear in the earliest of his published writings and

[41] Ibid., 223. Langer states: "The elements of music therefore are sensuous images of the tensions and resolutions which constitute *passage* for us; and those sensuous images, creating the semblance of passage, are tonal forms in virtual motion. By these the illusion of time is achieved and its experiential character set forth—its complexity, density, and volume, its interwoven elements and indivisible flow."

[42] Ibid., 228.

[43] Langer, *Philosophy in a New Key*, 153.

continued to play a role throughout his entire career. Thus, in several short pieces that appeared in the 1979 volume of *Assembly*, Searle introduces the definition of liturgy as "rehearsal of Christian attitudes," and therefore was recognized among the post–Vatican II scholars who focused primarily on the pastoral project of illuminating the meaning of liturgy in the life of the Christian community. Rather than exerting his energy on proposing ways to change the liturgy, Searle sought to articulate the need for a deeper internalization of the liturgy itself.

In the March edition of the 1979 volume of *Assembly*—a publication of the Notre Dame Center for Pastoral Liturgy for which Searle himself functioned as editor—an article titled "The Sacraments of Faith" appeared in which he concretely defines liturgical celebration in terms of "rehearsal of attitudes."[44] Here Searle concisely portrays all of the sacraments in terms of their ability to help Christians surrender to the new life that is bestowed in death. His contention is that all Christian liturgical practice teaches the art of dying to self, as we enter into Christ's self-gift. Searle writes:

> When we participate in the sacraments of faith we identify with Christ in his own commitment of his whole self freely to God. . . . The sacraments of faith are not painless alternatives to the faithful obedience which is perfected in suffering. *They are rather instances of learning-by-doing, rehearsals of attitudes of obedience and surrender, exercises and celebrations of our self-abandonment to God in Christ.* . . . The liturgy enacts this paradox: it is a celebration of life because it is a rehearsal of death.[45]

At a point in the post–Vatican II renewal when liturgical celebration was often an experiment in attaining temporal joy and personal satisfaction, Searle offered a theology of celebration rooted in Christian surrender.[46] Moreover, he emphasized the attitudes of "obedience"

[44] See Mark Searle, "The Sacraments of Faith," *Assembly* 5, no. 5 (1979): 54–55.

[45] Ibid., 54. Emphasis mine. See also Searle, *Eight Talks on Liturgy*, 87–88. He states: "Our Christian faith should produce in us an attitude to death which clearly differentiates us from our unbelieving contemporaries. . . . In former times and in less advanced cultures, death was a public, or at least a family, celebration; now it is a private obscenity. . . . This has resulted in attitudes to sickness and death which are profoundly unchristian."

[46] See Searle, "The Sacraments of Faith," 55. Searle concludes the article with this statement: "Our liturgical celebrations, so parochial and demure, are heavy with unnoticed irony: the life-giving waters only resuscitate those

and "surrender" as paramount to the nature of liturgy precisely because these are the attitudes held by Christ as he suffered death on the cross in offering himself to the Father.

Several months later Searle wrote an editorial for *Assembly* titled "Active Participation" in which he once again stated that liturgy is about practicing the art of self-surrender to contemplate what it means to be part of Christ's own suffering, death, and resurrection.[47] Instead of viewing liturgy in terms of what "builds" community, Searle contends that liturgy is where our oneness in Christ is realized again and again, since community is already established in Christ through baptism. He writes:

> Active participation is nothing more or less than the realization and activation of the common life of Christ into which we are initiated by baptism. The right and duty of active participation is the right and duty to discover the immeasurable dimensions of our life together in the Spirit of Christ. It is the right and duty to lose one's life in order to find it in the common life of the one Body.[48]

Thus, he states quite succinctly: "We learn who we are by doing what we do."[49] As early as the late 1970s—just a little more than a decade after the close of the Second Vatican Council—Searle began calling for the need for a corporate contemplation of liturgy to conquer a growing sense that how one participates in worship is a matter of personal choice. "The enemy of 'active participation,'" Searle writes, "is not interiority or a dislike of noisy celebrations. The real enemy is individualism, i.e. egotism in all its forms."[50]

---

whom they first drown; the bread of life is the condemned man's nourishment; the sacrament of unity celebrates a unity we hardly suspect and desire even less; the comfortable congregation gathers dispassionately under the sign of the Crucified to pray for the blessing—not promised in the Gospel—of never being asked to change, to suffer or to surrender. Yet the irony, hanging like a vulgarism in polite conversation, remains to disquiet us and even, on occasion, to drive a saint to that insanity we call faith."

[47] See Mark Searle, "Active Participation" (Editorial), *Assembly* 6, no. 2 (1979): 65, 72.

[48] Ibid., 72.

[49] Ibid.

[50] Ibid. He continues: "Too often, what passes for community celebration is little more than the indulgent 'self-expression' of a group of people who 'like that kind of thing'—until they tire of it. Similarly, the refusal of the 'new

Finally, in the December 1979 edition of *Assembly*, Searle wrote an editorial titled "Liturgical Gestures," in which he again discusses liturgy in terms of the "rehearsal of attitudes" and specifically credits Susanne Langer as the source of this idea.[51] Here he deals with the issue of "authenticity," as he contends that the introduction of the vernacular into the liturgy as well as the mandate to reform the rites according to the goal of making things understandable served to uncover the search for meaning and authenticity.[52] Authenticity in the liturgy is not about the revelation of one's own personal feelings in the moment, but rather is about expressing what the ritual demands of us. Searle writes:

> Yet it is precisely in the area of integration, and of authenticity which is its moral dimension, that problems seem to arise for people in regard to liturgical celebration. Often the question is posed in terms of feelings and emotions. *Liturgical rites and texts invite us to express emotions*

---

liturgy' may be, for all its apparent piety, a refusal to give up attachment to familiar forms. In either case, there is an inability to move beyond one's own ideas of God, Church and the economy of salvation. In either case, the result is the arrested spiritual development of the individual and the disintegration of the ecclesial community."

[51] See Mark Searle, "Liturgical Gestures" (Editorial), *Assembly* 6, no. 3 (1979) 73, 80. Here Searle defines liturgy as "rehearsal of *right* attitudes," in keeping with Langer's earlier contribution. However, in subsequent works, he will change this definition to "rehearsal of *Christian* attitudes."

[52] Ibid., 73. Searle writes: "Before the coming of the vernacular liturgy, Catholics had enjoyed a reputation for cultivating the non-rational, for moving in a world of symbols and beliefs which mediated between the Transcendent and simple humanity in ways which placed comparatively little emphasis on intelligibility. With the introduction of the vernacular, however, the expectation has arisen that everything should be simple to understand (and thus to explain) at the risk of otherwise failing to be authentic. *This double quest, for meaning and authenticity, has shifted the balance in favor of the written and spoken word and away from non-verbal forms of participation*. Statue and icon give way to the printed banner; incense is out, commentary is in; the congregation of spectators becomes an audience drilled in programmed responses. This, in turn, is producing its own reaction in some circles. There is a sudden hungering for the visual, the expressive, the tactile, the olfactory. Dance is in: either in the form of a solo performer offering an 'interpretive dance,' or in the form of simple movements that everyone can join in and that often smack of nothing so much as first-grade play sessions. New rituals are being invented: linking hands for the Lord's Prayer; burning written lists of sins in the paschal flame; solemnly (or gleefully?) turning on the popcorn machine to 'symbolize' the resurrection." Emphasis mine.

30

that are not necessarily ours. We are called upon to express contrition and humility when we feel neither particularly sorry nor particularly humble. We are called to be alternatively joyful and repentant, to say "I believe" to things we are not sure of, to stand, to kneel, cross ourselves and genuflect, whether that is the way we feel or not.[53]

Thus, Searle turns to the example of rituals of etiquette and suggests that just as such simple actions involved in greeting and leave-taking are indispensable for the well-being of society, so too must "programmed responses" be trusted in the liturgy. It is not a matter of "going through the motions" but rather practicing and articulating who we are at prayer. "In fact, they are a form of discipline in which we express attitudes rather than emotions."[54]

Perhaps for the reason that "attitudes" can sometimes be mistaken for "feelings," Searle labors to provide an exact definition for what constitutes attitudes. Attitudes express a worldview; they represent a deeply-held conviction about an outlook on life. "Attitudes," according to Searle, "represent more or less habitual ways of thinking, judging, and acting; more or less stable and reiterated ways of relating to ourselves and to the world around us. . . . They are, in short, our response to life itself."[55] Therefore, using Langer's definition of ritual as the "rehearsal of right attitudes," Searle contends that what is necessary for liturgical enactment is the practicing of objective attitudes that are sometimes mistakenly overrun by the desire to express subjective emotions. He writes:

> The gestures of the faithful during the course of the liturgy represent expression of attitude rather than of emotion. In fact, not the least important aspect of liturgical ritual is that it helps to shape our attitudes instead of letting ourselves be tossed around by the fickle gusts of feeling. They are not so much meant to be spontaneous reactions to the here and now as disciplined approaches to the Always and Everywhere. As Susanne Langer has pointed out, "a rite regularly performed is the constant reiteration of 'first and last things'; it is not a free expression of emotions, but a disciplined rehearsal of right attitudes." What the

[53] Ibid. Emphasis mine. See also Searle, *Eight Talks on Liturgy*, 64. What he writes concerning contrition may be applied to the project of liturgy as a whole: "It is more concerned with God and with his purpose and with getting back into the stream of what God is doing. It is more concerned with that than with oneself and with one's own feeling."

[54] Searle, "Liturgical Gestures," 80.

[55] Ibid.

liturgical gesture can do, therefore, is help us to discover the proper way of being-with-others and of being-before-God. *Whether or not they meet our moods, they discipline us and rehearse us in right attitudes.* Indeed, the very conflict of gesture and emotion may on occasion provoke insights into who we are and who we are called to be. Liturgical celebration not only expresses faith, but can form us as men and women of faith . . . if we enter into its actions.[56]

What Searle will later develop as his concept of "liturgical spirituality," here he articulates as the demand to rehearse the attitudes of the liturgy with "attentiveness," not to oneself or even to the gesture performed but rather "that to which the gesture points us"—namely Christ.[57] Clearly, this kind of "attentiveness" requires that the liturgical assembly must practice praying as the Body of Christ, to pray in such a way so that every spoken word, every enacted gesture, every moment of silence reveals Christ's own attitudes toward the Father in surrendering himself in perfect love.[58]

One of the places where the use of "rehearsal of Christian Attitudes" appears very early on in Searle's writings is in the area of Christian

[56] Ibid. Emphasis mine.

[57] Ibid. Searle states: "We need to 'dwell in' the gesture, whether it be a genuflection or the sign of the cross, to get the feel of it, to try it on. . . . By putting ourselves into the prayerful postures of the liturgical tradition, we might discover their direction, discover who God is and who we are together before him. In other words, even the simplest liturgical gestures do not merely express the things of which we are already conscious, but they serve to deepen our consciousness and to strengthen 'right attitudes.'"

[58] For a similar theology on "attentiveness" as fundamental to liturgical prayer see Evelyn Underhill, *Worship* (New York: Harper & Brothers, 1936), 27. She eloquently writes: "Habit and attention therefore co-operate in the life of worship; and it is a function of cultus to maintain this vital partnership. Habit alone easily deteriorates into mechanical repetition, the besetting sin of the liturgical mind. Attention alone means, in the end, intolerable strain. Each partner has his weak point. Habit tends to routine and spiritual red-tape; the vice of the institutionalist. Attention is apt to care for nothing but the experience of the moment, and ignore the need of a stable practice, independent of personal fluctuations; the vice of the individualist. Habit is a ritualist. Attention is a pietist. But it is the beautiful combination of order and spontaneity, docility and freedom, living humbly—and therefore fully and freely—within the agreed pattern of the cultus and not in defiance of it, which is the mark of a genuine spiritual maturity and indeed the fine flower of a worshipping life."

initiation and faith development.[59] Like core attitudes that govern our behavior and outlook upon the world, Searle believed that baptismal faith must be understood more as a matter of *discovery* than of *decision*.

Thus, in a short piece titled "Conversion and Initiation into Faith Growth," which appeared in 1981, Searle began to speak of faith in terms of a "fundamental attitude toward existence."[60] Here Searle demonstrates that faith development in an individual is inseparable from the faith of the Church and ultimately the faith of Christ. Therefore, what is initiation if it is nothing but the expression of the attitude of Christ (i.e. "his total submission to the will of the Father, even to death on a Cross")?[61] Searle writes:

> Faith, in the last analysis, is what a person lives by and lives for. It is the sum total of the attitudes which motivate us, the values we opt for,

[59] See Mark Searle, *Christening: The Making of Christians* (Great Britain: Kevin Mayhew Ltd., 1977). This book was republished in the United States by the Liturgical Press in 1980. Hereafter all citations will be from the Liturgical Press version.

[60] See Mark Searle, "Conversion and Initiation into Faith Growth," in *Christian Initiation Resources Reader*, vol. 1, *Precatechumenate* (New York: William H. Sadlier, Inc., 1981), 65.

[61] Ibid., 67. Searle argues that the most fundamental liturgical attitudes that are rehearsed are "obedience," "trust," "self-surrender," and "confidence in God's truthfulness." See Mark Searle, "Faith and Sacraments in the Conversion Process: A Theological Approach," in *Conversion and the Catechumenate*, ed. Robert D. Duggan (New York: Paulist Press, 1984), 68. Searle continues: "Christian faith is therefore something open-ended, and this in two ways. It is open-ended in the sense that it is a surrender to being led by God into an unknown future; and it is open-ended in that we cannot give our lives totally and entirely over to God in a single momentous decision, but must continually, day by day, take up the opportunities and confront the vicissitudes of life in ways that express and affirm our faith in God" (68–69). See also Mark Searle, "Infant Baptism Reconsidered," in *Alternative Futures for Worship*, vol. 2, *Baptism and Confirmation*, ed. Mark Searle (Collegeville, MN: Liturgical Press, 1987), 42. He writes: "Paschal faith is the faith which was Christ's, the faith whereby he was made perfect through suffering and consistently surrendered his life into the hands of the God who alone could save him out of death (see Heb 5:7-8). Such a pattern, as something lived out by the community of the baptized, is what constitutes the faith of the Church. *By baptism we have been fitted into a pattern of surrender and exaltation, of self-abandonment and deliverance, of dying and being raised.*" Emphasis mine.

the personal relationships we establish in pursuit of those values. Since none of us has the purity of heart—or single-mindedness—of Jesus' dedication to the Kingdom of God, our faith and our religious beliefs do not so completely coincide. The psalmist says, "Some put their faith in horses and chariots, but we put our faith in the name of the Lord" (Psalm 20:8). Reality is not so clear-cut: there is the bettor as well as the believer in all of us. We live by various faiths. We have religious convictions, but our attitudes, lifestyle, sense of priorities, and reactions to the events of the day often reveal a set of loyalties which are hard to square with demands of the obedience of faith.[62]

Thus, to live according to the "obedience of faith" is to resist the temptation to believe that our conversion to Christ is ever complete, that we have come to know him fully, or that our attitude no longer needs to be conformed to his. What is true for a catechumen is true for the entire Church: "The understanding of the gospel and the teaching of the church are things we come to gradually in the experience of trying to live the Christian way."[63]

CONCLUSION

"What is the point of liturgy?"[64] This is the underlying question that subtly guides the principles for liturgical reform contained in the *Constitution on the Sacred Liturgy*.[65] And yet, at the time of the promulgation of *Sacrosanctum Concilium* on December 4, 1963, new discoveries

---

[62] Ibid., 68.

[63] Ibid., 72.

[64] See Searle, "What Is the Point of Liturgy?," 26–27.

[65] See the many descriptions of the nature of liturgy in the introduction and first chapter of *Sacrosanctum Concilium*. According to the plan of renewal envisioned by the Fathers of the Second Vatican Council, the ascertaining of knowledge as to what liturgy is must accompany the work of restoring or creating new prayer forms. See, for example, Annibale Bugnini, *The Reform of the Liturgy 1948–1975*, trans. Matthew J. O'Connell (Collegeville, MN: Liturgical Press, 1990), 48. In keeping with the call for "full, conscious, and active participation" as mandated in *Sacrosanctum Concilium* 14, Bugnini writes: "The pastors of local Churches, along with all their pastoral workers, are urged to start the process of educating the faithful in the liturgy, familiarizing them with the Scriptures, and getting them actively involved in the celebration through listening and singing and through acclamations, prayers, and responses. In addition, they are to begin the work of translating the liturgical books; this a completely new field, full of difficulties and responsibilities."

continued to be asserted as to what "the very nature of the liturgy" means.[66] Mark Searle became one of the liturgical scholars who would make an important and challenging contribution to the understanding of liturgy. Launching his study of the liturgy from the perspective of ritual behavior, Searle maintained that exploring the human dynamics of ritual would help to provide greater insight into the liturgy than could be provided by theological and historical methods alone.

Searle was convinced that the liturgy reveals God's "attitudes" toward the world; that prior to our response, the liturgy expresses God's love for creation. However, if the liturgy is revelatory of God's "attitudes" toward us, then our faith response must involve "rehearsing" those same attitudes, learning to see the world as God sees it. Thus, liturgy is the "rehearsal of Christian attitudes." The liturgy is the locus for the celebration and appropriation of "right" attitudes, the place where the Christian community practices over and over again the worldview of God's reign. It is the event in which individual Christians rehearse surrendering their individuality in order to be fashioned into the Body of Christ. It is where the pattern of redemption is lived out, experienced bodily, and appropriated for the transformation of all of life.

As will be demonstrated in the subsequent chapters of this study, liturgy as the "rehearsal of Christian attitudes" is a fundamental key in unlocking Searle's method for liturgical studies and of his vision for liturgical reform in general. This mantra becomes the basis for Searle's project of leading worshipers into a deeper sense of what it means to participate in the liturgy. His aim is to demonstrate that, in all things liturgical, "rehearsal" demands deep attentiveness, while the "attitudes" practiced necessitate a willing surrender of self. If enacted with alert attentiveness and contemplative care, the liturgy itself becomes the revelation in our world of the "justice of God."

[66] See, for example, *The Study of Liturgy*, ed. Cheslyn Jones, Geoffrey Wainwright, and Edward Yarnold (New York: Oxford University Press, 1978). See especially the first essay by J. D. Crichton, "A Theology of Worship," 3–29.

Chapter 2

Liturgy as the "Justice of God"

When the Fathers of the Second Vatican Council proclaimed in *Sacrosanctum Concilium* that the liturgy is "the summit toward which the activity of the Church is directed" and "the source from which all its power flows,"[1] they implicitly reaffirmed the indispensable relation between the Church's corporate work of prayer and its involvement in the redemption of the world. Far from being an escape from the world's anxieties and miseries, the liturgy is a primary means of experiencing the ways of peace and justice. Liturgy and the pursuit of justice do not put forth competing agendas, for liturgy that is separated from the world becomes a myopic waiting for a perfect society in heaven, whereas the agenda of justice without a grounding in the liturgy risks forgetting God's role in establishing a Kingdom of right relationship and peace.

The attempt to define clearly the intrinsic link between liturgy and life was the work of the nineteenth- and twentieth-century liturgical pioneers whose vision of worship produced what is well known as the "liturgical movement."[2] In his classic work *Liturgical Piety*, Louis Bouyer offers the following definition of this phenomenon: "The liturgical movement is the natural response arising in the Church to the perception that many people have lost that knowledge and understanding of the liturgy which should belong to Christians, both clergy and laity, and in consequence, have lost the right use of the liturgy also."[3] In other words, the liturgical movement must be spoken of according to a two-fold aim: to "rediscover" the liturgy, and at the same

---

[1] *Sacrosanctum Concilium* 10 in Flannery, *The Basic Sixteen Documents*.

[2] For an overview of the development of the beginnings of the "liturgical movement," see Olivier Rousseau, *The Progress of the Liturgy: An Historical Sketch from the Beginning of the Nineteenth Century to the Pontificate of Pius X* (Westminster, MD: Newman Press, 1951).

[3] Louis Bouyer, *Liturgical Piety* (Notre Dame: University of Notre Dame Press, 1954), 39.

time to "renew" the Church's life of prayer.[4] Similar to Bouyer, Bernard Botte once described the liturgical movement as a necessary reaction to the following dilemma: "Left to themselves, the faithful became more and more isolated in a religious individualism and narrow moralism whose ideal was to have each one work on personal salvation by avoiding mortal sin."[5] In short, the liturgical movement was born out of the conviction that greater comprehension of the meaning of liturgy would help Christians see worship as intertwined with all aspects of life.

For his own part, Mark Searle wrote of *two* liturgical movements. The first focused on establishing a greater understanding of what liturgy is, "weaning nineteenth- and twentieth-century Catholics from their culturally accommodated devotions and their individualistic piety and bringing them back to the liturgy."[6] The second worked in the reverse direction to reform the liturgy itself and was based on the premise that the "liturgy had to be accommodated to the people."[7] Searle summarizes his interpretation of the history of the liturgical movement as follows:

[4] Ibid. See Henri Daniel-Rops, ed., *The Liturgical Movement*, trans. Lancelot Sheppard (New York: Hawthorn Books, 1964), 9. Here there appears an excerpt from a 1940 letter from Romano Guardini to the bishop of Mainz, in which he outlines the major objective of the liturgical movement in terms of restoring the relevance of worship (and religious thinking in general) to a world marked by the effects of Modernity: "The liturgical movement came into being because it was necessary. Under the influence of modern individualism and rationalism, the worship of the Church with its magnificent forms, lofty considerations and concentration on the totality of revealed realities, had been increasingly relegated to the background. Spiritual life had assumed very largely a subjective and private character. It therefore became necessary that from within the Church should arise the desire to regain what had been thus set aside. Scientific and historical research was then carried out in an endeavour to revive the liturgy in its purity and to restore to it the place belonging to it in religious life."

[5] Bernard Botte, *From Silence to Participation: An Insider's View of Liturgical Renewal*, trans. John Sullivan (Washington, DC: The Pastoral Press, 1988), 8. See also Gerald Ellard, *Men at Work at Worship: America Joins the Liturgical Movement* (New York: Longmans, Green and Company, 1940).

[6] Searle, *Called to Participate*, 1.

[7] Ibid.

Historians usually see the liturgical movement that led to the reforms of Vatican II as unfolding in several phases: First, the monastic phase, associated with Solesmes and Beuron and Maria Laach; second the pastoral phase, associated with Lambert Beauduin, Pius Parsch, Virgil Michel, and others between the wars; and finally, the reform phases culminating in the liturgy constitution of the Second Vatican Council. . . . If instead of focusing on places and personalities, however, the historian were to focus on agendas, the history of the liturgical movement would seem less evolutionary, more discontinuous. . . . The first movement was driven by the strong belief that liturgy could re-form Catholics as a People of God to be reckoned with socially and politically. The second recognized that for liturgy to have an impact on the people, it would have to be brought closer to them, for example, through the use of the vernacular.[8]

According to Searle, the first liturgical movement, with its emphasis on a renewed understanding of the liturgy, would attempt to produce a new sense of being Catholic (along with a worldly mission), while the second liturgical movement, which called for a renewal of the liturgy itself, aimed at improving participation in worship. Thus, Searle describes the first movement as "bringing people to the liturgy" and the second movement as "bringing the liturgy to the people."[9]

While Searle believes this second liturgical movement culminated in the work of the Second Vatican Council with its Constitution on the Sacred Liturgy, he concentrates on three important pioneers of the first liturgical movement: Prosper Guéranger, OSB (1805–75), Pius X (1835–1914), and Virgil Michel, OSB (1890–1938).[10] "Unlikely as it must have seemed to most of their contemporaries," Searle writes, "they saw the best chance for such a (social) transformation to lie with the ancient, encrusted, largely ignored, and almost entirely fossilized

[8] Ibid.

[9] Ibid., 11–12. Searle provides the following summary: "Thus we have had two liturgical movements, both of which have made important contributions to the life of the Church, much as multiple movements enrich and deepen a symphony. The first focused on liturgical formation and social transformation, *bringing people to the liturgy* so that they might be empowered to go out and change the social order. The second focused on liturgical change and ecclesial renewal, *bringing the liturgy to the people* so that they might participate fully and help bring the Church into the modern world." Emphasis mine.

[10] Ibid., 2–8.

public worship life of the Church."[11] A brief word about the writings of Guéranger, Pius X, and Michel will help to situate the importance of the century-long work of liturgical investigation and reinvigoration that took place prior to Vatican II.

Prosper Guéranger's contribution to liturgical reform flows from his work to restore the Benedictine abbey at Solesmes in 1833 as well as his ongoing publication of *Institutions liturgiques* (beginning in 1840) and his reflections on the liturgical year (beginning in 1841).[12] In the aftermath of the French Revolution and government-sponsored attack against the Church as well as the rise of the Enlightenment, Guéranger sought to revitalize faith in the Church and in the tradition of its liturgy. He believed that the liturgy provided society with a trustworthy and stable pattern for living that moved away from the temptation to rely on the power of the individual.[13] Thus, he stressed the importance of communal prayer over individual devotion. In his study of Guéranger, biographer Cuthbert Johnson writes:

> It was the social aspect of Liturgical prayer that Guéranger stressed as being of fundamental importance. . . . He actually went so far as to say that the social dimension of the Liturgy is "the basis of all divine worship." . . . The Church is a visible society and since the social dimension of the Liturgy is the common exercise of the virtue of religion, Guéranger pointed out that it was impossible to consider this virtue simply as a matter of concern for the private spiritual well-being of the individual.[14]

[11] Ibid., 2.

[12] See Cuthbert Johnson, *Prosper Guéranger (1805–1875): A Liturgical Theologian, An Introduction to His Liturgical Writings and Work* (Rome: Pontificio Ateneo S. Anselmo, 1984), 428–32. See also R. W. Franklin, "The Nineteenth Century Liturgical Movement," *Worship* 53 (1979): 12–39.

[13] See, for example, Mary David Totah, ed., *The Spirit of Solesmes* (Petersham, MA: St. Bede's Publications, 1997), 164–68. See also Louis Soltner, *Solesmes and Dom Guéranger, 1805–1875*, trans. Joseph O'Connor (Orleans, MA: Paraclete Press, 1995), 89–110. Soltner writes: "In giving back to his century the profound meaning of liturgical prayer, the abbot of Solesmes fought against two forms of individualism: a personal individualism, by upholding the superiority of ecclesial prayer; and a national or regional individualism, by emphasizing the importance of this unity—never to be confused with uniformity" (91).

[14] Johnson, *Prosper Guéranger (1805–1875)*, 256–57.

Therefore, by restoring a sense of beauty in liturgy, as seen in his reintroduction of the Gregorian chant at Solesmes, worshipers would recognize and contribute to the aesthetic dimension of society, for as Guéranger wrote: "*La Liturgie, cette divine esthétique de notre foi.*"[15] According to Guéranger, confidence in and care for the Roman liturgy would help to correct the materialistic attitude that marked mid-nineteenth-century France; true understanding of the liturgy would promote a balance between the individual and the communal, between devotional and liturgical prayer.[16]

The second significant pioneer of the liturgical movement, according to Searle, is Pius X, who succeeded Leo XIII in 1903 and reigned until 1914. During his pontificate, Pius X encouraged frequent reception of Communion, restored the use of chant, reworked the breviary, and promoted the active participation of the assembly in liturgical celebration. While displaying a desire to restore interest in the liturgy itself, Pius X took a skeptical approach to theological scholarship in general by condemning the trend of "Modernism." Critical of scientific developments and historical-critical methods, he identified the liturgy of the Church as the "indispensable fount" from which flowed the true "Christian spirit"—only the liturgy would move the Church away from the attraction of secular movements to a position of prophet in the world. In his *Motu Propio* on restoring sacred Music, *Inter Plurimas Pastoralis* (November 22, 1903), Pius X writes:

> We are filled with a burning desire to see the true Christian spirit flourish in every respect and be preserved by all the people. We therefore are of the opinion that before everything else it is necessary to provide for the sanctity and dignity of the temple where the faithful assemble for no other purpose than that of acquiring this spirit from its primary

[15] Ibid., 262. "The Liturgy is the divine aesthetic of our faith."

[16] See R. W. Franklin, "Guéranger: A View on the Centenary of His Death," *Worship* 49 (1975): 327–28. Franklin sums up Guéranger's contribution to the liturgical movement as follows: "Balancing reactionary politicians and utopian socialists, Guéranger urged that the community not reject existence in the contemporary world. But the choking life of materialism would be transcended only if men adopted a system of values whose end was not man himself but reached beyond man and mere concern with the standard of living. The community is formed by that act of reaching beyond. That act is the mass liturgy. The liturgy expresses the authenticity, austerity, simplicity, and dignity which overcome the stuffy bourgeois world."

and indispensable fount, that is, the active participation in the most sacred mysteries and in the public and solemn prayer of the Church.[17]

For Pius X, liturgical reform did not mean a radical reworking of liturgical texts and rituals; rather, it meant promoting the "active participation" in the liturgy necessary for a retrieval of a "true Christian spirit" in the world. His understanding of the duty for the Church to "restore all things in Christ" (*instaurare omnia in Christo*) meant that the world order must be thoroughly Christianized; he believed that submission to the Church's ancient liturgy would unify the Church in its mission to bring the world to Christ.[18]

The third pioneer of the liturgical movement, identified by Searle, was Dom Virgil Michel, OSB, who sought to awaken the Church in the United States to a deeper understanding of the liturgy.[19] The early twentieth century in the United States witnessed both the economic collapse, which brought about the Great Depression in the 1930s, and the rebound generated by the industrial needs of the Second World War. The triumph of a capitalistic market in the United States not only increased social disparity in many facets of life but also served to crown individualism as an American ideal. A free enterprise system would go hand-in-hand with the pursuit of self over society. Thus, Michel saw the liturgy as means of practicing the ideals of Christianity that would counter the rise of unbridled individualism.[20] Endorsing the theological principle that participation in the "Mystical Body of Christ" produces a practical solidarity in life, Michel writes:

[17] Pius X, *Motu Propio on the Restoration of Sacred Music* (November 22, 1903), in *All Things in Christ: Encyclicals and Selected Documents of Saint Pius X*, ed. Vincent A. Yzermans (Westminster, MD: Newman Press, 1954), 200.

[18] See Pius X, *The Restoration of All Things in Christ* (October 4, 1903), in Yzermans, *All Things in Christ*, 3–13. "To re-establish all things in Christ and to lead men back to submission to God is one and the same aim. We must therefore labor to bring men back to the dominion of Christ, and when this is accomplished, we shall have then have brought them back to God" (7).

[19] See Keith F. Pecklers, *The Unread Vision: The Liturgical Movement in the United States of America: 1926–1955* (Collegeville, MN: Liturgical Press, 1998).

[20] See Virgil Michel, "The Liturgy, the Basis of Social Regeneration," *Orate Fratres* 9 (1935): 537. See also Paul Marx, *Virgil Michel and the Liturgical Movement* (Collegeville, MN: Liturgical Press, 1957), especially 49–71.

Similarly the liturgy of the Church not only makes and keeps us members of this fellowship, but it always puts the idea of fellowship in Christ into full practice. Just insofar as we participate in the liturgy after the mind of Christ do we also live and breathe this supernatural social unity of all members in Christ. This is why the liturgy is so truly the primary and indispensable source of the true Christian spirit: it not only teaches us what this spirit is but also has us live this spirit in all its enactments. In the liturgy the teaching is inseparable from the putting into practice.[21]

Michel believed in the promotion of an "intelligent return" to the liturgy, which would provide the necessary practice for living a Christian life in general.[22] In his words, "The Christian who drinks deep at the liturgical sources of the Christ-life will appreciate the seal of Christ with which he was indelibly marked at his baptism, and he will endeavor to put this same seal on everything with which he comes in contact throughout his daily life."[23] For Michel, this sort of intelligent appropriation of the liturgy's spirit in all areas of life will ensure that concern for society will prevail over the tide of rampant individualism.

Clearly, Prosper Guéranger, Pius X, and Virgil Michel shared the conviction that changing people's approach to the liturgy would assist in the overall transformation of society. Reinvigorate the desire to understand the liturgy and the result would be an awakening of the proper means of participating and influencing the social order. However, after the Second World War, the emphasis of the liturgical movement shifted to focusing on the refurbishing of the liturgy in order to help transform the Church. Emblematic of such a shift is the work of Pius XII in his restoration of the Easter Vigil in 1951 and the restored Holy Week liturgies in 1955. In addition, the National Liturgical Weeks (1940–75) served to realize the need that in order to increase liturgical

[21] Michel, "The Liturgy, the Basis of Social Regeneration," 542. Michel concludes the article with the following syllogism: "Pius X tells us that the liturgy is the indispensable source of the true Christian spirit; Pius XI says that the true Christian spirit is indispensable for social regeneration. Hence the conclusion: The liturgy is the indispensable basis of Christian social regeneration" (545).

[22] See Virgil Michel, "The Scope of the Liturgical Movement," *Orate Fratres* 10 (1936): 490.

[23] Ibid.

participation, it would be necessary to make changes to the liturgy itself. Whereas the early pioneers of the liturgical movement believed that what needed updating was appreciation of the ancient liturgy, reformers of the second half of the twentieth century believed that liturgy itself was insufficient for real participation. Such is the spirit that would imbue the work of the Second Vatican Council, which sought a restoration of the liturgy that would allow the graces of the liturgy to be more accessible to those who celebrate its mysteries. Whether the liturgical movement emphasized transforming society or transforming the Church, at its very foundation was the consistent need to demonstrate the indivisibility of liturgy from life.

IN THE FOOTSTEPS OF SAINT FRANCIS

With his training in the Franciscan worldview, in which respect for all of God's creation is central, Mark Searle believed deeply in the connection between liturgy and life.[24] At a time in the history of the US Church when its hierarchy was devoting much attention to issues of peace and justice,[25] Searle recognized that Christian liturgy is a privileged setting for wrestling with the issues that threaten the very survival of the world. The liturgy is not a form of activity that adds the dimension of the sacred onto life, but rather, it is the practice and the discovery of a particular way of life. He once wrote in an unpublished talk: "What this means for us, as it meant for Francis, is that the sanctification of life is not so much something the Church *does*, but rather something the Church *is*. Christian life is life lived in such a way that

[24] Searle's first detailed exposition on the connection between liturgy and life can be found in his 1974 piece titled *Eight Talks on Liturgy*. He writes: "In the documents of Vatican II we see the Church looking reflectively at a world now alienated from her, a world which feels it has outgrown the Church and does not need faith. This, in turn, led to the Church's reassessment of her own identity as a community of faith, love and hope in an unbelieving and despairing world. But the Church cannot, anymore than the individual, discover her identity simply by defining it. She has to discover it in the experience of her life in the world" (6–7).

[25] See, for example, *The Challenge of Peace: God's Promise and Our Response* (Washington, DC: United States Catholic Conference, May 3, 1983) and *Economic Justice for All* (Washington, DC: United States Catholic Conference, November 18, 1986).

its holiness is revealed."[26] Therefore, the connection with the definition of liturgy as the "rehearsal of Christian attitudes" becomes immediately clear: the liturgy does not transport worshipers to a different (i.e. "holier") world, but rather, it immerses them in the worldview of Christ that pervades the very identity of what the Christian community is already all about, albeit usually unrecognizable, by virtue of the baptismal waters and the eucharistic feast.

Thus, Searle believed that a major stumbling block in realizing the inseparability of liturgy and life is that Christians mistakenly believe they "come to" Church for Sunday Mass rather than understand that they "belong to" Church as a people.[27] The result is that the liturgy is seen as something "other-worldly."[28] However, it is precisely because Christians recognize themselves to be a people belonging to Christ that they are one with the world in all its joys and its suffering. "The trouble is," writes Searle, "that most people do not think of themselves as belonging to this Church, but rather of themselves as coming into contact with the Church at Sunday Mass. . . . Sunday worship appears as totally other-worldly, irrelevant to the concerns of the age, a haven for people who happen to like that kind of thing."[29]

Searle found in Scripture two "great types or models" for countering such an approach to liturgy, models that demonstrate how the Sunday

---

[26] Mark Searle, "The Hallowing of Life," 8. Although it is uncertain as to when Searle wrote this paper, he states in the introduction that the talk is being given "in the very year in which we celebrate the eight hundredth anniversary of the one man who, perhaps more than any other, exemplifies what it means to hallow life: Francis of Assisi." Thus, it is likely that this talk was written in 1981.

[27] See Mark Searle, "Liturgy as Critical of Society" in MSP, B16, Folder "Liturgy + Social Justice Papers." See also Mark Searle, "The Church Celebrates Her Faith," *Life and Worship* 43 (1974): 6.

[28] Searle, "Liturgy as Critical of Society," 1–2. For Searle, the connection between liturgy and life is based on the Incarnation of Jesus Christ: "Yet surely the liturgy of the Church is no more other-worldly than Jesus Christ himself—and no less this worldly. We confess Jesus to be truly God and truly man, believing that the divinity is to be found in his humanity, present and active in his historical and fully human involvement with the world. Such is the pattern, not only of the incarnation of the only-begotten Son of God, but of all God's dealing with men: the divine presence is found in historical human form."

[29] Searle, "Liturgy as Critical of Society," 1.

liturgy is an expression of belonging to a people.[30] First, he suggests that the Exodus story, and more specifically the forming of an assembly in the desert of Sinai, reveals how a band of refugees can reconstitute its identity by recognizing themselves as God's chosen people.[31] "The revelation given in this act of deliverance from slavery," Searle writes, "was such as revealed the deepest aspirations of man himself: aspirations to freedom, dignity, equal access to the fruits of Creation."[32] Thus, the gathering at Sinai, far from being simply a religious experience, was necessarily political in nature, as it grounded a people in a particular worldview, one at odds with the Israelites' experience in Egypt.

The second "model" of belonging, as established in Scripture, is the Last Supper, which witnesses to "the gathering of a group of people at a critical moment in their life as a group: the end of their three years on the road, the imminent arrest and execution of their leader, the beginning of a new phase which would have repercussions far beyond that little group."[33] Searle suggests that this scene is a dual celebration of all that has taken place in a community's history as well as the establishment of a future destiny. He writes:

> When Jesus said, "Do this in memory of me," he was not implying that the historical events associated with that particular celebration were the only events ever worth celebrating and that the rest of human history is meaningless. On the contrary, we were to celebrate "this" in memory of him on any and every occasion precisely because everything we experience has meaning and is worth celebrating.[34]

Thus, Searle contends that every celebration of Christian liturgy provides meaning for the Christian community: it reveals God's presence in the past events of a community's life, and it provides hope for a

---

[30] Ibid., 2.

[31] See Exodus 19:3-8. Here God commands Moses to tell the Israelites: "You have seen for yourselves what I did to the Egyptians and how I carried you away on eagle's wings and brought you to me. So now, if you are really prepared to obey me and keep my covenant, you, out of all peoples, shall be my personal possession, for the whole world is mine. For me you shall be a kingdom of priests, a holy nation." This is the translation provided by Searle in "Liturgy as Critical of Society."

[32] Searle, "Liturgy as Critical of Society," 2.

[33] Ibid.

[34] Ibid., 3.

community's future. "What we have forgotten," Searle maintains, "is that liturgy is the celebration of the presence of God in the community of men and its affairs, of the fact that God calls communities as well as individuals, of the fact that communities, groups, families, even nations, must *as such* seek his will and submit to it."[35]

For Searle, God's "intervention" in human history is directly related to the establishment of a people in his name. Therefore, he identifies liturgy as the "celebration of the life of a congregation as life with God who is reconciling the world to himself,"[36] which means that the liturgy not only proclaims God's peace as a future-oriented goal but also as the present-lived experience of the assembly at prayer. He continues:

> The liturgical assemblies of the Old Testament and of the early church developed a strong sense of identity vis-à-vis the people among whom they lived and a strong sense of vocation to further God's plan for the world. The celebration of the Eucharist should have a similar effect. It should spur us to look more closely at what goes on in the world around us, to understand it in the light of faith, and to celebrate the presence of God in our times.[37]

Thus, the influence of the liturgy on society is not only that participants' hearts might be changed in the midst of celebration but that all of the world's inhabitants who witness the Church collectively surrendering itself in love might be drawn to God. The image of "belonging to a people" serves to underscore the indispensable link between liturgy and life. It is this sense of belonging—this fundamental attitude—that liturgy rehearses in the gathering of a Christian people, and in the enactment of its foundational story, its life in Jesus Christ.

"SERVING THE LORD WITH JUSTICE"

Beginning with an editorial he wrote for the June 1979 edition of *Assembly*, Searle depicts the bond between worship and justice through the story of the medieval knight Parsifal and his quest for the Holy Grail.[38] His rendition of the story is quoted here in full:

[35] Ibid., 3–4.
[36] Ibid., 4.
[37] Ibid., 4–5.
[38] See Mark Searle, "Liturgy and Social Action," *Assembly* 6, no. 1 (1979): 57. Note that the cover art of this book depicts Parsifal's search for the Holy Grail. It is the work of Edward Burne-Jones.

Wolfram von Eschenbach's thirteenth-century version of the story of Parsifal tells of a knight who, looking for adventure, stumbled upon a castle where the Holy Grail was kept. Before his astounded eyes were borne first the bloody Lance and then the life-giving grail. He wondered at the sadness of the company, but asked no questions. Next morning he awoke to find the castle empty: the wounded king and all his sorrowful court disappeared, and with them the Holy Grail. The land around lay desolate and bereft of life.

Parsifal returned to a life of adventuring and, thanks to the strange sword he had been given at the castle, his reputation spread far and wide. Yet, beneath his success, he was tormented with the memory of the Grail. Wherever he went he made inquiry as to its whereabouts, but no one could tell him anything of it. Then, one Good Friday, he was directed to seek out a hermit to whom he made his confession and with whom he prayed and fasted for forty days in search of divine guidance. At the end of that time he set off again, but soon found himself led to the Grail castle. As he drew near, two questions began to stir in his heart. Entering humbly into the castle, he approached the wounded king, and kneeling before him, put those questions to him. "Uncle," he inquired, "what is your sorrow? Who does one serve, in serving the Grail?"

With that the wounded king arose, radiant and whole, the burden of grief was lifted from the whole company, and the lands and waters for miles around sprang to life anew, teeming with living things.[39]

Searle suggests that the connection between the call to worship and its association with daily life is captured in Parsifal's two questions: attention must be given to the world's pains and injustices ("What is your sorrow?"), and fitting worship must be rendered unto God ("Who does one serve, in serving the Grail?"). "Liturgical renewal without social concern," writes Searle, "degenerates into pious aestheticism. Social concern without liturgical celebration loses sight of the Source of life. . . . If, as Vatican II taught, the liturgy is the source and summit of Christian life, this means that it must be rooted in, and relate back to, the daily struggles of Christians and their neighbors in society."[40]

The story of Parsifal serves as the introduction to the keynote address Searle gave at the eighth annual Notre Dame Conference on

[39] Ibid. In a later work, Searle acknowledges that his telling of Wolfram von Eschenbach's *Parzival* is based on Ann Himmler's "The Fisher King," as found in *Parabola* 3, no. 2 (1978): 16–22.

[40] Searle, "Liturgy and Social Action," 57.

Pastoral Liturgy held in June of 1979.[41] In the published version of this address, titled "Serving the Lord with Justice," Searle uses the story of the Holy Grail to show that "there has always been a certain tension between the inner life and social reform."[42] The proven historical danger is that liturgy can provide an escape from the reality of life, while concern for alleviation of society's ills can often overshadow commitment to prayer, reducing it to a "self-indulgent luxury."[43] Countering such commonly-held worldviews, Searle writes:

> The story of Parsifal offers us a symbolic image in which pursuit of the Grail and concern for the suffering neighbor are intrinsically and inseparably connected, without either being reduced to the other. We have to ask of the needy, "What is your sorrow?" Yet, at the same time we must also raise the question, "Whom does one serve in serving the Grail?" It is not so much a matter of the first question relating to the active dimension of the Christian life and the second to its contemplative dimension, for the Grail is a symbol of total healing—personal, social, spiritual, and communal. Somehow the questions are more closely linked than that. Each is a dimension of the other.[44]

However, Searle is not content with simply arguing that liturgy and the social dimension of Christian life must necessarily go hand in hand, rather, he desires to help redefine what justice means when it is held in relationship with liturgy. In other words, Searle believes that in order to renew the Church's understanding of the inseparability of liturgy from life, it is necessary to clarify what justice means as stemming from the liturgy and governing the way Christians live in the world.

Given the climate of rapid social and ecclesial change following the Second Vatican Council, Searle was very much aware of the sus-

---

[41] See Mark Searle, "Serving the Lord with Justice," in *Liturgy and Social Justice*, ed. Mark Searle (Collegeville, MN: Liturgical Press, 1980), 13–35. While Searle's address appears as the opening piece in this collection, other contributors include J. Bryan Hehir, Walter Burghardt, Edward Kilmartin, and Regis Duffy. "Serving the Lord with Justice" also appears as the first essay in A. Koester and B. Searle, *Vision*, 4–22. Two years earlier, Christopher Kiesling addressed this topic at the January meeting of the North American Academy of Liturgy. See Christopher Kiesling, "Liturgy and Social Justice," *Worship* 51 (1977): 351–61.

[42] Searle, "Serving the Lord with Justice," 14.

[43] Ibid.

[44] Ibid.

picion held by those leery of the Church's place in politics or in the promotion of social justice. In "Serving the Lord with Justice," he acknowledges the confusion that exists around the concept that liturgy demands justice:

> The question we want to ask is this: What has all this liturgical activity to do with the cause of justice? For some people, the answer would be "Nothing." Others would see an indirect link insofar as they believe that churchgoing is a stabilizing influence in society and that religion helps people to keep the law and to live as conscientious citizens. Others again would like to see religion more explicitly endorse specific political options, and the ritual of the Church take on the role of deliberate social consciousness-raising.[45]

Thus, Searle concerns himself with the project of defining the word "justice." He argues that in a pluralistic society, such as the United States, justice ends up being interpreted in a variety of ways, most of which point to legal justice, in which "the struggle for justice means seeking legal redress or Constitutional amendment for situations felt to be unjust."[46] Even such things as fundamental human rights—i.e. freedom and the right to life—become equated with adherence to civil law. However, this is not the understanding of justice that the liturgy supports.

"The liturgy celebrates the justice of God himself," Searle writes, "as revealed by him in history, recorded in the Scriptures, and proclaimed in the assembly of the faithful."[47] Herein lies Searle's masterful insight regarding the interconnectedness of liturgy and life: justice is found in the liturgy because it is about divine revelation. In Searle's own words:

> For its own part, the justice of God is not to be understood, as it often is in the popular imagination at least, as a matter of legal enactment or as the expression of a certain divine wisdom in tailoring exquisitely fitting punishment to the crimes of the inescapably guilty. *The justice of God is ultimately God himself, just as he is. It is a justice that is revealed in all that God does to reveal himself.*[48]

[45] Ibid., 15.
[46] Ibid.
[47] Ibid., 15–16.
[48] Ibid., 16. Note that from this point forward the words "justice of God" will be placed within quotation marks to identify it as a specific term used by Searle. Emphasis mine.

It is helpful, therefore, to distinguish human justice, which Searle says "is at best a bridle on evil," from God's justice, which is "the flowering of the good."[49] The "justice of God" is revealed whenever all created things are receptive to God's revelation and correspond to their created purpose. "In short," Searle writes, "the justice of God is satisfied when things conform to the purpose for which he made them."[50]

A PRIVILEGED ENCOUNTER WITH THE "JUSTICE OF GOD"

Thus, Searle not only equates the "justice of God" with divine revelation, he contends that liturgy is the arena in which the "justice of God" is enacted and celebrated; this kind of justice is not proclaimed simply as a future possibility but as a lived reality for the liturgical assembly.[51] This is so because it is a work achieved and manifested in Christ, for as Searle writes:

> The justice of God has been revealed among us in many and various ways throughout the course of human history, but above all it has been seen in all its dimensions in the person of Jesus. He was the Just One. He not only spoke about the coming Kingdom, speculatively as it were, but he embodied it in his own person. In his life and activity he modeled the radically different justice which is that of the Kingdom of God. . . . Jesus lived the justice of God. . . . But the fact that such divine justice has been realized in human form upon this earth means that it is no escapist utopia but a real possibility and the object of a well-founded hope. And the fact that the same Spirit that animated him has been poured out upon the rest of humanity means that the realization of such justice may henceforth always be looked for and worked for.[52]

[49] Ibid. He continues: "That is why God's justice must transcend legal justice: 'I tell you, if your justice goes no deeper than that of the scribes and the Pharisees, you will never get into the kingdom of heaven' (Matt 5:20). God's justice is done when arbitration is transformed by reconciliation; when people become more than objects of desire, manipulation, and profit; when poverty is confronted by asking, not how much the poor require, but how much the rich need; when the goods of the earth are looked upon, not as sources of private profit, but as sacraments of divine and human intercommunication."

[50] Ibid.

[51] Ibid., 17. Searle draws the connection in this way: "For the justice of God that the liturgy proclaims *is* the Kingdom of God."

[52] Ibid.

It is through baptism, therefore, that Christians become responsible for revealing the "justice of God." In other words, because the followers of Christ have been refashioned into his person, they share in the mission of revealing God's Just Kingdom.[53] Thus, the "justice of God" is not a matter of "vague optimism" but rather "is a matter of hope because it has already happened."[54]

Thus, what liturgy does is to help Christians practice that hope. For Searle, liturgy demands that all participants be caught up in a world-view in which all relationships are rightly ordered and in which all of creation is one with God.[55] The starting point for such a vision must

[53] Ibid., 17–18. Searle describes the "unenviable responsibility" of Christians in the following manner: "In every generation some people are called by name consciously to serve this Kingdom and its justice as revealed in Jesus. They are called Christians, and together, as a new humanity, they have the unenviable responsibility of representing the hope of a higher justice and working for its realization. It is not that the Kingdom and Justice of God are to be found only among them, but they are called and commissioned in its service. The form in which they receive that commission is the ritual known as baptism, in which they are called to surrender themselves to the God who revealed himself in Jesus and whom they acknowledge as the Creator of the world and the Lord of history. These disciples of Jesus, who die to the man-made and demonically disjointed world of their times, begin to live according to a new order and according to a new principle: the Spirit of God who enables them to do the works of God."

[54] Ibid, 17. See also Mark Searle, *Liturgy Made Simple* (Collegeville, MN: Liturgical Press, 1981), 26. Searle writes: "Either to act as if all were accomplished and all were well with the world, or else to act as if the world and all its affairs had nothing to do with a Kingdom that will only be established after death and out of time would be to misunderstand both the nature of Christian life and the nature of Christian liturgy. The liturgy is of the present, but it points to the future. It is of this world, but it points to a reality which transcends present experience. It is of the present, because it celebrates and makes real the presence among us of the God who is saving the world in Christ, but that very presence makes us painfully aware of how far we are from the Kingdom of God. It constitutes a call to live and work for the values of God, which are not the values of a society which takes for granted inequality, competitiveness, prejudice, infidelity, international tension, and unbounded consumption. *The liturgy celebrates the presence of God's Kingdom, but it is a presence which contradicts us in many ways and calls us into a future that is of God's making and not a construct of Western civilization.*" Emphasis mine.

[55] Searle, "Serving the Lord with Justice," 21.

necessarily be the perfection of God. Searle states clearly: "This is not a justice, then, that begins with human rights abstractly conceived, but with a divine economy in process of realization."[56] What the liturgy intends to do, then, is to rehearse relationships (with God, others, and the material world) as God intends them. Searle writes:

> For the members of the worshiping community, relationships with one's fellow human beings are based not simply upon their common humanity but upon their common humanity as assumed and redeemed by the love and obedience of Jesus, and raised to a new level by the Spirit of Jesus at work in the world. . . . *The liturgical assembly, at least in its ideal form, offers a model of such interaction. It is not a community of equals but a community of God-given and complementary charisms,* gifts that cannot be identified *a priori* by categories of the secular community—age, sex, race—but are distributed by God indiscriminately among all for the sole purpose of building up the community in perfect justice.[57]

There are to be no artificial, social distinctions that promote separation within the assembly; instead, the worldview of "perfect justice" establishes how relationships are to unfold. In other words, the liturgy "presupposes a group of people who can reach across the social, political, and economic barriers that structure our world to say 'Our Father' and to speak of themselves as a 'we.'"[58]

Given the fact that liturgy rehearses right relationships, it is possible to say that it makes the Kingdom of God truly present. This is not to say that the Kingdom of God is limited to the celebration of the liturgy, but rather, it is the Church's means of sacramentalizing the "justice of God." In other words, it is a privileged encounter with God's Just Kingdom. As Searle poignantly states:

> All this may sound idealistic and remote, indeed so remote as to be useless as a guide to action. On the other hand, the justice of God presented in the liturgy is anything but an abstraction, for the liturgy sacramentalizes the presence of Christ, the Just One. *For that reason, and for that reason alone, we can say that the liturgy not only proclaims the justice of the Kingdom of God as something to be done but actually renders it present, not as an achievement of ours but as a gift of God. In its presence*

[56] Ibid.
[57] Ibid., 24. Emphasis mine.
[58] Ibid., 25.

52

we are confronted with that which we are called to be, with that which God would make us be, if we permit it. Thus the liturgy not only provides us with a moral ideal but confronts us with an ontological reality in the light of which the ambivalence of our own lives is revealed for what it is.[59]

Searle's logic here is clear: because God is revealed in Jesus Christ, and because the liturgy of the Church is the sacramental celebration of the Lord, then the liturgy must necessarily be a living encounter with the Kingdom of God as God intends it. Searle continues: "It (liturgy) proclaims and realizes the saving presence of the Spirit in the world, brings the presence of the Kingdom, and enables us to realize where this is happening even outside the liturgy. *Celebrating the liturgy should train us to recognize justice and injustice when we see it.*"[60]

It is important to understand that this does not mean that the liturgy is to be used as a forum for exploiting the agenda of social justice issues, rather liturgy in and of itself imbues participants with an understanding of a way of life based on the Kingdom of God. Thus, Searle compares the liturgical assembly to a "rehearsal room" in which participants practice their assigned roles again and again. In a vital paragraph of "Serving the Lord with Justice," he writes:

> The liturgical assembly, then, is the place where justice is proclaimed, but it is neither a classroom nor a political rally nor a hearing. It is more like a rehearsal room where actions must be repeated over and over until they are thoroughly assimilated and perfected—until, that is, the actors have totally identified with the part assigned to them. *The liturgical action is a rehearsal of the utopian Kingdom first enacted upon the human stage in the meals that Jesus shared with outcasts and sinners.* In it we learn to understand the drama of God's justice as it unfolds in our world and to identify with the role assigned to us so that we may play it effectively in our lives and eventually before the throne of God for all eternity, when his justice will be established beyond all compromise.[61]

---

[59] Ibid., 28–29. Emphasis mine.

[60] Ibid., 29. Emphasis mine.

[61] Ibid., 32. Emphasis mine. Writing almost ten years after Searle, Edward Foley echoes the concept of liturgy as a "rehearsal" of justice. See Edward Foley, "Liturgy and *Economic Justice for All*," in *Living No Longer for Ourselves: Liturgy and Justice in the Nineties,* ed. Kathleen Hughes and Mark Francis (Collegeville, MN: Liturgical Press, 1991), 116–23. Foley writes: "This is what it means to call liturgy a 'rehearsal' of the Christian life. Rehearsal, in this sense,

In another place, Searle reiterates this by saying: "I want to suggest that the liturgy we have inherited is an actual rehearsal of the way of life foretold in the prophets and realized in Christ; not a talking about justice and peace, but a doing of justice and peace."[62] Once again, the key to Searle's thinking is that the outline of God's Kingdom can be found in the doing of liturgical celebration.

A simple illustration of rehearsing the "justice of God" involves the practicing of the attitude of charity which underlies all liturgical action. In a 1978 article titled "The Washing of the Feet," Searle traces the historical development of the foot-washing rite and connects it to the charitable custom in monasteries of providing hospitality to the poor and to the stranger, hospitality that often included washing the feet of travelers.[63] He suggests that this sense of care was naturally drawn into the liturgical gesture of symbolizing the Lord's act of washing his disciples' feet, thus providing "a vivid reminder of the relationship between liturgy and life, between ritual prayer and the life of charity."[64] Furthermore, he contends that the ritual washing of feet on Holy Thursday contains both a "word of revelation" and a "word of judgment":

> As a word of revelation it speaks to us, as Jesus' original action spoke to his disciples, of the unimaginable condescension of our God. As a word of judgment, it calls into question the clerical domination of the community and challenges the community itself to examine the quality of its own ministry to the world and to one another. Perhaps while retaining the Holy Thursday ritual, we would do well to associate it with other ways of fulfilling the Lord's command and showing effective care for the poor.[65]

---

is not simply a dramatic enactment of some long-finished historical event. Nor is it an imperfect repetition of some act in order to get it right. Rather, it is a continual reentry into and further appropriation of a rich and inexhaustible reality. Rehearsal so imagined is neither artificial nor preparatory; it is, rather, ritual engagement with the truth. . . . [O]ur entry into the Christian mysteries is a rehearsal of the call offered to us in faith as well as a foreshadowing of what our response is to be" (121).

[62] Searle, "Grant Us Peace . . . Do We Hear What We Are Saying?," 7. He concludes this thought be stating that liturgy "is a momentary realization of the peaceable kingdom of justice in a torn and savage world."

[63] See Mark Searle, "The Washing of the Feet," *Assembly* 4, no. 5 (1978): 14–15.

[64] Ibid., 15.

[65] Ibid., 16.

Thus, the foot-washing rite rehearses and enacts right relationships, in which is demonstrated the "effective care for the poor." In an editorial that appeared in *Assembly* two years later, Searle suggests that the gesture is not so much a social critique as it is an opportunity for contemplation in which the assembly is invited "to enter into it to discover there the 'divine disclosure' of the One who humbled himself for our sakes."[66]

Such rehearsal of right relationships is not limited to the annual celebration of Holy Thursday; rather it is a part of assembling for Eucharist in general. In transcending divisions and in overcoming social boundaries, the "justice of God" is made manifest, albeit a justice to be perfected in an age yet to come. Searle states succinctly: "We have not yet become what we already are: a new creation."[67] Furthermore, gathering as an assembly in Christ demands that the relationships established and renewed therein are translated into an overall way of life. Searle states:

> The liturgy is a rehearsal of the roles we are called to take upon ourselves throughout life. We are to become what we are. The liturgy puts us into the position we are called to adopt, and week by week rehearses us in our parts as members of the one Body. If we were already perfect, if we had our parts down pat, we would not need the rehearsal: the whole of life would be a celebration of Eucharist, a realization of our identity as the reconciled People of God. But rehearse we must, and each part of the liturgy is part of the vision of peace and a rehearsal of our roles as peacemakers.[68]

The entire celebration of the Eucharist "leads us to rejoice in our relationship with God, with one another and with the material creation."[69] Thus, the assembly practices the "delight" that marks right relationships, relationships as they exist in God's Just Kingdom.[70] Searle concludes: "The Eucharist is not merely a brief weekly prayer: it is rather

[66] Mark Searle, "Holy Thursday: Opening of the Paschal Feast," *Assembly* 6, no. 4 (1980): 88.

[67] Searle, "Grant Us Peace . . . Do We Hear What We Are Saying?," 8.

[68] Ibid.

[69] Ibid., 10.

[70] Ibid. Searle writes: "At the Eucharistic rehearsal for the Kingdom, we are taught not merely to observe the proprieties of justice, but to delight in our God and in the order he is establishing. The primary expression of this delight

a rehearsal of the mood in which a Christian is to live in the world under God, a pervasive attitude coloring the Christian life, both personal and communal."[71] The Eucharist thereby "sensitizes" the Christian community to a life of justice and to a rejection of all that is not of God's will.[72]

THE CHURCH AS BEARER OF A "UTOPIAN TASK"

In its enactment, the liturgy is nothing less than the realization of hope for the world. "The Christian attitude toward the world, then," writes Searle, "is not one of condescension, but one of witnessing to the hope of exaltation."[73] As demonstrated above in the example of the Holy Thursday footwashing, Searle believed that the liturgy is where the "values of the Kingdom" are not only proclaimed as something to strive for in hope but as something to be realized in the act of worship itself.[74] Ultimately, Searle recognized the recognition that such "sacramentality" is not simply a principle of worship but a way of life, for as he states in a 1977 piece on the Eucharist:

> The liturgy assumes these signs (drawn from experience of the world) and endows them with new meaning, but does not destroy their natural human significance. . . . What the reform of the liturgy ultimately points to . . . is the sacramentality of life itself. What it asks of us is a humble, prayerful, yes, even contemplative receptiveness to the all-pervasive and saving presence of God in the material creation and in the lives of men. In the last resort, it is a matter, as someone once said, of not letting the liturgy go to your head, but of really taking it to heart.[75]

---

is the great prayer of thanksgiving, the blessing of God for his creation, which God has wonderfully made and more wonderfully restored."

[71] Ibid.

[72] Ibid., 10–11.

[73] Searle, "Serving the Lord with Justice," 33.

[74] Ibid.

[75] Mark Searle, "Eucharist and Renewal through History," *Liturgy* 1 (1977): 19. See also Karl Rahner, "Secular Life and the Sacraments: The Mass and the World," *The Tablet* 225 (March 13, 1971): 267. The following quote from Rahner clearly sparked Searle's imagination and appears in his *Called to Participate*, page 78: "The world and its history is the terrible and sublime liturgy, breathing death and sacrifice, that God celebrates for himself and allows to be held throughout the free history of men, a history which he himself sustains through the sovereign disposition of his grace. Throughout the whole

Here Searle identifies several important attitudes of the Christian life: humility, prayerfulness, and contemplation. These attitudes are fundamental to those who seek the "justice of God" and strive to fulfill the purpose for which they were created. The rehearsal of Christian attitudes in the liturgy enacts the worldview of God's Kingdom, and as Searle once wrote: "in our liturgical renewal, we should be more concerned to re-think our basic attitudes towards the liturgy and its relationship to life-in-the-world than to re-vamp our services."[76]

A "revamped" Christian worldview assists in moving the world in the direction of God, thereby allowing the world to see its injustices for itself. Searle looks to the writing of Alexander Schmemann and to his notion that the world is returned to God through the Lord's ascending to the Father.[77] Schmemann writes:

> Christianity begins to fall down as soon as the idea of our going up in Christ's ascension—the movement of sacrifice—begins to be replaced by His going down. And this is exactly where we are today: it is always a bringing Him down into ordinary life, and this we say will solve our social problems. The Church must go down to the ghettos, into the world in all its reality. But to save the world from social injustices, the need first of all is not so much to go down to its miseries, as to have a few witnesses in this world to the possible ascension.[78]

Again, the link between worship and the world, for Searle, is that they both move in the direction of God; neither is about absolute perfection in this life but about final perfection in the life of God. This "Godward" movement prevents the Christian from having to make a dubious choice between the practice of social concern and the performance of liturgy, as both are directed to future life in God. As Searle states

---

length and breadth of this colossal history of birth and death, a history on the one hand full of superficiality, folly, inadequacy and hate—and all of these 'crucify'—a history, on the other hand, composed of silent submission and joy, heights and sudden falls: throughout all this there takes place the *liturgy of the world*." Emphasis original. See also Kevin W. Irwin, "A Sacramental World—Sacramentality as the Primary Language for Sacraments," *Worship* 76 (2002): 197–211.

[76] Searle, *Eight Talks on Liturgy*, 9.

[77] See Searle, "Serving the Lord with Justice," 33.

[78] Alexander Schmemann, "Sacrifice and Worship," *Parabola* 3 (Winter 1978): 65. See also Alexander Schmemann, *Sacraments and Orthodoxy* (New York: Herder and Herder, 1965), especially 32.

in his 1981 article "Attending (to) the Liturgy": "What the traditional words and gestures of the congregation do is not express our personal faith and feelings, but discipline and shape them in such a way that we are enabled to relate rightly to our God, our neighbors, our world and ourselves."[79]

All of this raises the question: how does the liturgy teach so as to "discipline" and "shape"? In his 1981 article titled "The Pedagogical Function of the Liturgy," Searle contends that liturgy is an educational tool that provides formation based on "socialization" rather than on "exhortation." He criticizes the traditional method of teaching when he writes:

> If education is conceived of in terms of the classroom transmission of information, then a dichotomy is immediately assumed between the teacher (who has knowledge) and the taught (who do not). Education is then conceived to be an exercise in transmitting those educational commodities which the teacher decides the learners need. Correspondingly, the liturgy will be seen as an opportunity for those who claim to understand the things of God to instruct those who do not and to tell them what they need to know. The primary focus will be on such opportunities as the liturgy provides for explicit teaching: introductions, Scripture readings, commentaries, sermons, exhortations. This focus may also be expanded to incorporate prayers and hymns, which can serve as supplementary resources for inculcating moral and doctrinal truths.[80]

However, if the primary teaching function of the liturgy is to form participants in their identity as one in the Body of Christ, it must be admitted that there exist many other means of socialization that compete for influence and adherence.[81] Searle's concern is that while the litur-

---

[79] Mark Searle, "Attending (to) the Liturgy," *New Catholic World* 224, no. 1324 (1981): 157.

[80] Searle, "The Pedagogical Function of the Liturgy," 333.

[81] Ibid. Searle writes: "For one thing, the Christian living in a pluralistic society belongs to a plurality of communities and is consequently subject to a plurality of competing socializations. We are far removed from the 'total community' of the medieval village, where the liturgy served to structure people's lives so much more pervasively than can ever be the case today and where, in turn, so many nonliturgical areas of life lent their support to the same 'world of meaning.' Today, by contrast, the weekly celebration of the liturgy represents for many an isolated oasis of contact with the ethos of the believing community."

gical reform of the Second Vatican Council "was undertaken precisely in order to communicate Christian values and to shape Christian attitudes more effectively," the liturgy has not succeeded in socializing a people who turns to the liturgy as a source of identity; instead, participants are often "manipulated" by "authorities" (the ones with knowledge to impart and thus the keepers of power).[82] For the liturgy to be understood and experienced as the "rehearsal of Christian attitudes," it must be a source of freedom rather than a means of manipulation.

However, in surfacing the "pedagogical function of the liturgy," Searle argues that the liturgy has mistakenly been viewed for centuries as the vehicle through which the Church passes on a "monopoly of truth" to those in need of socialization.[83] In describing the way in which the liturgy served to maintain this monopoly, Searle writes:

> On the one hand, its obligatory character, together with its being identified as the exclusive source of contact with the other-worldly which was "really real," served to ensure the legitimation of the status quo, the "unchanging" dominance of the elite who ruled, taught, and sanctified—and a denial of the relevance or authentic religious values of the secular experiences of the many. On the other hand, when—as always happens—the individual failed to measure up to the expectations determined by the hierarchical Church (for example, by sin, doubts of faith, or simply by suggesting that religious observance was not very satisfying) then the only recourse such persons might have to resolve their anxiety or frustration was to return to the sacraments—thereby further interiorizing the system.[84]

[82] Ibid., 334. Searle asks: "Is the liturgy really neutral? Is it in fact manipulative? More specifically, is the claim that the liturgical reforms have given the liturgy back to the people an accurate reflection of the current state of affairs, or is it simply an example of the way new rhetoric can camouflage old attitudes?"

[83] Ibid., 342–43. See also Mark Searle, "Notes on an Educational Policy" in MSP, F28. Searle writes of the Church's self-understanding: "The supposition was that revelation was something confided to the (hierarchical) Church who thereby had a monopoly of 'truth' which it was her duty to 'teach' and 'pass on' by instruction and authoritative definition. . . . This whole system rested upon the concept of 'sacred truths' and 'sacred mysteries'—or 'grace'—standing over against the experience of life in the 'world'" (2–3).

[84] Searle, "The Pedagogical Function of the Liturgy," 343.

Moreover, the resolution of such an experience of alienation on the part of the faithful "will be overcome not by more aggressive instruction and discipline of Christian people, but by giving the faithful back their voice, in the sense of recognizing their life experience as an authentic source of Christian reflection on the world."[85] In others words, as stated throughout this chapter, there can be no separation of liturgy from life; the liturgy informs life experience, and life experience informs the liturgy.[86]

Certainly, Searle is realistic and honest about the ways in which the liturgy can become an "ideological tool," particularly when it withdraws from society and thereby "sacralizes" salvation and "privatizes" sin.[87] However, it is also his belief that liturgy can become "critical" and can serve as a critique of political, economic, and social structures that are not emblematic of the "justice of God" (namely when people and creation are prevented from becoming who or what God created them to be). Searle writes:

> In short, Christianity is faithfully understood as "utopian praxis" insofar as it is about the Kingdom of God being "at hand" and thereby calls all other kingdoms ("reality constructs") into question. However, history shows that Christianity is always in danger of being subverted by other views of what is real which claim to be "natural," thereby masking their cultural relativity which the Gospel message and evangelical liturgy should proclaim. The result is that liturgical celebrations

[85] Ibid., 344.

[86] Ibid., 345. Searle writes: "Consequently, revelation and salvation are available to all in their experience of life, if only they can recognize it and respond to it. . . . From this premise, three consequences follow. First, it means that a person's own experience of life in the world is a valid Christian experience and that the 'true' and the 'really real' are not to be located elsewhere as the monopoly of the few. Second, theologizing, or the articulation of faith-experience, is not the occupation of professionals alone and is not restricted to the manipulation of certain imposed patterns of thought and speech. Third, the sacramentality of grace is no longer confined to specific acts confided to the jurisdiction of one class, but escapes the narrow confines of liturgical celebration to permeate all Christian life. In short, all Christians share the functions of Christ as prophets, priests, and rulers, so that these can no longer be conceived as functions simply exercised by some (who have) in favor of others (who have not)."

[87] Ibid., 342–43.

provide a forum for "naïve socialization" into these cultures and not into the Christian community with its own vision and task.[88]

Therefore, Searle believes that the liturgy provides a critique only when it is willing to dialogue with life experience; in other words, his liturgical pedagogy is one that promotes reflection and critique, inward not simply outward. Simply put, he suggests that if the liturgy is to reveal God's Just Kingdom then it must be a product of critical reflection on all the social dimensions of relationships—with God, with others, and with all creation.

Liturgy may never be understood, therefore, as a means of escape from the realities of the world in which we live. Rather, participation in liturgical prayer demands the realization that its ritual expressions and spoken words are about "the fundamental and universal human themes which enter into every human life."[89] Searle maintains:

> If the God whom we worship is the God who fathers and pervades all human life; if the Christ in whom we worship is the one who sums up in himself all humanity, redeeming all human experience; then the liturgy we celebrate is not off in a world of its own. *Liturgy, like*

---

[88] Ibid., 357. Here, Searle uses the phrase "utopian praxis." The phrase "utopian task," which appears in the heading of this section, is found in on page 354 of this article. Searle borrows the term "utopian" from Paulo Freire, *Cultural Action for Freedom*, Monograph Series 1 (Cambridge, MA: Harvard Educational Review, 1970), 20. See also Searle, "The Church Celebrates Her Faith," 11. Here he writes of the "revival of political liturgy": "We suffer, too, from an excessively individualistic and spiritualistic approach to life. This means that the Gospel and the liturgy have been interpreted in terms of how I am to save my soul, instead of in terms of what God is doing for the world as such. It is interesting that until the high middle ages Christian eyes were fixed on the second coming and the general or universal judgment, even though it was generally realized after the first few years that His return was not necessarily going to be soon. After the high middle ages, however, all our attention has been fixed on the death of the individual and his personal judgment. For us to restore the balance we must recover a faith which relates to what God is actually doing in and for the world. We will then need a kind of celebration which is the celebration of God speaking to us and active among us here and now, today, this week, this year, in what is happening to us. We may see the revival of political liturgy!"

[89] See Mark Searle, "On the Art of Lifting Up the Heart: Liturgical Prayer Today," *Studies in Formative Spirituality* 3 (1982): 406–7.

contemplative life, is not a withdrawal into some other world, but an encoun-
ter in depth with the world in which we live. To join in the celebration of
the liturgy is to acknowledge that we belong to the world that God
is redeeming, that we share the common human condition and that
the whole of humanity is the object of his reconciling and redeeming
love.[90]

As suggested earlier, primary among the Christian attitudes revealed
and rehearsed in the liturgy is a basic hope in humanity and in the
world in general.[91] Liturgy confronts us with the reality of who we are
and who God intends us to be—namely, a people "who have learned
to recognize the disparity between the values of the Kingdom and the
values by which our world is organized, and who have learned to surrender to the former and break with the latter."[92]

CONCLUSION

This chapter has explored Searle's desire to connect liturgy to life
through his notion that liturgy reveals the "justice of God." More than
a platform for an agenda of justice, the Christian liturgy is the stage on
which the attitudes of just relationships are practiced and perfected.
Searle's view of liturgy as a privileged encounter with the "justice
of God" serves to provide support for his contention that the liturgy
simultaneously forms the celebrating community in the attitudes of
Christ; this is its pedagogical function. The liturgy thereby serves not
only to critique the values of the world order but seeks to critique itself
as a means of leading Christians to greater freedom by forming participants in "Kingdom" behaviors and skills. Searle believed wholeheart-

[90] Ibid., 406. Emphasis mine.

[91] Ibid., 407. Searle writes: "Liturgy, then, invites us to a new perspective
on human life and draws us to adopt certain attitudes toward life." To "adopt
certain attitudes toward life," however, requires that one is engaged in the
world and seeks to understand it. Searle continues: "Paradoxically, then, what
the liturgy requires is precisely knowledge of life and of the world, the ability
to transcend our individual fortune and misfortune and to identify ourselves
with the whole human race with whom and for whom we articulate the deep
longings, struggles, dreads and joys of human existence in prayers of thanksgiving and entreaty. . . . The liturgy celebrates faith as a way of being in the
world, as the surrender to the God of life who alone is capable of redeeming
our lives."

[92] Searle, "Serving the Lord with Justice," 33.

edly that the rehearsal of Christ's worldview would reveal God's will, allowing us to "be in a position to take up our vocation to be priests and prophets and peacemakers in the society in which God has placed us."[93] Such a rehearsal depends on a willingness to discern the "justice of God" as it exists in the "new order" God has redeemed in Christ. We now turn to the rhythm and structure of the Eucharist understood as the chief "rehearsal room" for the Church's "utopian task." Here we will come to comprehend precisely why Searle was fond of saying that Christianity "is more caught than taught, and the model for learning is closer to that of an apprenticeship than that of a classroom."[94]

[93] Searle, "Grant Us Peace . . . Do We Hear What We Are Saying?," 12.
[94] Searle, "Infant Baptism Reconsidered," 49.

Chapter 3

The Rehearsal of Gathering

What does it mean to gather together as the Body of Christ? This question seems so very straightforward, and yet providing an answer is quite a difficult task indeed. *Sacrosanctum Concilium* 7 offers the following definition of the liturgy as the action of the mystical body of Christ, both "the Head and his members":

> The liturgy, then, is rightly seen as an exercise of the priestly office of Jesus Christ. In the liturgy the sanctification of women and men is given expression in symbols perceptible by the senses and is carried out in ways appropriate to each of them. In it, complete and definitive public worship is performed by the mystical body of Jesus Christ, that is, by the Head and his members.
>
> From this it follows that every liturgical celebration, because it is an action of Christ the priest and of his body, which is the church, is a preeminently sacred action. No other action of the church equals its effectiveness by the same title nor to the same degree.[1]

A theological understanding of the liturgy as the work of the mystical Body, the Church gathered into the *totus Christus*, was still considered revolutionary at the time of the Second Vatican Council. For it was, in fact, the work of the German Benedictine, Odo Casel (1886–1948) half a century earlier, whose 1932 *Das christliche Kultmysterium* (*The Mystery of Christian Worship*) would plant these seeds of a "mystery theology" that would not truly germinate until their use by Pius XII in his encyclicals *Mystici Corporis* (1945) and *Mediator Dei* (1947) and subsequently blossom in the text of the Constitution on the Sacred Liturgy (December 4, 1963).[2]

The essential key to Casel's "mystery theology" as well as to the understanding of the liturgy as the action of the mystical Body of Christ is rooted in a proper theological conception of grace: grace is

---

[1] *Sacrosanctum Concilium* 7 in Flannery, *The Basic Sixteen Documents*.

[2] See Aidan Kavanagh, "Introduction," in Odo Casel, *The Mystery of Christian Worship* (New York: Herder & Herder, 1962), vi–xii.

not *given* in the sacraments of the Church, rather, grace is a matter of being *conformed* to Christ's Body. Thus, grace is not compiled or accumulated as one might stockpile reserves in a bank account; grace is gradually *discovered* as one is introduced to Christ and comes to recognize his presence in relationship. A theology based on the mystical Body of Christ rests upon the axiom of Pope St. Leo the Great, namely, "what was visible in Christ has passed over into the sacraments of the Church."[3] Aidan Kavanagh offers the following summation of this theological perspective on liturgical celebration:

> Christ is present not just as the object of our pious memory but present in his saving acts—he dies not again but *still*, rises not again but *still*— in us, by us, and through us for the life of the world. Christ does not pass out graces to those who follow him if they behave themselves. *He gathers them lovingly into himself* as he conquers from the Cross and rises from the grave, in the liturgy as in the Church. This is the Mystery the liturgy celebrates, the Mystery the Church cherishes as its source and center.[4]

If the mystery that is at the center of our contemplation is that of Christ *gathering* the Church into himself, then the manner by which the liturgical assembly gathers and forms the worshiping Body of Christ has sacramental value. This action bears the weight of revealing Christ's desire to bring his own together in himself. Furthermore, each new gathering, with the unique experiences and dispositions of all its members, demonstrates that Christ's offering takes place in us, that "we may complete in ourselves for the Church's sake what is lacking in the sufferings of Christ."[5] As the eminent ecclesiologist Yves Congar

---

[3] Leo I, *Tractatus* 74:2, CSC, *Series latina*, vol. 138A, 457. See also Mark Searle, "Liturgy: Function and Goal in Christianity," in *Spirituality and Prayer: Jewish and Christian Understanding*, ed. L. Klenicki and G. Huck (New York: Paulist Press, 1983), 94. Here Searle interprets this axiom of St. Leo as follows: "Jesus did not simply announce the Word of God, in all he was and did, he *was* the Word of God. Similarly, the Church does not simply celebrate the sacraments, but is itself in a prior sense a sacrament of God's activity in the world."

[4] Kavanagh, "Introduction," xi. Emphasis mine.

[5] This phrase is based on Colossians 1:24 and is found as the concluding sentiment of the Prayer after Communion for September 15—Our Lady of Sorrows. See also John Paul II, *Salvifici Doloris* (February 11, 1984), http://www.vatican.va/holy_father/john_paul_ii/apost_letters/1984/documents/hf_jp-ii_apl_11021984_salvifici-doloris_en.html. The Pope writes, "In the Paschal

succinctly states, "The church fulfills in the body what had already been offered by the head."[6]

For his own part, Mark Searle desired to translate the theology of the Mystical Body into a question of community and thus communion. He would describe the Mass itself as a "series of graduated steps" into communion with Christ which culminates in the gathered community's pledge of our inseparability from Christ and one another. Searle writes:

> The terms *corpus Christi* and *communio* were originally used as much of the Church as of the Eucharist: indeed, in both instances, the reference to Church is prior—a fact which only serves to underline the ecclesial dimension of Eucharist and the Eucharistic identity of Church. Thus Eucharistic communion is essentially rooted in an existential communion of life which allows of, indeed necessitates, other forms and degrees of communion. What is interesting, perhaps, is that some of these forms and degrees of communion are themselves represented in the liturgy of the Mass and this in such a way that the unfolding of the rite gradually draws us into deeper and deeper unity until we 'find ourselves at one' in the breaking of the bread.[7]

Mystery Christ began *the union with man in the community of the Church*. The mystery of the Church is expressed in this: that already in the act of Baptism, which brings about a configuration with Christ, and then through his Sacrifice—sacramentally through the Eucharist—the Church is continually being built up spiritually as the Body of Christ. . . . The sufferings of Christ created the good of the world's redemption. This good in itself is inexhaustible and infinite. No man can add anything to it. But at the same time, in the mystery of the Church as his Body, Christ has in a sense opened his own redemptive suffering to all human suffering. In so far as man becomes a sharer in Christ's sufferings—in any part of the world and at any time in history—to that extent *he in his own way completes* the suffering through which Christ accomplished the Redemption of the world."

[6] Yves Congar, "The Structure of Christian Priesthood," in Paul Philibert, trans. and ed., *At the Heart of Christian Worship: Liturgical Essays of Yves Congar* (Collegeville, MN: Liturgical Press, 2010), 105. Congar continues: "She brings Christ to fullness within her, all the while receiving from him the very grace by which she adds her own contribution to this fullness. This is how the body experiences the maturation and the growth of the One who, after having achieved everything and contained everything fully in himself, now desires that we should do the same *with him*."

[7] Mark Searle, "Rites of Communion," *Assembly* 7, no. 4 (1981): 126.

Note Searle's choice of words in the final sentence above. He does not say that we *build* "deeper and deeper unity" but rather that we *find ourselves as one*. Thus the celebration of the Eucharist entails the discovery of our identity in Christ; it is about realizing who we truly are at the deepest core of our beings—knit together in Christ's Body.[8] Therefore, within the ritual of the Mass, the Gathering Rite takes on special significance as an exercise in being formed as the Body of Christ. The specifics of *how* we begin this task of discovering anew our oneness in Christ may be summed up fundamentally as the rehearsal of the attitude of surrender, surrender to myself and my preoccupations in order to experience "an existential communion of life" which is nothing less than life in Christ.

Therefore, the physical, historical assembly that is called by God and led by the Spirit to form the Body of Christ has sacramental value far beyond the visible manifestation of a mere collection of individuals; it signals forth the recognition that our very way of life in God is a communion. In other words, the act of assembling demonstrates an active response, a fundamental willingness, to be guided by the will of God. In his 1983 article "Liturgy: Function and Goal in Christianity," Searle describes the symbolic nature of the assembly in these terms:

> We are called and saved, not as individuals, but as a people. God's salvation is for the human race as a whole, not just as an accumulation of individuals, and the Church understands herself as a first sign of a new beginning of human life lived under the rule of God. The Church, strictly speaking, becomes Church when the faithful assemble in *ecclesia* (congregation), and her liturgy is not the action of some individuals on behalf of others so much as a celebration of the whole body. *In the weekly assembly, the Christian becomes aware of his place in the scheme of things, as part of something larger that God is working in history and in this place and time.*[9]

[8] See Ephesians 4:16. "If we live by the truth and in love, we shall grow completely into Christ, who is the head by whom the whole Body is fitted and joined together, every joint adding its own strength, for each individual part to work according to its function."

[9] Searle, "Liturgy: Function and Goal in Christianity," 100. Emphasis mine. Searle continues by manifesting the rehearsal-nature of the assembly: "The practice of common prayer, addressing God as 'Our Father,' the performance of common gestures, the asking of forgiveness from one another, the exchange of the kiss of peace and, above all, the sharing of the one bread and the one cup at the weekly Eucharist are meant to shape our Christian consciousness

Elsewhere, Searle states the objective of the assembly as that of being drawn out of "preoccupation with ourselves and feelings," which from the Christian perspective "appear trivial, if not positively narcissistic."[10] Thus, the assembly itself becomes an act itself—the act of re-membering Christ, meaning more than a cognitive recollection, but a reordering all relationships in him.[11] The act of gathering entails immersing oneself so fully in the Body that one can simply not remain the same; assembling means that relationships are forged, renewed, and restored. Searle writes:

> The Christian liturgy is what the Christian assembly does when it gathers: it remembers Christ. This remembering or anamnesis is no mere imaginative recall, however. To remember Christ is to identify with Christ in his submission to God, to identify with his sacrifice and self-surrender in order to become, like Christ, the objects of God's saving remembrance. . . . The assembly, remembering Christ in a profound act of recollection, discovers its own mystery, its identity as the Body of Christ in the world, continuing his surrender to God and to the work of God, until the end of time, ("ready to greet him when he comes again"). The liturgy itself is essentially an act of remembering into the future, in which we submit ourselves again and again to the plan of God for human history and commit ourselves to its realization.[12]

---

about the quality and meaning of our relationships with one another and our fellow human beings." Such shaping of the Christian consciousness revolves around the deep discovery that the Christian life is no solitary endeavor.

[10] See Mark Searle, "Assembly: Remembering the People of God," *Pastoral Music* 7, no. 6 (1983): 16.

[11] See Megan McKenna, *Rites of Justice: The Sacraments and Liturgy as Ethical Imperatives* (Maryknoll, NY: Orbis Books, 1997), 4. McKenna writes: "To remember does not mean merely to bring to mind; it means 'to remember,' to put back together again, to make present again."

[12] Searle, "Assembly: Remembering the People of God," 17–18. Shortly thereafter Searle writes: "We come to the liturgy, not so much to express ourselves as to find ourselves; not to vocalize the faith we already feel, but to be drawn into the faith and fidelity of Christ himself; not to create a sense of community, but to discover the unimaginable mystery of our common life in Christ and in his Spirit; not to be instructed by songs and sermons, but to open ourselves to the instruction of the Spirit."

Therefore, the formation of the Christian assembly for prayer is an act of "profound recollection"[13] because it involves, not the simple work of remembering my accomplishments, my faults, and my failings—the ways in which I have personally excelled in Christian virtue and the times that I have fallen short—but rather the far more difficult task of seeing Christ present in our midst, seeking to reknit his broken Body into one. Such attentiveness, such "profound recollection," comes neither naturally nor easily, and it is for this reason that the Church's liturgy devotes a significant amount of time and energy on gathering, before it asks the assembly to lift up its heart to God in the Opening Prayer.[14] We first discover who it is we are before who we can profess to be.[15] We turn now to the ritual components that comprise the rite of gathering.

AN ATTITUDE OF SACREDNESS

One of the first elements of ritual "language" that forms the assembly as its members prepare for worship is the unspoken language of the church building itself. While it is undeniably true that opinion will vary greatly with regard to the style of construction and to the genre

---

[13] Ibid., 18.

[14] See Alexander Schmemann, *For the Life of the World* (Crestwood, NY: St. Vladimir's Seminary Press, 1998), 26–27. Schmemann describes the action of gathering as that of a "journey or procession." He writes: "The Liturgy of the Eucharist is best understood as a journey or procession. It is the journey of the Church into the dimensions of the Kingdom. . . . The journey begins when Christians leave their homes and beds. They leave, indeed, their life in this present and concrete world, and whether they have to drive fifteen miles or walk a few blocks, a sacramental act is already taking place. . . . For they are now on their way to *constitute the Church*, or to be more exact, to be transformed into the Church of God. They have been individuals, some white, some black, some poor, some rich . . . and now they have been called to 'come together in one place,' to bring their lives, their very 'world' with them and to be more than what they were: a *new* community with a new life."

[15] See Mark Searle, "The Shape of the Future: A Liturgist's Vision," in *Sunday Morning: A Time for Worship*, ed. Mark Searle (Collegeville, MN: Liturgical Press, 1982), 141. Searle states: "The importance of the Sunday assembly is not that it can, of itself, create community, but that it continually reminds us of who we are and invites us to reaffirm our commitment. A sense of community is one of those things which will be given those who seek first the kingdom of God. The Church is not something that exists for its own sake: it is a by-product of life in the kingdom of God."

of liturgical art, the foundational concern must be for what truly facilitates individual worshipers to become, and to show reverence for, the corporate Body of Christ. Before ever a word is uttered in the liturgy, the building in which we gather has already spoken to us. Does the given house for worship project an attitude of sacrifice, or does it merely provide reassurance and comfort? In 1983, Searle provided the following reflection:

> What is not always fully recognized, however—either by those involved in church building and renovation or by those who object to spending for such ventures—is the degree to which a community is shaped by the building it occupies. . . . No church building is ecclesiologically innocent: it expresses—and forever thereafter impresses—a sense of what it means to belong to the church, the respective roles of different ministries, the wealth or poverty of the Christian imagination, the sense of where Christ is to be found and so on. It is more than a sermon in stone: it is a multimedia communication of a version of the Christian Gospel, communicated in the shape of the building, its interior arrangements, its decoration and appointments, the kind of interaction it fosters or prohibits among the worshippers. Everything speaks, everything tells us who we are (for better or worse) and what our place is.[16]

No matter the design of the physical building, the fundamental outlook of reverence for the "sacred" allows worshipers to interact gracefully with the environment, be it a contemporary post–Vatican

---

[16] Mark Searle, "Church Building," *Assembly* 10, no. 2 (1983): 225. See also Mark Searle, "Foreword," in Regina Kuhn, *A Place for Baptism* (Chicago: Liturgy Training Publications, 1992), iv. Searle writes: "The building was a *sign*. Often enough it was, admittedly, a sign of ethnic pride, of Catholic chauvinism, or of simple affluence. But, for all its ambivalence, it was also a monument to the people's faith in the reality of the other world and, by that very fact, a sacrament or outward sign of God's presence among and concern for the local population." See also Gerard Lukken and Mark Searle, *Semiotics and Church Architecture* (Kampen, The Netherlands: Kok Pharos Publishing House, 1993). This is a technical application of the science of Semiotics for interpreting the meaning of a particular church building, and in the final sentence of the book, Searle concludes: "Semiotic analysis of church architecture will serve, it is hoped, to raise the level of awareness among both architects and church people of how buildings have a voice of their own and may 'speak' in ways not foreseen or intended by those who planned and erected them" (130).

ll structure or a lavish Gothic cathedral. This is precisely because "reverence" for Christians must mean the search for the "wholeness" in God's good creation. Entering into this search is the task of the assembly, as its members take account of where they are and with whom they are gathered. Searle writes:

> If Christianity is what Christianity claims to be—a religion of incarnation and a religion of redemption—then the house of the church must be a place of wholeness, of reconciliation with God, with our fellows, with the natural world. It must be a place where all these things come together again, a sacred place. . . . For Christians . . . sacredness is not a quality inherent in places or things. Rather it is a quality associated with the way we experience them. Sacredness is a way of doing things, a way of relating. . . . This attitude towards life and towards the world in which we live *should* characterize the whole Christian life. . . . In short, a house for the church must be the kind of place that dreams are made on, a place where vision is fostered, a place where the Spirit's presence might be felt, renewing the face of the earth.[17]

Thus, Searle articulates here a fundamental attitude, or worldview, that is communicated in any physical space designed to shelter the assembly and to fashion them into the gathered Body of Christ: "sacredness." "Sacredness" is not as subjective as one might first suspect, meaning it does not correspond to the idea that "beauty is in the eye of the beholder." *"Sacredness is a way of doing things, a way of relating."*[18] This way of relating is determined by life in God's Just Kingdom, where all relationships are in harmony, where domination is quelled by true communion. When entering the Church building, this search for the discovery of "sacredness" is a liturgical duty that is to be performed by each and every member of Christ's Body.

Before continuing with the ritual elements of our liturgical prayer, it might be helpful to examine the important role of warm-up exercises in team sports, or the tuning of instruments before a band concert. In order for the team to play as a whole, in order for the tunes of each individual instrument to coalesce as a sound that can be distinguished as music, a time of preparation is necessary. This time, both mentally and bodily, allows individuals to be attentive to the others participating in the performance. It moves a person into a bigger world; one

---

[17] Mark Searle, "Sacred Places," *Assembly* 10, no. 2 (1983): 228.
[18] Ibid. Emphasis mine.

71

literally can now be defined by the whole. In an editorial on "The Introductory Rites," Searle draws precisely such a comparison:

> There is a popular children's book about a symphony orchestra. It begins with some hundred people, scattered throughout the city, rising from their afternoon naps, going through their various ablutions, getting themselves dressed, setting out for the orchestra hall on various modes of transportation, arriving in their locker rooms, taking their places, tuning their instruments . . . and it concludes with the first, glorious, totally harmonized opening chord of the symphony. Perhaps it is not too far-fetched to think of gathering for the Eucharist in these terms, the introductory rites being everything that precedes and enables us to total and harmonized prayer.[19]

As important a role as preparation has in any performance, whether individual or corporate, there is no denying that preparation is generally treated as secondary to the actual performance, whether that be a sporting event, a musical concert, or a time of liturgical prayer. Consequently, the Introductory Rite can be mistakenly understood as an add-on to the more indispensible material of the Mass. As Ralph Keifer writes: "The entrance rite is not treated as though it were a part of the mass significant in itself but only as a modest prelude to the more important twofold liturgy of word and eucharist."[20] As Keifer subsequently argues, the Gathering Rite is much more than a dispensable add-on to the celebration of the Eucharist, one that merely sets the stage for what is to follow. Rather, this time of corporate action is a necessary step in establishing an identity as the Body of Christ. If this period of "warming up" is not attended to with great care, it will not successfully draw the assembly into the attitudes of the liturgy; we will exist as individuals at prayer—like instruments that may be sounding the notes of the written score but unaware of the music produced by the orchestra as a whole—rather than as fully united in the prayer of Christ.

Thus, the General Instruction of the Roman Missal (hereafter GIRM) states: "The rites that precede the Liturgy of the Word, namely, the Entrance, the Greeting, the Penitential Act, the *Kyrie*, the *Gloria in excelsis* (*Glory to God in the highest*) and Collect, have the character of

---

[19] Mark Searle, "The Introductory Rites," *Assembly* 11, no. 1 (1984): 257.
[20] Ralph A. Keifer, "Our Cluttered Vestibule: The Unreformed Entrance Rite," *Worship* 48 (1974): 271.

a beginning, an introduction, and a preparation."[21] However, the instruction that follows is even more helpful in defining the importance of such a beginning: "The purpose is to ensure that the faithful, who come together as one, *establish communion and dispose themselves properly to listen to the Word of God and to celebrate the Eucharist worthily*."[22] In his 1981 *Assembly* piece "Rites of Communion," Searle simply states that "assembling is the first step in the making present of the body of Christ."[23] In addition to taking account of our surroundings, as members of the assembly take their places and make the deliberate search for "sacredness" by the commitment to reestablish relationships as intended by God, the entrance song plays a particularly valuable role in forming the assembly. The GIRM suggests that the entrance song (actually called the "Entrance Chant" in the GIRM) has three major purposes: it is to foster unity, it is to lead the assembly into the mystery of the celebration, and it is for the practical purpose of accompanying the procession of ministers.[24] Unfortunately, many in the assembly interpret the inclusion of an entrance hymn as a disposable and unnecessary component of the liturgy, meaning that they see this piece of ritual just as "filler." As a result, the decision to fully participate becomes an option for many worshipers from the very opening moment of the liturgy. If worshipers believe that this segment is unnecessary, then why take part in it?

The purpose and nature of ritual music was a very important component of liturgical renewal for Searle. While acknowledging that liturgy has both canonical (prescribed) and indexical (flexible) elements, he believed that music was an area that had become too unpredictable for the assembly and therefore had become a hindrance to corporate formation. In a 1985 article titled "Ritual and Music: A Theory of Liturgy and Implications for Music," which appeared in *Assembly* and was later reprinted in both *Church* and *Pastoral Music*, Searle writes:

---

[21] GIRM 46, in *The Roman Missal, Third Edition*, United States Conference of Catholic Bishops (Collegeville, MN: Liturgical Press, 2011).

[22] Ibid. Emphasis mine.

[23] Searle, "Rites of Communion," 126.

[24] GIRM 47. "When the people are gathered, and as the Priest enters with the Deacon and ministers, the Entrance Chant begins. Its purpose is to open the celebration, foster the unity of those who have been gathered, introduce their thoughts to the mystery of the liturgical time or festivity, and accompany the procession of the Priest and ministers."

If we have 500 hymns, all equally usable, none having any special claim to function in the rite, then it is hard to see how the selection of any piece rather than another makes much difference. The result is trivialization. On the other hand, if the set pieces of the Mass are chanted or sung, that can actually serve as a safeguard against their trivialization. . . . I realize this goes somewhat against the grain for those who have a vested interest in greater, not less, variety; but I would suggest that the failure to recognize the importance of the fixed elements of the rite will only lead to the trivialization of the role of music in the rite. It's my taste against everyone else's: There is no "music of the Church" properly so called. So, since it is a matter for each individual's taste, it cannot make any claim to loyalty or love. Furthermore, music seen to be matter of personal taste in fact divides the Church. Is this acceptable? Can we tolerate the Body of Christ being divided into those who like folk and those who like hymns and those who like polyphony?[25]

Searle's critique that liturgical music is often too flexible and unpredictable, and therefore, incapable of becoming a canonical dimension of the ritual, is perhaps even more important today than it was just twenty years after the close of the Second Vatican Council. Searle continues in this article to argue that liturgical singing would be improved if the assembly knew the music by heart.[26] The question for consideration must be one of ownership: is corporate song, particularly the entrance hymn that serves the goal of surfacing the presence of Christ in the assembly from the opening moments of the liturgy, something that flows from the heart of the assembly or is it something imposed upon it? Does the music selected for the entrance hymn allow the assembly to best rehearse the role of revealing (or sacramentalizing) the oneness of Christ? In terms of the rehearsal of attitudes, does liturgical music foster sacredness?[27]

[25] Searle, "Ritual and Music: A Theory of Liturgy and Implications for Music," 317.

[26] Ibid. He writes: "From time to time my family and I attend the liturgy of a small Melkite community in South Bend. The whole liturgy is in English and it is sung from beginning to end: only the sermon is spoken. Yet there are rarely more than 25 people in attendance, and there is no organ, no cantor, no choir, no guitar group. The point is: the liturgy is almost invariable, so that people know it by heart. Why can't we do the same?"

[27] See Mitzi J. Budde, "The Church's Song as Response to the Divine Mystery," *Worship* 86 (2012): 199. Budde writes: "Music unites the words of

Thomas Day, in his study *Why Catholics Can't Sing: The Culture of Catholicism and the Triumph of Bad Taste*, offers this simple piece of advice: "Good congregational singing begins with a sense of beloved familiarity."[28] Applied to the entrance hymn, a "sense of beloved familiarity" suggests that music would be more about forming the assembly in unity than it would be about providing a glimpse into a particular "theme" from the liturgy. The question that surfaces is, once again, to what degree are members of the assembly able to take ownership of the music that is sung, thereby making it their own? The assembly needs to be trained in the art of ritual music and must understand the art of surrender that is behind the act of corporate song.[29] Searle writes:

> Why are we putting so much time, energy and money intro producing new music instead of in training people in liturgical prayer? The question, then, is not "How can we get the people to learn new and different music, or even how to sing better, but how do we sing in such a way that "the eternal hymn which is sung throughout all ages in the halls of heaven" and which Christ introduced to earth, is heard in our assemblies? *How do we sing in such a way that it is not we who sing, but Christ who sings in us?*[30]

The attitude of "surrender," by which I put my voice at the disposal of the assembly, calls for the contemplative sense of hearing much more

---

worship with the desire for God within our hearts. It expresses the mystery of faith and the faith of the generations. Ideally, the hymns should resonate throughout the coming week, to call the people into remembrance of prayer and to empower them for life in the world until they are back in the worshiping community."

[28] Thomas Day, *Why Catholics Can't Sing: The Culture of Catholicism and the Triumph of Bad Taste* (New York: Crossroad Publishing Company, 1990), 170.

[29] Ibid., 172. Day suggests that the reform of liturgical music depends on an attitude of humility on the part of the congregation. He concludes his work with the following statements: "It may also be impossible for musical 'good advice' to get past the front door of thousands of Catholic churches and chapels where the message of liturgy goes something like this: 'I am here, God, and I am great. I have loved myself with an everlasting love. And all of us here are one big I, formed by rapport into a gathered community which offers itself to you. Now let us all share the whole-wheat bread.'"

[30] Searle, "Ritual and Music: A Theory of Liturgy and Implications for Music," 317. Emphasis mine.

than a collection of individuals singing, of singing something greater than music that comes from my design alone. Just as the time of warm up prior to an athletic competition strives to remind and inform individual athletes that they play as a team (the objective of warming up is shattered if it is interpreted as a time for showing off one's own prowess), so too is the entrance hymn meant to de-center myself from myself so that I can discover the communion that is gradually unfolding.[31]

The singing of the entrance hymn accompanies the procession of the presider and other ministers to the sanctuary, from where the very first ritual gestures are enacted for the assembly on behalf of the priest and the deacon, namely, a bow and the kissing of the altar, as well as the ritual gesture of incensing the altar. These are important signs of sacredness and reverence that serve to hone our attention to the symbolic presence of Christ in his gathered assembly (the altar) and also indicate the arrival of "the people"[32] summoned by God. Dominic Serra suggests that the actions of bowing, kissing, and incensing comprise "one act of veneration in three modes of expression."[33] Furthermore, Serra argues that the proper execution of these gestures is paramount: "When executed in close succession, these rites—powerfully drawing attention to the altar—will not appear to be disjointed,

---

[31] Although what has been stated here about liturgical singing suggests that *every* member of the assembly has a responsibility to "join in," Searle willingly admitted that the attitude of "surrender" is something learned not forced. See Searle, *Called to Participate*, 19–20. Here he acknowledges that every liturgical celebration will contain various levels, or degrees, of involvement: "Unlike a movie or theater audience, however, even the most passive assembly is not entirely passive. They will be engaged in some sort of performance, even if it is sometimes not strictly of a piece with the main performance or consistently in step with it. I have observed, for example, that those seated in the front pews of a church invariably join in the singing and in everything else. Those in the middle may or may not join in the singing, but they are likely to join in the responses and to stand up and sit down at appropriate times. Those in the back pews, however, are much more likely to read the bulletin than they are to join in the singing and the responses, but they will invariably stand up and sit down when it is appropriate to do so. *Liturgy clearly allows for different degrees and levels of involvement, but (and because) it remains the action of the whole assembly.*" Emphasis mine.

[32] See OM. No. 1 states "When *the people* are gathered . . ." Emphasis mine.

[33] Dominic E. Serra, "The Introductory Rites: Theology of the Latin Text and Rite," in *A Commentary on the Order of Mass of* The Roman Missal, ed. Edward Foley, et al. (Collegeville, MN: Liturgical Press, 2011), 127.

separate actions but rather three expressions by which Christ is greeted."[34]

Is the meaning of a tripartite veneration apparent to the assembly? The answer is most likely "no." In the first place, incense is rarely used at the opening of the liturgy (if at all) to indicate that Christ is with us and that we are in Christ. Applying the empirical data from the Notre Dame Study of Catholic Parish Life (1983–85) to the Introductory Rites, Searle believes that these opening gestures, when not rehearsed, demonstrate a "tilt away from the non-verbal and from the 'ceremonies of respect'" and represent a "cultural attitude that does not stand on ceremony, preferring informality to formality."[35] For example, Searle questions the omission of the use of incense on a regular basis at the opening of the Sunday liturgy: "incense was not used in any of the Masses in the parishes surveyed. . . . The option to reverence the people with incense, of course, no longer exists, but the option to incense the altar was never used."[36] Clearly, the preference for informality serves to change the very nature of the greeting of the altar, and the question remains as to whether or not the assembly is contemplatively drawn into this intimate greeting. There is no denying that the general attitude toward the use of incense in our culture is negative—most people do not like their sense of smell to be invaded by smoke, and most worshipers would simply interpret the use of incense as unnecessary pomp. Such an attitude is contrary to the very nature of the liturgy.

Conversely, the ritual gestures of bowing, kissing, and incensing—when understood as a unified act of reverence and as an unspoken

---

[34] Ibid. Serra suggests that the unity of these three expressions is best articulated when the presider bows to the front of the altar, kisses it from there (before walking about to the other side) and begins incensing from the front of the altar. He writes: "This may also heighten the sense that the altar is approachable from all sides, not just from the side usually occupied by the priest. God's holy people gathered around the altar should sense that the altar belongs to the whole church, a community hierarchically ordered and gathered around Christ, our altar, priest, and sacrifice. This attention to the altar and its centrality in the midst of the assembly will help establish it as a symbol of Christ's presence in our midst."

[35] Mark Searle, "*Semper Reformanda*: The Opening and Concluding Rites of the Roman Mass," in *Shaping English Liturgy: Studies in Honor of Archbishop Denis Hurley*, ed. Peter Finn and James Schellman (Washington, DC: The Pastoral Press, 1990), 84.

[36] Ibid.

expression of awe for the One in whom we have been gathered—
opens the Mass with an attitude of "humility." The assembled Body of
Christ silently greets the Lord with the body. With a bowing down of
the torso, with a kiss of the lips, and with the fragrant gift of incense,
the Church rehearses an attitude of humility—all things that follow
are to be done out of reverence for Christ. Regarding the attitude of
humility in the bodily enactment of bowing, Searle offers these poetic
words:

> "Zedekiah was one and twenty years old when he began to reign. . . .
> And he did that which was evil in the sight of the Lord his God, and
> humbled not himself before Jeremiah the prophet speaking from the
> mouth of the Lord . . . but he stiffened his neck and hardened his
> heart from turning unto the Lord God of Israel."
>
> Unbending, unyielding,
> unacknowledging of God or man.
>
> Without a supple neck
> how could I greet a neighbor in a crowd?
> how could I tell my child she is doing well?
> how could I express my grief and shame?
> how could I assent without interrupting?
> how could I show sadness in the face of suffering?
> how could I show solidarity with one who speaks?
> how could I offer my silent respect to a great lady?
> how could I honor an eminent man?
> how could I accept the verdict of my peers?
> . . . simply, silently, wordlessly?
>
> how could I surrender to the blessing
>   of the One who alone can deliver me out of death?
>
> how could I acknowledge
>   that there is only one Name
>   by I which I can be saved—
>   the name of Jesus?[37]

Because the assembly participates in the gestures of reverence through
the actions of the priest presider, the deacon, and the other ministers,
the responsibility is great for carrying out this ritual with care and

---

[37] Mark Searle, "Bowing," *Assembly* 6, no. 3 (1979): 79.

poise. However, local parishes ought to search for ways to engage members of the assembly in the acts of bowing and greeting the altar with a kiss. For example, have our contemporary assemblies truly been formed in understanding the meaning of the bow or genuflection they enact on entering the pew? Do they actually take the time to focus such a bow on the altar, or is this act of reverence done hastily, carelessly, and without a true connection to the one who stands at the head of the assembly? For the priest and the deacon, who regularly kiss the altar, this gesture can embody personal surrender, but how do members of the assembly experience this in their bodies if they themselves have never approached the altar with such focused attention?

This concern for focused attention may be applied as well to the next ritual gesture that involves the physical participation of the entire assembly: the Sign of the Cross that accompanies the words "In the name of the Father, and of the Son, and of the Holy Spirit." If our very first moments of the liturgy have been focused around greeting the presence of Christ in the gathered assembly, now we move even deeper into mystery as the assembly marks itself in the triune life in which it is created and lives every moment of every day. As in the gesture of bowing, Searle interprets the Sign of the Cross with poetry:

> At the beginning and end of this Mass;
> at the beginning and end of our lives;
> at the beginning and ending of all we do
> stands the sign of the cross, saying:
> this place, this space of time, this life,
> this child, these people, this corpse,
> belongs to the Lord and will not be snatched from Him
> who bears indelibly in his body
> the marks of that same cross.[38]

In a very real sense, the communal tracing of the cross on the body denotes the identity by which this gathered body now operates; it is no longer a diverse group of random individuals, it is a sacramental assembly. "Thus, this assembled people is itself the primary sacrament of Christ," writes Searle, "the outward and visible sign of the presence of Christ in and to the world, the medium of his own continuing mediatorship for the glorification of God and thus the sanctification

---

[38] Mark Searle, "Sign of the Cross," *Assembly* 6, no. 3 (1979): 75.

of the human race."[39] If the communal gesture of the Sign of the Cross is entered into seriously and with ritual care, it can be clear within the assembly that the Body of Christ is being rehearsed in an attitude of surrender: "In a sense they cease to be themselves, or at least they surrender their claim to uniqueness in the face of something much larger."[40]

The ratification of a new corporate identity in Christ can be found not merely in the "Amen" uttered by the assembly at the conclusion of the Sign of the Cross, it is confirmed in the greeting exchanged between the priest and the assembly. "Grace to you and peace from God our Father and the Lord Jesus Christ," utters the priest, to which the assembly responds "And with your spirit." This is a formal greeting that is meant to verbally express our encounter with the divine. And yet, as Searle suggests in an editorial entitled "Ritual Dialogue," the importance of a formal greeting between the priest and the assembly is often misunderstood and even mistrusted:

> How can they (ritual dialogues) ever be more than an unthinking, automated response to a given cue? a conditioned reflex void of any human intentionality? . . . This leaves us with distinctly uncomfortable memories of our early years in school when we learned by rote, chanting together, "Two times one is two, two times two is four . . . " or read together off the board, "The square of the hypotenuse is equal to the sum of the squares of the other two sides." As children we were mostly too unselfconscious about that sort of thing, at least, to let it bother us, but as adults it is a different matter. "The Lord be with you. And also with you. And with your spirit," is disturbingly reminiscent of "Good morning, children. Good morning, teacher." (Not so disturbing to some celebrants, apparently, who begin their liturgical ministry in exactly that way, finding it more meaningful!)[41]

[39] Mark Searle, "Collecting and Recollecting: The Mystery of the Gathered Church," *Assembly* 11, no. 1 (1984): 258. He continues: "Thus we may speak of the assembly as the primary and indispensable source of the sacramentality of the sacraments so-called. They are acts of the Church: they are acts of Christ. Consequently, the process by which people gather for Mass and enter into the rite is actually the process of people-becoming-sacrament."

[40] Ibid. Continuing, Searle writes: "Like John the Baptist, each of us can say: 'He must increase, I must decrease.' Or with Paul: 'It is no longer I who live, but Christ who lives in me.'"

[41] Mark Searle, "Ritual Dialogue (Editorial)," *Assembly* 7, no. 3 (1981): 113.

Although the formality of the greeting at the opening of the Mass may tap into distant memories of our childhood formation, it serves the very important purpose of articulating that a new relationship has been established in this present act of liturgical prayer—it manifests the commitment to pray as one body in the triune life. The greeting "invite(s) us to take up a position vis-à-vis ourselves, our God and one another, offering us the opportunity together to confront, concur, confess, acclaim, assent, convert and, not least, connect."[42]

AN ATTITUDE OF CONTRITION

After identity in Christ has been established both in gesture and in word, the community further articulates its humility in a "penitential act." It is important to remember that before the 1970 Missal of Paul VI, the penitential rite was a form of private preparation that involved only the priest and the servers. In its public format, it must be interpreted as a further expression of humility as the assembly continues its preparation. The GIRM suggests that the penitential act is composed of three elements: silence, confession, and absolution: "The Priest calls upon the whole community to take part in the Penitential Action, which, after a brief pause for silence, it does by means of a formula of general confession. The rite concludes with the Priest's absolution, which, however, lacks the efficacy of the Sacrament of Penance."[43] Searle provides the following interpretation:

> The penitential rite . . . provides for a moment of silent recollection—recollection of who we are and who we are called to be as members of the Body of Christ. It is not so much a moment for asking forgiveness for our personal sins as for asking God to forgive our failure to live together as a sign to the world, as the Body of Christ.[44]

Elsewhere, Searle suggests that the penitential act allows for the recognition of "collective guilt" for not living as the Body of Christ:

> As soon as the community has assembled, its purpose is not so much the forgiveness of the sins of individuals as the community's acknowledgement that it has not been what it is called and empowered to be: the body of Christ. It is thus a confession of our collective guilt, made

[42] Ibid., 120.
[43] GIRM 51.
[44] Mark Searle, *Liturgy Made Simple*, 36.

as the body comes together in the presence of its head and prepares, with and through him, to confront the Father. We are his body, yet we are estranged from him and from one another: "Lord, have mercy." We are bonded together in our confession of shared guilt, in the common invocation of Christ's merciful forgiveness.[45]

Thus, Searle indicates that the penitential act serves to "recollect" who we are and to stir up in us a sense of contrition for failing to keep this memory alive and active. The presider's invitation, now to be treated as a standard formula in the new Roman Missal, provides a clue: "Brethren (brothers and sisters), let us acknowledge our sins, and so prepare ourselves to celebrate the sacred mysteries." The point here is not so much to plead for God's forgiveness as it is to recognize ("acknowledge") that we come together in humility, as sinners not the sinless. "Notice," comments Serra, "that the acknowledgment of our sins, not the forgiveness of our sins, will make us well suited for the celebration of the mysteries."[46]

In Searle's language, the penitential act rehearses the assembly in the attitude of "contrition," of confessing that we are not self-sufficient but always in need of God. "Being contrite," writes Searle, "means repudiating one's Godless past as a basis for future action, opting instead to make God one's future."[47] The penitential act expresses an attitude of contrition with complete confidence that mercy will follow; however, such mercy entails the commitment to seeing life anew. Searle expresses the intrinsic relationship between contrition and mercy in the following poetic reflection:

> Lord, Christ, Kyrie:
> > you before whom alone we bow
> > before whom the cherubim bow
> > before whom the earth is silent
> Have mercy on us:
> > mercy, reprieve, relief;
> > another chance, new lease on life,
> > new dawn, new day, new age;
> > repair of the broken,

---

[45] Searle, "Rites of Communion," 126.

[46] Serra, "The Introductory Rites: Theology of the Latin Text and Rite," 129.

[47] Mark Searle, "Penance," in *Pastoral Liturgy*, ed. Harold Winstone (London: Collins, 1975), 195.

quickening of the dead,
grin of the defeated,
the breath of life given back
to those crushed in the winepress
we call "living."

Have mercy on us.[48]

Every act of liturgical prayer bears witness to the newness of life that is established when all things are humbly subjected to God's loving will. When it is God alone before whom we bow, then right relationship is established. "True contrition," writes Searle, "thus differs from the kindred sentiments of remorse and regret in that it is (a) forward-looking rather than backward-looking, and (b) more concerned with the other, God, than with oneself and one's feelings."[49] Thus, the penitential act, as a ritual gesture, declares that the assembly desires to live into God's reconciling life in the world rather than to remain dependent on itself. In Searle's words, "Genuine contrition includes not only the negative resolution not to sin again, but a positive adherence to God and to his plan of reconciliation."[50] Such is the rehearsal of God's Just Kingdom.

Continuing to become gradually aware of its identity as the Body of Christ, the assembly now turns its attitude of contrition into an act of praise as it sings the *Gloria*.[51] Such a shift makes particular sense if the penitential act is seen as an exercise in making "God one's future," in rehearsing an openness to the vision of the Kingdom that the Word of God will proclaim and reveal. Thus, the *Gloria* is the verbal articulation of the willingness on the part of the gathered Church to see the world as totally saturated by divine life. Although sometimes the singing of the *Gloria* with exuberant joy seems to provide a stark contrast to the *Kyrie* immediately prior, the point is to employ corporate singing once again in order to assist the assembly in its surrender to God. Searle writes:

[48] Mark Searle, "Lord, Have Mercy," *Assembly* 7, no. 3 (1981): 114.
[49] Mark Searle, "Penance," 195.
[50] Ibid.
[51] See Catherine Vincie, "The Introductory Rites: The Mystagogical Implications," in *A Commentary on the Order of Mass of* The Roman Missal, ed. Edward Foley, et al. (Collegeville, MN: Liturgical Press, 2011), 148. Vincie writes: "Penitence makes way for praise."

When the liturgy requires us to sing, "Glory to God in the highest and peace to his people on earth," [ICEL2010 translation: "Glory to God in the highest and on earth peace to people of good will"] it does not matter all that much whether or not we feel on top of the world. If we do, and the prayers and rites provide us with an outlet for expressing our mood and emotions, that's good; but if the ground does not shake and the heart does not quake, the exercise is not invalidated in the least. What matters is that we follow the indications of the rite and try to make its attitudes our own.[52]

What are the attitudes that are verbally expressed in the singing of the *Gloria*? The answer can be found in the second sentence of the new (2010) English translation of this ancient hymn: "We praise you, we bless you, we adore you, we glorify you, we give you thanks for your great glory, Lord God, heavenly King, O God, almighty Father." What may seem to be an exaggerated series of verbs directed to the Father actually get to the heart of the matter: from the recognition of God's mercy and reordering of relationships, the Church cannot contain the joy that bursts forth. Furthermore, this joy is the expression of Christ who has taken away the world's sins and intercedes for the world at the Father's right hand, who alone is "the Holy One," "the Lord," "the Most High." The historical occurrence of the Church assembled in prayer at this very moment receives the assurance of the angels that peace is given to the world. Contrition and mercy culminate in adoration; the *Gloria* rehearses a confident renewed worldview: all of God's creation attuned to the glory of God.

AN ATTITUDE OF SILENCE

The final element of preparation involved in the Introductory Rites is the Collect, which is ritually composed of four elements: (1) the invitation to prayer, (2) silence, (3) the uttered prayer, and (4) the "Amen" of the assembly. Of these four elements, the role of silence deserves special consideration. In opening the liturgy, many words have been used to foster a sense of humility and a fundamental openness to God, but in the end, the best expression of our common life before God is silence, a profound nothingness that desires the fullness of the Spirit. Using an abundance of words himself, Searle provides the following reflection on this Christian attitude, which he entitles "Keeping Silence":

[52] Searle, *Called to Participate*, 25.

Speech must die to serve that which is spoken.
                    Paul Ricoeur

There is the silence of boredom, fretful and fidgety,
    the uneasy space between things happening,
    unrestful waiting for something to occur.

There is the silence of being, of centered repose,
    where process is suspended and things are allowed to be:
    the silence of the first sabbath
    when God rested from his work of creating
    to relish the goodness of it all.

There is the silence of old friends:
    a wordless, mutual presence;
    the being together out of which
    occasional words fly like sparks
    from silence into silence,
    slow born, slow digested.

There is the silence of memory and recollection,
    the savoring of words and images,
    remembrance of things done and experience shared:
    the relishing of the past that quickens longing
    the assimilation of what is known
    that deepens understanding.

There is the silence of speechlessness,
    of being lost for words in the face
    of shock, delight or wonder:
    the strange, disorienting experience
    of groping for words that stretch and strain
    and break under the weight they cannot bear.

There is the silence of solemn respect,
    of listening carefully to another's words that matter,
    of knowing there is a time for speaking
    and that it is not now,
    that one must quiet oneself and listen
    for the word that may shape one's life.

The Lord is in his holy Temple:
let the earth keep silence before him.[53]

---

[53] Mark Searle, "Keeping Silence," *Assembly* 6, no. 3 (1979), 76.

Silence between the invitation to prayer and the spoken Collect is not an option, and, in fact, the rubrics of "The Order of Mass" state clearly: "And all pray in silence with the Priest *for a while*."[54] Dominic Serra substantiates this instruction: "When the silence between the invitation to prayer and the collect is omitted, the text will seem to be the priest's prayer rather than the congregation's, and the delicate balance between the ministry of the whole people and that of the priest will be missed."[55] Nonetheless, without proper catechesis and practice with the art of silence, the assembly is likely to interpret this time as "unrestful waiting for something to occur."[56]

Writing more than thirty years ago, Searle foresaw the complications of introducing "genuine liturgical silence" into modern-day congregations, assemblies that are largely products of what he called a "noise-intoxicated age."[57] He believed that true silence is at the heart of theology itself and deserves to be mastered in liturgical celebration. He writes:

> Silence, of course, is more than mere absence of noise, or suspension of speech or a pause from activity. . . . As the human word is not to be identified with chatter, so human silence is more than absence of speech. Rather it is the ground from which the word emerges, the home to which it returns. In this sense, human silence and human speech both model and reflect the deep silence of God and the efficacy of his eternal Word. It is from the silence, paradoxically, that the word derives its power, its depth, its import, and it is in the silence of the hearer's heart that it finds its proper soil. For words that ultimately matter, like the Word of God himself, stretch and strain to speak of that which lies too deep for words and succeed only to the extent to which they fall into the ground and die.[58]

This deep silence is the attitude—the worldview—that the assembly rehearses as it ultimately readies itself to be confronted with the Word of God; in the end, all the words we possess cannot adequately express our humility and openness as can real silence. Thus, the Collect is not an attempt to make sense of what will follow, or even an opportunity

---

[54] OM 9. Emphasis mine.
[55] Serra, "The Introductory Rites: Theology of the Latin Text and Rite," 131.
[56] Searle, "Keeping Silence," 76.
[57] See "Silence," *Assembly* 9, no. 1 (1982): 177.
[58] Ibid.

to sum up what has been, but rather the ritual commitment to be emptied before God. "The prayer recited," Searle writes, "must echo the silence, hinting in its mode of recitation at the movement of the Spirit out of and back into the stillness of God."[59]

In his 1988 article "Forgotten Truths about Worship," Searle identifies silence as one of four "participatory skills" that "every Christian needs to develop if liturgical prayer is to be accessible."[60] In fact, he will go so far as to say that liturgy is not just dependent on silence, but it is itself "silence accompanied by words and stillness accompanied by gestures."[61] Searle continues:

> It is from the silent depths of our innermost being that the Spirit rises, and it is into that Spirit-filled depth that the Word enters and there resounds. Thus, at the beginning of any liturgy, or in response to the invitation "Let us pray," we need to settle down and still the clamor of our preoccupations and distractions, to reach down even beyond the depths of our personal silence into those depths of silence where we are all one. . . . [A]ctive participation, in which the Word of God will pierce our innermost being and the prayer of Christ will surge up from the depths of the Spirit, requires first and foremost a profound self-emptying. This self-emptying is to expose us to the depths of the real self, *so the silence is not a privatistic, individualistic withdrawal from the presence of the community so much as it is a moment of recollection in which the community itself is re-collected in a common coming-to-consciousness of the depths at which we are all one.*[62]

Thus, it is this last dimension of silence—the self-emptying that contemplates "the depths at which we are all one"—that is particularly to be mastered by the assembly in coming to the brink of being prepared

[59] Searle, *Called to Participate*, 57.

[60] Mark Searle, "Forgotten Truths about Worship," *Celebration* 17 (January 1988): 8. The remaining three "participatory skills" Searle mentions are "action," "speech," and "music and song."

[61] Ibid. See also Joseph Dougherty, "Silence in the Liturgy," *Worship* 69 (1995): 142–54. This article provides a worthwhile description of silence as "language." For example, Dougherty writes: "Silence betokens, then, the anti-structural elements on the continuum between society and individual, and thus silence enables the individual's appropriation of the communal. Silence also verifies the individuality of the person and the existence of the Other to whom worship is addressed" (154).

[62] Searle, "Forgotten Truths about Worship," 8. Emphasis mine.

to hear the Word of God. Returning to his earlier *Assembly* editorial on silence, Searle calls this the "silence of awe," and maintains that "it is not the silence of facing the void, but a silence of encountering Presence: dreadful yet thankful, joyful yet sober, awesome yet somehow reassuring."[63]

All of this suggests that there is much work to be done in leading congregations into the meaning of the silence that follows the invitation "Let us pray." Clearly, members of the assembly have not been taught the value and meaning of this silence as an indispensible liturgical component, for if truly enacted as silence, it generally leads to restlessness and impatience within the Body. This is largely due to the fact that the members of contemporary assemblies struggle with the very concept of "centering" the self, of living into the self that is Body of Christ, and ultimately is the life of God. It is work to "center" oneself on others and *the* Other, as Searle writes:

> There is a necessary exercise of silence in which the participants, as individuals and as congregation, "center" themselves, allow the inner noise to settle and prepare to put down roots into the deep Self. Very often, such an exercise is conceived of in highly individualistic terms, which would seem to run counter to the communal character of our worship: as if each of us is withdrawing beneath an invisible cowl of private introversion. There is a place for such interior withdrawal, but it is not the liturgy of the Church. Liturgical silence as a centering exercise means a shared silence. . . . In liturgical silence it is the Body which centers itself in the silence, enters into the silence to become aware of itself precisely as Body animated by the one Spirit.[64]

Modeling such silence is indeed the role of the presider and ought to be considered as important a ritual detail as pronouncing the "words of institution" correctly. However, the assembly also must be informed as to the nature of this silence and rehearsed in its execution. Such formation of the assembly echoes the attitude of sacredness, whereby participation in the liturgical assembly is viewed in terms of commitment to a "way of relating" in which Christ acts to draw individuals out of solitary confinement into his view of the world as one. As Searle writes: "Potentially, at least, (for the old self does not, like old soldiers, just fade away), the hopes, thoughts, images, aspirations, desires that

---

[63] Searle, "Silence," 184.
[64] Ibid.

well up from the region of my deepest self, are no longer those of my own unregenerate nature, but the hopes, thoughts, aspirations,—yes, the prayers—of Christ himself."[65]

Thus, the ultimate goal of the Gathering Rite is to pray in Christ, to contemplate the reality that it is not we who pray, but Christ who prays in us.[66] The utterance of the opening Collect is the confident recognition that the assembly is centered in Christ. God may be approached precisely because the assembly has grown into Christ through its surrender and response to mercy. Being recommitted to the Kingdom, it may be gathered into Christ's prayer. Searle writes:

> The only really indispensable part of the Introductory Rites is the collect or opening prayer. This is the point to which everything else leads, the point at which this crowd of people, who have just come from their homes or workplaces, or from shopping or partying or whatever, can find themselves together as a community. The idea is that, wherever we have come from, whatever we've been doing, we come together now as the Body of Christ. We lose our individuality to find our common identity; we let the noise and preoccupations of our lives die away as we become aware of him in whose presence we stand, and of those with whom we stand.[67]

Thus, the opening Collect demonstrates that transformation has already taken place in the gathered assembly. Reverence and surrender have been practiced so that Christ's presence may be tangible in his Body.[68] Searle labels such transformation as "growth": "Growth,

---

[65] Mark Searle, "Prayer: Alone or with Others?," *Centerlines* 1, no. 5 (1979): 19.

[66] See Mark Searle, "Participation and Prayer," *Music and Liturgy* 12, no. 5 (1986): 148. Searle writes: "The liturgy is an exercise of the priestly office of Jesus Christ: 'may the Lord Jesus pray in us and holy Spirit': to participate in the liturgy requires that we so empty ourselves of our own agenda and preoccupations that we can reach the depths where the holy Spirit of Christ is praying in us and hymning God through us. That, I think, is what is meant by the Council when it requires the 'full, conscious and active participation' of the faithful and when it further suggests that the liturgy can only achieve its effect if we are properly disposed, if our thoughts match our words and if we are open to the working of grace."

[67] Searle, *Liturgy Made Simple*, 36.

[68] See Janowiak, *Standing Together in the Community of God*, 78. Janowiak writes: "Faithful practice, attentive preparation and enactment, and the contin-

then, is indeed something the liturgy is about: it is about growth in openness to the Spirit, growth in assimilation to Christ, growth in self-forgetfulness. In the life of the Spirit, more is indeed less; he must increase and I must decrease, and for there to be growth I must shrink in importance."[69]

Furthermore, an important dimension of the Collect is its universality. While it may be argued justifiably that the new English translation of the *Roman Missal* presents faith communities with prayers that move toward uniformity at the expense of intelligibility,[70] potential frustration with the prose and the cadence of the translation may serve as a challenge for even greater surrender on the part of that gathered Church. Like the world of the psalms, which can seem quite foreign to modern ears, the opening Collect leads us deeper into ambiguity and mystery. In Searle's words:

> In considering the collects, we see that being able to pray them presupposes the sort of training provided by the psalter, for they are equally alien. They pray for graces of rather abstract kind: "show us the way to peace in this world"; "protect the good you have given us"; "may we live the faith we profess and trust your promise of eternal life." . . . It will never be specifically relevant because it is always the prayer of the larger Church. If it is made relevant, by the presider praying spontaneously for example, something will be gained, but something equally will certainly be lost. What will be lost is what is produced by the very fact that the prayer itself says (i.e., communicates to us) little or nothing about ourselves.[71]

Shortly thereafter, Searle reiterates precisely why objectivity is an important characteristic of the opening Collect: "Like all solemn prayers of the liturgy offered by the presider in the name of the Church, the collect is a faint and distorted echo of the prayer of Christ before the throne of God."[72] Our words do no justice to the prayer that wells up

---

ual pause to stand in reverent acknowledgment of the grace and mercy being offered here give deeper meaning to the term for the praying and singing assembly that the liturgy documents often employ: 'the faithful.'"

[69] Searle, "Participation and Prayer," 151.

[70] See, for example, Thomas O'Loughlin, "A Vernacular Liturgy Versus a Liturgy in the 'Vernacular'?," *Worship* 86 (2012): 244–55.

[71] Searle, *Called to Participate*, 55.

[72] Ibid., 56.

in the heart of Christ, yet we make them known, because to remain utterly silent would be to fail to participate in Christ's priestly work to heal the world and to restore all things to the Father.[73]

CONCLUSION

From the outset, in order to understand the liturgy as the "rehearsal of Christian attitudes," and therefore as the enactment of the "justice of God," it is necessary to take account of *how* the community gathers. On one level, this means exploring the disposition of each individual heart that enters into worship (i.e. is a person in a position to be open to the Word of God speaking to the assembled Body?). At another level, the *how* of gathering is a matter of facilitation, meaning what are the corporate conditions that make worship possible? While the first level question is extremely elusive, the second question is more objectively verifiable. For the task of forming a group of disparate individuals into the praying Body of Christ, the Mass contains rituals that shape our outlook and allow the world to be perceived in Christ.

On entering the worship space, all who have come to pray are invited to rehearse the attitude of *sacredness*, trying to see all elements of worship (living and inanimate) as striving to reveal the wholeness that serves as the foundation of God's reign. Sacredness is rehearsed in allowing one's voice to blend in song with others; it is visibly pinpointed in the veneration of the altar; and it is verbally ratified in the greeting between presider and the assembly. Further preparation to manifest identity in Christ is found in the ritual rehearsal of the attitude of *contrition*, whereby the assembly commits itself to seeing all relationships of creation as washed anew by God's love and as participants in the work of offering praise and glory to God. Finally, the Gathering Rite concludes with an attitude of *silence* in which the assembly is immersed in Christ's presence and seeks to overhear the prayer of his heart. Therefore, the goal of the Introductory Rite is to form the Body of Christ by a ritual "emptying" of all called by God into the project of worship. In this movement, we commit ourselves anew to God's Just Kingdom. Having begun this surrender, the Body is now ready to practice the skill of listening as it encounters the Lord in his Word.

---

[73] Ibid., 81–82. Searle writes: "Whenever we celebrate the liturgy, therefore, it must not be for our own benefit so much as an exercise of our vocation to represent humanity before God. We must learn to pray the prayer of the liturgy with the voice of the whole Church."

Chapter 4

The Rehearsal of Listening

One of the greatest debates on the floor and behind the scenes of the Second Vatican Council concerned the preparation and eventual promulgation of *Dei Verbum*, the Constitution on Divine Revelation (November 18, 1965).[1] The underlying point of division among the Council Fathers in preparing their teaching on "The Word of God" essentially resided in the relationship between Scripture and tradition, with the minority camp proposing that tradition contains truths which are not found in Scripture. Maintaining that "tradition and scripture make up a single sacred deposit of the word of God, which is entrusted to the church,"[2] *Dei Verbum* affirms that the proclamation of scripture has a "venerable" place in the life of the Church:

> The church has always venerated the divine scriptures as it has venerated the Body of the Lord, in that it never ceases, above all in the sacred liturgy, to partake of the bread of life and to offer it to the faithful from the one table of the word of God and the Body of Christ. It has always regarded and continues to regard the scriptures, taken together with sacred tradition, as the supreme rule of its faith. For, since they are inspired by God and committed to writing once and for all time, they present God's own word in an unalterable form, and they make the voice of the holy Spirit sound again and again in the words of prophets and apostles. . . . In the sacred books the Father who is in heaven comes lovingly to meet his children, and talks with them.[3]

The Council clearly reestablished for the Church the understanding that the proclamation of scripture is God's communication of loving presence to his people. Remarkably for the time, the Word of God is

---

[1] See John W. O'Malley, *What Happened at Vatican II* (Cambridge, MA: Belknap Press of Harvard University Press, 2008), 277–82.

[2] *Dei Verbum* 10 in Flannery, *The Basic Sixteen Documents*.

[3] *Dei Verbum* 21.

described in *Dei Verbum* as "the church's support and strength"[4] and as "nourishment" to "enlighten the mind" and "strengthen the heart."[5] Liturgical proclamation of God's Word is true encounter with the Living God. Therefore, the quality and concern regarding *how* the encounter is enacted within the liturgical assembly is deserving of great attention and care.

As discussed in chapter 1, Mark Searle believed liturgy itself to be the localized expression of the Word of God, "the self-communicated intervention of God in perceptible form in the world of men."[6] Searle's earliest writings, as well as his later works that were focused on semiotics, reveal his concern for revitalizing the search for meaning in the act of communication. In other words, "word" is to be understood as any means by which, on the one hand, self-expression takes place, and on the other, that self-expression is interpreted. As Searle writes, "The Word of God is not, in the first instance, a spoken word but an event comprising many human words and gestures which, taken together and in their entirety, reveal the God who saves us."[7] When speaking of the Liturgy of the Word, therefore, it is much more than the words that come forth from the ambo, it is the entire complex of words, gestures, movements, and postures of the listening people that comprise God speaking and revealing himself to the world.

Perhaps another way of stating this is that there is much more to "listening" during the Liturgy of the Word than simply hearing the words of Scripture spoken aloud. In fact, the "listening" that is involved in the liturgical act is precisely what separates the liturgical Word of God from the reading of Scripture in private or in a nonliturgical gathering. The liturgical Word requires attentiveness to the interaction of words proclaimed and words received. The question to be discerned is how is God confronting his people at this very moment? Searle writes:

> It seems a pity that, in fact, the practice of the Church has resulted in the Word of God being almost exclusively identified with the

[4] *Dei Verbum* 21 concludes: "It is eminently true of holy scripture that: 'The word of God is living and active' (Heb 4:12), and 'is able to build you up and to give you the inheritance among all those who are sanctified' (Acts 20:32; see 1 Th 2:13)." Here the Word of God is described as active presence.

[5] *Dei Verbum* 23.

[6] Searle, "The Word and the World," 2.

[7] Ibid., 3.

Scriptures themselves. They are only the Word of God in so far as their proclamation in the *ecclesia* confronts the hearers with the presence of God now and enables them to recognize and respond to his activity in all spheres of life. . . . It is the proclamation of the Word *now*, not remembrance of its proclamation in the past which is essential.[8]

While the Word of God, which is found in Scripture, is meant to inform and influence the living of life in this world in general, the liturgical work of "listening" to God's spoken Word takes on a particular importance. The liturgy itself is quite simply the arena of awe and wonder at being confronted by the encounter with the Living God. "If the liturgical assembly," writes Searle, "in its words and actions, is to be credible in its claim to reveal the profoundest truth about human existence, then we, who are part of that assembly, and thereby part of the event which is God's Word to the world, must live by that truth and be seen to live by that truth."[9]

Although appearing somewhat similar to participation as spectators, such as movie goers in a theatre or sports fans in a stadium, participation in the liturgical event by which God "comes lovingly to meet his children" (DV 21) requires overcoming the temptation of passivity. It requires learning to listen "actively." But how? Searle himself was quite realistic that the cultural pattern of being bombarded with words provides a difficult challenge to the act of "listening" to the Word of God. As he writes in a January 1979 editorial for *Assembly*:

> How can we really hear the Word, we who are drowning in an ocean of devalued words and dishonest language? How can we hear the Word amidst the clamor of the advertising media, CB radios, talk shows, and the incessant trivialization which pervades our news programs and even that last bastion of public eloquence, the pulpit? As Christians, we have a responsibility to work to restore the credibility of the spoken word and to recover the discipline of listening.[10]

Searle continues in this editorial to suggest that two things are necessary here: first, he argues that we must "clean up our speech" and ensure that the liturgical word is heard differently from "the irrelevant and unworthy drivel against which we learn to inure ourselves"

---

[8] Ibid., 6–7.
[9] Ibid., 8. See also Searle, "The Word and the World," 5.
[10] Mark Searle, "The Word of the Lord," *Assembly* 5, no. 4 (1979): 41.

(meaning that care should be taken for each word spoken), and second, the assembly must prepare itself to listen worthily to the Word.[11] "Restoring" the credibility of the spoken word and "recovering" the discipline of listening in the Liturgy of the Word demonstrate well how the "justice of God" (restoration of credibility) is to be found in the "rehearsal of Christian attitudes" (discipline of listening).[12] We now turn to the liturgical ritual of encountering God in his Word.

AN ATTITUDE OF "TRUSTING IMAGINATION"

Having been brought to the depths of silence in the opening Collect, the assembly sits together for the Liturgy of the Word. If the work of the Gathering Rite is about surrendering oneself to the Body of Christ and reestablishing one's identity as an active member of corporate prayer—thereby recognizing the presence of Christ in the assembly—the Liturgy of the Word broadens this presence by rooting the community in the greater story of salvation. The biblical readings, together with accompanying song, demonstrates the dialogical nature of this story, in which God first calls in order to solicit the response of his people. In other words, in the proclamation of the liturgical Word, the assembly seeks to "listen" as God's chosen people, not as individual hearers. As Searle writes in "Rites of Communion":

> The *Hearing of the Word* is likewise a collective activity, an exercise in communion, for as in the past God calls us together to address us *as a body*. This is quite different from reading the Scriptures privately. Here we are made aware of our identity as a people of God's choosing, a people with a common story and a common vocation, saved not as individuals but as part of the body of Jesus raised from the dead. When Moses proclaimed God's word at Sinai, Israel came to be; when God spoke to us through his Word, Jesus Christ, the new Israel was born. From week to week we gather to hear the Word he addresses to us today and thereby discover our common, God-given, identity.[13]

---

[11] Ibid.

[12] See Searle, "The Shape of the Future: A Liturgist's Vision," 143. Searle writes: "Serious attention to the conditions for a more effective hearing of the word may well be a significant factor in determining the shape of the Sunday assembly in the future."

[13] Searle, "Rites of Communion," 126.

The GIRM affirms this corporate nature of the Liturgy of the Word (i.e., of "listening" as one Body):

> For in the readings, as explained by the Homily, God speaks to his people, opening up to them the mystery of redemption and salvation, and offering spiritual nourishment; and Christ himself is present through his word in the midst of the faithful. By silence and by singing, the people make this divine word their own, and affirm their adherence to it by means of the Profession of Faith; finally, having been nourished by the divine word, the people pour out their petitions by means of the Universal Prayer for the needs of the whole Church and for the salvation of the whole world.[14]

This description of the Liturgy of the Word is simple and straightforward enough, but in practice there is great ritual detail that must be attended to in order to facilitate the contemplation of the Lord's presence in the intersection of Word and the life of the community. For example, the GIRM suggests that the first ritual detail is the silence of the assembly: "The Liturgy of the Word is to be celebrated in such a way as to favor meditation, and so any kind of haste such as hinders recollection is clearly to be avoided."[15] What is clearly intended here is for the incorporation of a posture of deep silence that undergirds and pervades the entire event of being "grasped by the heart" by the Word of God.[16]

For his own part, Searle believed that before the biblical texts are able to be heard by the assembly, the metaphorical nature of liturgy must be understood, thereby opening the assembly to the dynamics of a "communications event."[17] "Scripture readings, prayers, chants, preaching, . . ." writes Searle, "are not separate elements, but a series of increasingly intense and immediate proclamations of the presence

---

[14] GIRM 55.

[15] GIRM 56. The instruction continues: "In the course of it, brief periods of silence are also appropriate, accommodated to the assembled congregation; by means of these, under the action of the Holy Spirit, the Word of God may be grasped by the heart and a response through prayer may be prepared. It may be appropriate to observe such periods of silence, for example, before the Liturgy of the Word itself begins, after the First and Second Reading, and lastly at the conclusion of the Homily."

[16] GIRM 56.

[17] See Searle, "Liturgy as Metaphor," 98–120. See also Mark Searle, "Christian Liturgy and Communications Theory," *Media Development* 31:3 (1984): 4–6.

of God in the world of men."[18] In an attempt to break with the long-standing interpretation that the purpose of the biblical readings in the liturgy is to educate by the transmission of information, Searle suggests that the liturgy is best interpreted according to a "transactional model" dependent on the interaction of symbols.[19] The "transactional model" expands on a dialogical approach of call and response by focusing primarily on the change in relationships that occurs in the communications event. Searle writes:

> Here the focus is not so much upon the "sender" or on the impact of the message on the hearer as on the continuingly altering relationship between the conversation partners themselves, and between them and the situation they share. . . . In the process of communication, kaleidoscopic sets of relationships are continually defined, altered, even transformed, as the redescription of existing elements or the introduction of new elements make their impact felt upon the system as a whole.[20]

The challenge becomes helping communities to see the communications event in terms of the transformation of relationships at every level of being. Such recognition allows members of the Body of Christ to see their interconnectedness at a deeper level, precisely intertwined with the life of God. Thus, Searle will say that this communications event, in which relationships are necessarily transformed, is an "enacted parable" that functions positively "to offer a call rather than to impose moral imperatives."[21]

[18] Searle, "The Word and the World," 6.
[19] See Searle, "Christian Liturgy and Communications Theory," 5.
[20] Ibid.
[21] Searle, "Serving the Lord with Justice," 31. See also Mark Searle, "Images and Worship," *The Way* 24, no. 2 (1984): 112. He writes: "To transform the working of the religious imagination is to enable people to situate themselves differently in our world, to challenge their values, to bring them to question their accepted patterns of behavior. From this perspective, it can be envisaged that the liturgy might operate in Christian life rather like the parables of Jesus, indeed as enacted parable. By opening oneself to be receptive to the symbols of the liturgy, whether verbal or non-verbal, one risks discovery and encounter in confronting the True and the Holy. One risks growing in wisdom and holiness by developing a contemplative attention to words and actions even outside the liturgy. One risks losing one's comfortable ideas and familiar patterns of prejudice by learning really to listen and to act in the Spirit."

A bit more must be said regarding the idea of liturgy in general, and the liturgical proclamation of God's Word specifically, as an "enacted parable," as it is key to Searle's belief that metaphors work by offering a vision of the world that is quite different from the ordinary; in other words, symbols and metaphors are meant not to instruct but rather to provide insight.[22] Searle writes:

> The point about a parable is that when its character as parable is recognized, it is characteristically non-directive. Thus, the story that Jesus tells in response to a question or to a particular situation is one whose unexpected contrasts enable the listeners to come to an entirely different perspective concerning the matter at hand. . . . What is true of the parables and parabolic situations of Jesus in the Gospels is true for the liturgy also, though the liturgy has generally suffered the same fate as the parables in the hands of preachers and teachers, in being moralized and used to prove an ethical point. Yet the liturgy retains its parabolic potential to subvert all human perspectives and to offer us a way of seeing the world from the vantage point of God's justice revealed in word and sacrament. We are left to draw our own conclusions, or rather, we are left as a community to decide what appropriate forms of action might be called for in view of the newly recognized disparity between the order ordained by God and the order that actually prevails.[23]

As Searle suggests here, the success of parables depends on their ability to overturn expectations and to lead people into ambiguity rather than clarity.[24] For this reason, Searle believed that one of the chief

[22] See Theresa F. Koernke, "Introduction to 'Liturgy as Metaphor,'" in *Vision: The Scholarly Contribution of Mark Searle to Liturgical Renewal*, ed. Anne Koester and Barbara Searle, 23–26 (Collegeville, MN: Liturgical Press, 2004). She writes: "If everything means or signifies something, then Mark Searle is among the persistent heralds of attention to language and space and behavior in the public worship of the Church. The celebration of any of the liturgies of the sacraments is a speech act on the part of God and on the part of the assembly. Every celebration of any of the liturgies is an extended metaphor for the initiative of God in Christ through the Spirit and the response of Christians in Christ through the Spirit to the glory of God" (25–26).

[23] Searle, "Serving the Lord with Justice," 30–31.

[24] See John McKenna, "Symbol and Reality: Some Anthropological Considerations," *Worship* 65 (1991): 2–27. McKenna argues that symbols have suffered from literal interpretation since the Middle Ages. Furthermore, symbols work

enemies to listening to the Word of God is the prevalent attitude of "flatminded literalism,"[25] according to which "truth is best served by minimizing ambiguity, so that each word refers to one thing and one thing only."[26] Furthermore, Searle goes as far as to say that the project of all liturgical reform is to renew the imagination: "Liturgical renewal was, from the beginning, a function of ecclesial renewal, and ecclesial renewal meant a renewal of the Christian imagination."[27]

Therefore, the rejection of symbolic thinking in today's world of empirical fact led Searle to labor extensively in his academic career to extol the importance of symbol and metaphor and how we must be trained in how to approach them.[28] He argued, in fact, that entrance into the depths of the act of "listening" in the liturgical celebration, and particularly within the event of being confronted with God's

---

best when they are "ambiguous and imprecise." He writes, "Part of the richness of symbols is that they are *many faceted*. They are not limited to one meaning but are, rather, a 'bundle of meanings'" (24).

[25] See Searle, "Liturgy as Metaphor," 101. Searle quotes from John Shea's article, "The Second Naiveté: Approach to a Pastoral Problem," *Concilium* 81 (1973): 106–16. On page 110 Shea writes: "The scientific mode of knowledge is popularly considered the only way to the real. This cultural mood induces a flatminded literalism, where religious symbols are not allowed to flourish symbolically, but are frozen into statements about some ontological deity. They do not configure and mobilize human experience, but are considered solely as independent entities susceptible to a detached scrutiny. In this way religious symbols are victimized into literal language designating invisible objects. For most people religious language is a form of supernatural positivism. The first step to a second naiveté is away from a literal understanding of religious language and towards an awareness of the relationship between symbol and experience." See also Searle, "Images and Worship," 106–7.

[26] Searle, "Liturgy and Metaphor," 105.

[27] Searle, "Images and Worship," 104. See also Margaret Mary Kelleher, "Introduction to 'Images and Worship,'" in Koester and Searle, *Vision*, 122–25. She writes: "He was convinced that a significant step would be to attend to the gathered congregation itself as a visible sign of invisible realities. Among the suggestions he offers to foster such an awareness is the promotion of a contemplative approach to liturgical participation. His attention to the role of ritual repetition in liturgy as a way of rehearsing certain interactions and attitudes is also very pertinent for any exploration of liturgical spirituality."

[28] See Mark Searle and John A. Melloh, "Symbol: A Bibliography," in *Symbol: The Language of Liturgy*, ed. John B. Ryan (Washington, DC: Federation of Diocesan Liturgical Commission, 1983), 70–72.

Word, is through the cultivation of metaphor, which "lends a vocabulary in which to play out the insight."[29] However, how do metaphors succeed in producing insight in the first place? Searle answers this by stating:

> The most powerful metaphors in human language are those that touch on areas of experience which clearly engage our own mystery, opening up for us the wonder and ambiguity of human existence, yet there are two particular ways in which all metaphor lays claim on us. In the first place, metaphor requires the *engagement* of those who would understand it. . . . It thus constitutes an invitation to look at reality in a particular way. It requires an act of contemplation, rather than analysis which takes it apart and destroys it, dissipating its power. Contemplation, on the contrary, suggests an entering into that which is contemplated, a kind of in-dwelling. In this sense, metaphor calls for the hearer or reader to yield his ground, to part with his usual descriptions of variety, to move over onto the ground of the image, to live inside it, to look around and get the feel of it. It calls for a suspension of disbelief, a closure of critical distance, a commitment of trust to this ways of seeing. Once inside, when a metaphor yields up its secret, it demands a second kind of commitment: that of *loyalty* to the insight offered.[30]

Thus, a metaphor's ability to spark insight on the part of those who enter into the image is dependent on engagement and loyalty; as Searle states: "In short, a good metaphor not only carries cognitive content but it also has attitudinal import."[31] The example Searle employs here is helpful: a different attitude (outlook/worldview) is conveyed by describing old age as the autumn of life than by using the metaphor of an emptying hourglass—the former leaves room for understanding old age in terms of a beautiful season full of color, whereas the latter implies an impending emptiness and futility.[32]

While scripture is filled with rich metaphors and symbolic images, Searle contends that listening to the Word proclaimed in a liturgical context contains the enactment of one underlying metaphor, namely "that of the death and resurrection of Jesus as the disclosure, for those who will enter into it, of ultimate reality."[33] This "ultimate reality"

[29] Searle, "Liturgy and Metaphor," 106.
[30] Ibid., 110–11.
[31] Ibid., 111.
[32] Ibid.
[33] Ibid., 111–12.

might also be called the "truth," and thus the problem for contemporary assemblies is that "truth" is usually measured and constituted by literal statements and facts. Consequently, Searle contends that liturgy demands the rehearsal of what might be called "trusting imagination," in which participants willingly suspend the attitude of disbelief:

> We have to enter into the metaphor with a certain measure of sympathetic expectation and to linger with it until it yields up its secret. The dawning of insight, the gradual realization of disclosure, comes slowly and unpredictably to one who becomes immersed in the metaphor, plays with it, savors it imaginatively. . . . To us who have become distrustful of the word, the liturgy offers the opportunity to rediscover its power by submitting to the gesture as well. We kneel to confess, stand to salute and to praise; we bow, we beat the breast, we raise our hands, we genuflect, we make the sign of the cross—and in all this we discover the meaning of the rite by putting ourselves as best we can into what we are doing. In all these ways and more, the liturgy encourages us to try on the metaphor; not just to stand there, but to body it forth.[34]

Such "bodying forth" of the metaphor, and thus the "ultimate reality" of the Lord's death and resurrection, may seem particularly challenging when the assembly's liturgical role is that of attentive "listening" to the Word.[35] For instance, some people may contend that they are able to concentrate most effectively by listening with their eyes closed, while others may argue that they are able to understand the Word most fully when they are allowed to read the Word simultaneously with the

---

[34] Ibid., 114–15.

[35] See Searle, "Images and Worship," 110. Here he speaks of "listening" as learning a discipline or "the kind of self-control which frees one from distraction and preserves one from dissipation." He continues: "So there is a discipline of listening, looking and gesturing to be learnt: ways of standing, touching, receiving, holding, embracing, eating and drinking which recognize these activities as *significant* and which enable us to perform them in such a way that we are opening to the meaning (the *res*) which they mediate. In terms of the assembly, the primary signifier, there is a way of being together with others in the liturgy—a way of which all these ritual activities are a part— which goes beyond mere juxtaposition of bodies and beyond the pain or pleasure of orchestrated responses, and which leads to the loss of self in favour of profound union with the Body. One acts without acting, speaks without speaking, sings without singing: for it is Christ who prays, blesses, touches and sings in the Body to which my own body is given over."

liturgical proclamation (i.e., by using a missalette), while still others might say that attentive listening takes place only when a direct relationship of communication between the reader and the hearer, through eye-contact, is established. In other words, the question to be tackled is this: Is there a particular form of "listening" that is unique to, and therefore an acquired skill of, liturgical prayer, specifically the Liturgy of the Word? Or is "listening" so subjective that it transcends critique?

Searle's work suggests that the answer begins to take shape when assemblies understand what the Liturgy of the Word is all about and what it intends to do. The answer begins to form when the overarching attitude shifts from attending to the proclaimed Word specifically "get something out of it" versus "listening" to the Word in order to "enter into" a new (renewed) worldview. Searle writes:

> Is the Liturgy of the Word meant to be a period of religious instruction or edification? If so, perhaps discussion groups, filmstrips, and other things would do the job better. But the conclusion of each reading gives us a clue. "The Word of the Lord," the reader says. "Thanks be to God," we reply. The word of the Lord: not instruction about God, but the Word *of* God, the Word addressed to us by God himself. Now that is different from religious instruction—and a lot of priests have not yet learned the difference, for they turn their homilies into moral diatribes or financial appeals or doctrinal instructions or scriptural exegesis instead of helping us hear the Word of God. They talk about God instead of letting God speak to us.[36]

While Searle places great responsibility on the priest for clearing a path to helping the assembly to hear the voice of God, the greater responsibility is really on the shoulders of the assembly, before the presider ever opens his mouth to proclaim the Gospel and to preach. If the entire event of the Word is in fact God speaking to us, then from the very moment we are seated to hear this Word and to be confronted with the "truth," *how* we are engaged in this grand act of communication must entail the practice of "trusting imagination."

One of the particular ritual elements of the Liturgy of the Word that demonstrates substantial "ritual minimalism" for Searle, and thus may be seen as being incapable of sparking the imagination of the assembly, is the general execution of the procession of the Book of

---

[36] Searle, *Liturgy Made Simple*, 38–39.

the Gospels.[37] While ritual "listening" is designed to take on a particularly attentive dimension as the assembly rises to its feet, it must be questioned as to whether or not the reverence offered the Gospel Book summons the assembly to this level of heightened awareness? Does even the posture of standing truly express "the congregation's reverence for, and their readiness to receive, the One who is coming"?[38] The GIRM supplies ample instruction regarding the "marks of honor" that must accompany this ritual of welcoming the Lord:

> The reading of the Gospel constitutes the high point of the Liturgy of the Word. The Liturgy itself teaches the great reverence that is to be shown to this reading by setting it off from the other readings with special marks of honor, by the fact of which minister is appointed to proclaim it and by the blessing or prayer with which he prepares himself; and also by the fact that through their acclamations the faithful acknowledge and confess that Christ is present and is speaking to them and stand as they listen to the reading; and by the mere fact of the marks of reverence that are given to the *Book of the Gospels*.[39]

[37] See Searle, "The Notre Dame Study of Catholic Parish Life," *Worship* 60 (1986): 317. He writes: "There is little evidence of ceremony and ritual splendor in the Masses we observed. . . . The impression is one of ritual minimalism. . . . While the Alleluia was usually sung or recited before the reading of the gospel, there was a gospel procession at only three liturgies. If our parishes are typical, then the opportunities offered by the rite for solemnizing the liturgy are not much used in this country, even at the main parish Mass."

[38] Adolf Adam, *The Eucharistic Celebration: The Source and Summit of Faith* (Collegeville, MN: Liturgical Press, 1994), 40. See also David Philippart, *Saving Signs, Wondrous Words* (Chicago, IL: Liturgy Training Publications, 1996), 45. Philippart writes: "As the deacon lifts the beautiful book, we jump to our feet and sing the song of angels and saints: Alleluia! As the deacon carries the book through this room, we stand, and, if we cannot actually leave our seats to follow it in procession, at least we pivot in place to follow the gospel on its way to the ambo. We stand at attention to hear the good news; we stand ready to live by it and to give our lives for its purposes."

[39] GIRM 60. See also 62, which articulates the theology of singing the Alleluia prior to the proclamation of the Gospel: "An acclamation of this kind constitutes a rite or act in itself, by which the gathering of the faithful welcomes and greets the Lord who is about to speak to them in the Gospel and profess their faith by means of the chant."

Searle believes that for the assembly to "listen" to the Gospel, as followers confronted by Christ with the words of God's Kingdom, this has "to be translated into ritual action in ways analogous to those in which the presence of Christ in the Eucharist is made credible."[40] In other words, reverence shown the Book of the Gospels, through the manner in which it is carried, escorted, and eventually enthroned on the ambo, must match the quality of care surrounding the handling of the bread and wine at the altar. Searle states very clearly: "The point of showing respect for the book, for example, is to encourage reverence for the word of God, and reverence for the word of God must lead to the obedience of faith."[41] Furthermore, in his 1986 piece "On Gestures," Searle reflects on the formative posture of standing:

> Standing does not appear like a gesture at all, but in some circumstances it can be most significant. The prisoner stands to be sentenced, the soldier stands to receive his orders, the bringer of gifts stands to make the presentation, inferiors stand in the presence of a higher authority. Some or all of these are echoed in the way we stand for the entrance of the ministers, for the carrying out of the coffin, for the confession of sin at the beginning of Mass and especially for the hearing of the gospel. Standing for the gospel or the passion narrative

[40] Searle, *Called to Participate*, 52.

[41] Ibid. Searle concludes: "Ritualizing the word would fall into aestheticism or bibliolatry if it did not serve to foster an attitude of vulnerability before the word. . . . [B]eing vulnerable to the word implies a profound inner silence, in which all our preoccupations die away, in which all that we bring into God's presence falls away, in which we ourselves become hollow and receptive." See also Searle, "Participation and Prayer," 145. He writes: "If we yearn for contact with the holy, if we want to know the numinous again, if we need to face the mystery in awe and trembling and know that we have seen God or at least heard the still small voice, then we will have to learn new rules and new skills in implementing those rules. If that holy has indeed been relocated, it is not enough to be *told* where it is; we also need directions on how to get there and how to recognize it when we see it. And that, I think, is where we have been sold short these last twenty years. Or where we have all fallen short. For we all said that Christ speaks to us when the Gospel is proclaimed; that Christ is present when the community assembles; that Christ is present in the Eucharistic action of breaking and sharing the bread and drinking the common cup; but few of us have known how to hear him speak or how to glimpse his presence in what often looks like a very uninspired and uninspiring ritual performance."

is a token of respect, a sign of submitting ourselves to its orders: we stand at attention.[42]

If the "trusting" part of "trusting imagination" is to be rehearsed in the Liturgy of the Word, it is during the procession of the Gospel Book, the singing of the Alleluia, and the subsequent proclamation of the Gospel that this is enacted through bodily engagement. Standing at attention is a gesture of trust in the Lord and signals the assembly's readiness to follow him wherever he would lead. It is a mark of honor that deserves to be taught and practiced. Yet our assemblies have not been trained to contemplate the gesture surrounding the Gospel as action completely different from standing in line at a supermarket—the obedience of faith requires so much more.

Following the proclamation of the Gospel, with the assembly returning to a seated position, the attitude of "trusting imagination" is once again rehearsed in the homily, for it is here that the words uttered by the homilist are meant to lead the assembly deeper into the metaphors and images found in the proclaimed Word.[43] The GIRM states that the homily is "highly recommended," as "it is necessary for the nurturing of the Christian life."[44] However, it also states that the homily should be an "explanation" of the readings or of some other text from the Mass and should also "take into account both the mystery being celebrated and the particular needs of the listeners."[45] If the Liturgy of the Word is a communications event between God and the assembly, then it is very important that the word "explanation" be understood in

[42] Mark Searle, "On Gestures," *Liturgy 80* 13, no. 1 (1982): 6.

[43] See Searle "Images and Worship," 111–12. Here Searle argues that preaching understood as catechesis has too often attempted to "teach" rather than to tap into the imagination of the assembly. He writes: "Just as in our youth we were catechized as to the meaning of the sacraments without reference to the actual celebration of the rites (that, after all, was how theology itself proceeded); so in our own day preachers continue to read preconceived meanings (whether progressive or reactionary, it makes no difference) into the texts of scripture, and catechists take their cue for teaching the sacraments from any place other than the ritual image. In either instance, we have a survival of the idea that images are merely the wrappings of 'truth' and that they can be dispensed with, explained in other terms, and then reintroduced as illustrations of the teacher's remarks" (111).

[44] GIRM 65.

[45] Ibid.

terms of opening up the imagination of the assembly to the mystery of God's working in their lives.[46] In a 1980 editorial on the liturgical function of the homily, Searle elaborates on what this "explanation" entails:

> The homily, as part of the liturgy itself, is integral to our common worship. It is an act of the priestly office of Jesus Christ, part of the *sacrum commercium* between God and his people in Jesus Christ, through the empowering and uniting Spirit of holiness. It is no mere interlude for instruction, no occasion for a speculative monologue, but an act of worship shared by the speaker and the hearers, an act of magnifying the Lord, of recounting his marvelous deeds in the assembly of his faithful, an act of remembering the God who remembers his people. It partakes of the nature of sacrament. It is the word which, conjoined to the elements of human life and history—all the rich elements of birth and death, joy and pain, hope and despair, faith and faithlessness—makes manifest the sacramentality of all existence. It is a word of consecration spoken over the human species for the transubstantiation of our lives into the life of God in Jesus Christ. Through that original Word made flesh, the flesh of human affairs is made incarnate and eloquent of God's saving presence. The homily is the angel's declaration of God-with-us, a declaration taken to heart and enacted in the sacramental liturgy that follows.[47]

As with the liturgical readings that precede it, the homily is an act of God confronting his people through the medium of speech. Searle calls it "a word of consecration spoken over the human species" that is meant to reveal the reality that the assembly, as Christ's Body, shares in divine life.[48] This approach to the homily suggests that the assembly,

[46] "Explanation" might best be defined in terms of "becoming." The homily must be directed to helping the assembly "become" the Word. See Searle, "The Word and the World," 8.

[47] Mark Searle, "The Homily," (Editorial), *Assembly* 7, no. 2 (1980): 105.

[48] See Catherine Vincie, "The Liturgy of the Word: The Mystagogical Implications," in *A Commentary on the Order of Mass of* The Roman Missal, ed. Edward Foley, et al. (Collegeville, MN: Liturgical Press, 2011), 187–88. She writes: "In the liturgy, the Word of God is both proclamation and revelation. The church is formed by God's Word but also becomes a sacrament of God. It proclaims to others what it has seen and heard and, by the power of the Holy Spirit, mediates God's revelation of self and salvation. . . . God's gratuitous gift is a grace (often considered 'uncreated' grace); the ability to accept the gift is also a grace."

no matter how outwardly resistant to surrender and transformation, must strive to hear in the words spoken by the homilist a word that intertwines life with God's life.[49] Searle suggests that the homily is an epiphany—"the angel's declaration of God-with-us"—a reality that necessarily increases the seriousness of preparing for the preaching event on the part of both the preacher and members of the assembly. "By befriending the image," writes Searle, "and by working with it lovingly, it will yield a glimpse of the world invisible, a snatch of the song of the angels and saints, a momentary awareness of myself and the grocer as one Body, one Spirit in Christ."[50]

As Searle states in the quote above, the homily is "an act of magnifying the Lord," words spoken to a gathered assembly made holy by God in order to radiate back to God a reordered life. Therefore, the "listening" attitude embodied by the assembly plays a critical role in this moment of annunciation.[51] In his 1980 article titled "Below the Pulpit: The Lay Contribution to the Homily," Searle describes the role of active participation in which all members are "partners in a pro-

---

[49] See The Bishops' Committee on Priestly Life and Ministry, *Fulfilled in Your Hearing: The Homily in the Sunday Assembly* (Washington, DC: United States Catholic Conference, 1982), 8. Here the bishops describe the homily in terms of the intersection between the lives of people in the assembly and the life of God: "The community that gathers Sunday after Sunday comes together to offer God praise and thanksgiving, or at least to await a word that will give a meaning to their lives and enable them to celebrate the Eucharist. What the preacher can do best of all at this time and in this place is to enable this community to celebrate by offering them a word in which they can recognize their own concerns and God's concerns for them."

[50] Searle, "Images and Worship," 112.

[51] See Mark Searle, "Below the Pulpit: The Lay Contribution to the Homily," Assembly 7, no. 2 (1980): 110. Regarding the important role of listening in the preaching process, Searle writes that it is "our contention that there is an active ingredient involved in listening to a homily, and that this listening cannot be omitted from any adequate reflection upon the homily as event—for the event is an event of communication, which necessarily requires one who listens as well as one who speaks. Indeed, just as the development of listening skills has become a high priority in such diverse areas of modern life as industrial management and personal counseling, so we must ask whether the development of liturgical listening skills should not likewise become an integral component of the catechumenate and other forms of formation. *In short, to be silent is not necessarily to be passive; to be listening is a primordial form of active participation in human encounter.*" Emphasis mine.

cess of communication," a process that requires the development of "a certain asceticism" on the part of those listening to the homily.[52] He writes:

> There is, of course, a certain asceticism involved in going back, Sunday after Sunday, to submit to the inordinate amount of bad preaching that abounds, to put up with ill-prepared homilies, to suffer paternalistic perorations and clerical authoritarianism and well-intentioned but utterly impractical moralizing. That sort of thing is perhaps what first springs to a lay person's mind when there is talk about the impact of preaching: the sheer flood of inert ideas that washes over our Sunday congregations who are thirsting for the living waters of the Word of God. But there is more to the lay vocation than mere forbearance. The lay listener, like the ordained preacher, has the responsibility of looking for the Word of God which comes, as always, in human guise. God's revelation in the past was no monologue from the clouds, but came borne upon the flowing tide of human experience. Then, as now, the Word of God was not something one had simply to listen to, but something one had to listen for: it involved active human participation in the very event of revelation and its gradual assimilation in faith.[53]

But how do members of the assembly begin this active search for a Word which reveals? Like most other moments of the liturgy, Searle contends that the search begins with a fundamental openness. "The words of a sermon," he writes, "like the words of Scripture themselves, have to be received with an open and welcoming heart; but they also have to be wrestled with before they yield up their hidden dimension as communications of Ultimate Reality."[54]

But there is more to the search than a willing surrender of self and a fundamental openness. Interestingly enough, Searle argues that the assembly must learn how to "ignore the preacher"—"to attend *from* the preacher's words *to* the Word being preached."[55] Ignoring here does not mean "switching off" the homilist but attempting to make connections on one's own between the homilist's images and the images of the Word that strike to the heart. Beyond this, however, Searle provides an even greater challenge to contemporary assemblies called

[52] Ibid.
[53] Ibid.
[54] Ibid., 111.
[55] Ibid.

to be "partners in a process of communication"; he challenges them to learn from the listening behavior of little children. He writes:

> Little children are a most disconcerting audience, tending to react not to what we in our superior adult wisdom wish them to react to, but reacting to whatever strikes their little minds and imaginations. Similarly, ascetical hearers of the Word await in empty stillness the word or thought or image that "strikes." . . . [T]he Word of God that comes to us in listening to homilies comes as something that jumps out at us (often unbeknownst to the speaker) and claims our attention and forces us to submit our own lives and values to its judgment. The asceticism required of us as hearers of the Word is thus a certain kind of receptivity, even vulnerability, before this word of illumination and insight and judgment.[56]

Searle goes on to describe in greater depth what this vulnerability entails: it is "the willingness to be challenged, judged, stripped" but also "to let one's fears be overcome in the embrace of God."[57] In other words, listening to the Word of God as little children means not just openness but willing trust in the Word that lifts up and gives new life. An "ascetic hearer" of the Word needs to ask both "how am I being broken down by the Word?" and "how is God restoring me to life?" Herein is the metaphor of Ultimate Reality—the Paschal Mystery of death and resurrection.

Finally, beyond ignoring the personality of the homilist and becoming vulnerable to the Word in the spoken homily, Searle suggests that a third skill of the artful listener is to turn attention back to the preacher. If members of the assembly are truly open and vulnerable to God's challenge in the homily—thereby resisting the temptation to project feelings of anger and fear upon the messenger—then they are able to see through to the presence of Christ in the one doing the preaching. According to Searle:

> At this point there comes a reversal of the former attitude: instead of prescinding from the person of the preacher one comes back to the preacher again. But one is now in a position to recognize him not as a "functionary," but with compassion as a fellow-believer, fellow-sinner, fellow-struggler. Such compassion is the fruit of hearing the Word

[56] Ibid.
[57] Ibid., 112.

generously. The distance between the pulpit and the pew is then bridged by the recognition of one who is, to coin a phrase, "my brother, my self."[58]

In the end, recognizing the preacher through the outlook of compassion helps to seal the event of the homily as a communal activity and as a true act of worship. Listeners do not receive the homily as spectators; they are invited to form a new relationship with the one preaching, with others who have listened, and ultimately with God who has loved us through the means of human vocabulary. If the liturgical role of preacher is approached with an attitude of humility, and the assembly listens to the homily with openness and a willingness to be transformed, then Christ's presence will be apparent as he reaches out and heals the Body in his Word. As Paul Janowiak writes: "The harmony that results from what is spoken and heard, what is preached and received, and how the community then approaches the table in a continuing revelation of praise and thanks truly encompasses what we can honestly call *holy communion*, the 'well-spring' of our sacramental union with Christ, God's uttered Word of grace."[59]

AN ATTITUDE OF FAITH

After an appropriate period of silence that allows the entire event of the Word to be firmly grounded in the assembly's being, all stand together for the Profession of Faith. Given the dialogical nature of liturgical prayer, this is the spoken opportunity for the assembly to respond to God's revelation. The GIRM makes quite clear the meaning of this component of the Liturgy of the Word: "The purpose of the Creed or Profession of Faith is that the whole gathered people may respond to the Word of God proclaimed in the readings taken from Sacred Scripture and explained in the Homily and that they may also honor and confess the great mysteries of the faith by pronouncing the rule of faith."[60] It is important to underscore the communal nature of the profession of the Creed. It is our common confrontation with God's living Word that now enables the Body of Christ to re-vision its identity—to see itself drawn deeper into the life of God in order to heal the world as Christ.

---

[58] Ibid.

[59] Janowiak, *Standing Together in the Community of God*, 116.

[60] GIRM 67.

Thus, while the Creed is fundamentally a faith statement about the triune God as manifested in the world, its liturgical setting makes it a statement of commitment on the part of the Church. It is made with the same confidence of Joshua who stood before the tribes of Israel and boldly sang out: "As regards my family and me, we shall serve Yahweh" (Josh 24:15). If the Mass begins with ritual elements that seek to form a group of collected individuals into the assembled Body of Christ, and if the proclamation of God's Word re-members this Body, then the Creed, along with the intercessory prayer that follows, begins to rehearse a confident faith that prepares to be sealed in communion.[61] Perhaps it is fitting, therefore, that the Creed has baptismal origins, and is used to express the new relationship in which the one to be baptized is to be initiated. Searle writes:

> The Creed is actually a transplant. It belongs, really, not at Mass but at baptism. In fact the Apostle's Creed is the old baptismal formula of Rome, and the Nicene Creed developed out of the baptismal formula used in the early centuries in the Christian community at Jerusalem. It owes its place in the Mass to the desire to respond to God's works, as proclaimed in the readings, by an affirmation of faith in all God has done, is doing, and will yet do.[62]

Another way of stating this is to recognize the Creed as ritual proof that the Body of Christ is committed to the work of conversion that has been initiated in the proclaimed Word. "The summons of the gospel," writes Searle, "is not only to faith but to repentance, not only to belief but to conversion; or rather it is to a life of faith which cannot express itself but in the conversion of the whole person."[63] The Creed celebrates our being chosen by God and our willingness to engage in the work of conversion. "It is no simple admission of 'facts,' therefore but a confession of gratitude that all this was undertaken, as

---

[61] Searle, *Liturgy Made Simple*, 48–49. Searle writes of the Creed and the Intercessions as coming from the desire on the part of the assembly to respond to God's Word: "Both of these are in the liturgy because people have in the past found that what they wanted to do after taking the Word of God to heart was to give an assent of faith to what they had heard and to express their confidence in the God who had spoken to them, by commending to him the needs of the world."

[62] Ibid., 49.

[63] Mark Searle, *Christening: The Making of Christians*, 77.

St. Irenaeus puts it, 'because of his surpassing love for his creation' (*Adv. Haer.* III, vi, 2); or, as we say in the Creed, 'for us and for our salvation.'"[64]

Although the profession of faith in the context of the Mass may be understood as the articulation of a commitment to the worldview manifested in the liturgical readings and the homily, Searle believed, as was previously mentioned in chapter 1, that ultimately faith is a matter of *discovery* rather than *decision*. Within the eucharistic liturgy, the Creed as the profession of the Church's faith may be seen as this great moment of insight, "the discovery of being discovered, loved, and called to faith."[65] Borrowing a term from James Fowler, Searle frequently defines faith simply as a way of "leaning into life."[66] The Creed is the Body of Christ's opportunity to express in words the corporate act of "leaning into life"—a leaning perhaps even bodily enacted as the assembly bows during the words that announce the Incarnation, a looking at life and the world through a renewed vision of relationship with God.[67]

Furthermore, such an understanding of faith means, for Searle, that it encompasses the entirety of one's life—not just information and beliefs that one grasps but how one is grasped by life and approaches the world in general. "Faith," writes Searle, "is a holistic sense of who

[64] Ibid., 84.

[65] Ibid., 48.

[66] For example, see Searle, *Called to Participate*, 35. For Fowler's use of the expression "leaning into life," see James Fowler, "Perspectives on the Family from the Standpoint of Faith Development Theory," *Perkins Journal* (Fall 1979): 7. He writes: "In this way of thinking faith need not be approached as necessarily a religious matter. Nor need it be thought of as doctrinal belief or assent. Rather, faith becomes the designation for a way of leaning into life. It points to a way of making sense of one's existence. It denotes a way of giving order and coherence to the force field of life. It speaks of the investment of life-grounding trust and of life-orienting commitment."

[67] See Vincie, "The Liturgy of the Word: The Mystagogical Implications," 193. She writes, "During the creed, the community is invited to reverentially bow at the announcement of the birth of our Lord (GIRM2003, nos. 18–19). Bending low, we acknowledge the great *commercium*, the divine gift of the Son to humanity. A bow seems so small a gesture to respond to this divine offer of the incarnation. We can only hope that this small gesture trains our hearts and minds in gratitude and that we learn to offer ourselves."

we are, of the kind of world we live in, and integrated intuition of how things are and what it all means."[68] He continues:

> Part of the difficulty with much traditional theology of baptismal faith is a one-sided preoccupation with faith as a matter of cognitive understanding. Vatican II attempted to counter this with a return to the Pauline concept of the "obedience of faith," which it defined as that obedience "whereby a person commits himself totally and freely to the God who reveals . . ." (DV, 4). In this view, faith is essentially a way of being, marked by commitment to, and dependence upon, God. The articulation of belief can never be other than a reflection upon and a making explicit of that initial stance towards life.[69]

Although the new English translation of the *Roman Missal* restores the traditional sense of professing the Creed as a statement of one's individual faith—i.e., "I believe" instead of "we believe"—its location in the liturgy underscores the sense of the developing communion of the assembly. The Body of Christ is confronted by God's Word, and thus, the Church declares that it is a "household"[70] united in faith. As Searle states:

> The faith of the Church, therefore, is not just what if professes to believe. It is, fundamentally, its characteristic way of "leaning into life." The faith of the Church is more than any doctrine, more than anything the Church can say. *Ultimately, it is what the Church does in obedience to Christ and in conformity to the pattern of his own life, death and resurrection.* In brief, the faith of the Church is the faith of Christ: it is that existential subordination of itself to God which is the fruit of assimilating the Spirit of Christ and thus reproducing in this historical collective that same mind which was in Christ Jesus. Christ's own obedience of faith is the rock on which the Church is built, beginning with the apostles whose deaths so closely imitated that of their Master. From then until

[68] Mark Searle, "Childhood and the Reign of God: Reflections on Infant Baptism," *Assembly* 9 (1982): 186.

[69] Ibid.

[70] See Mark Searle, "Households of Faith" (Editorial), *Assembly* 8, no. 5 (1982): 169. Searle writes: "A household, traditionally, was more than a nuclear family—it usually included several families related by kinship or service. On the other hand, it was considerably less than the more or less anonymous conglomerates of isolated individuals and families which constitute our typical housing projects and even, sadly, our parishes."

now, the Church has found and continues to find its identity in its commitment to discovering and submitting to God's will and to carrying it out in the world. In this way, the Church, in being obedient to Christ, participates in Christ's obedience to God.[71]

The recitation of the Creed, therefore, is the ritual foreshadowing of what will take place in the Liturgy of the Eucharist that follows; it demonstrates that the Church is one with Christ in his obedience of faith.[72] The Creed, in a very real sense, moves the Word into the deeper realm of God's saving action in the Paschal Mystery of Christ, which is demonstrated by the words and actions of the Eucharistic Prayer that follows.[73] Thus, the Creed does not merely express the attitude of faith in response to God's Word, it also makes clear that the Church must now rehearse a self-emptying faith in order to renew itself in participating in Christ's priestly work of self-surrender.[74]

[71] Searle, *Called to Participate*, 35–36. Emphasis mine.

[72] See Jerome M. Hall, *We Have the Mind of Christ: The Holy Spirit and Liturgical Memory in the Thought of Edward J. Kilmartin* (Collegeville, MN: Liturgical Press, 2001), 145–46. Regarding the Church's participation in the faith of Christ, Hall writes: "The Church actualizes the Spirit of Christ's faith in gathering for prayer in Jesus' memory, in celebrating the Word proclaimed in their midst, and then in particular sacramental prayers and actions. In this process the Spirit gives the Church an accurate memory of the deeds of Jesus, gives the assembly and its particular members the saving attitudes of Christ, expressed in the official prayer texts and sacramental actions, and thus renews in them the covenant made in Jesus Christ. Those attitudes include trust, self-offering, love for God and neighbor, and thankfulness for God's self-communication. It was those attitudes which Jesus Christ expressed in his temporal acts and which were realized in the pinnacle of his personal history of faith and love on the cross" (146).

[73] Searle, *Called to Participate*, 36. Searle states: "Thus God, whose love and mercy were displayed and glorified when Jesus entrusted his life into God's hands, continues to be glorified when the Church, by its faith and obedience, gives new scope for the manifestation and glorification of God's will to save."

[74] Ibid. Searle contends: "To participate in the rite with that kind of self-emptying is to participate in the priestly work of Christ and to render visible and tangible here and now the eternal liturgy that Christ himself celebrates before the throne of God. We are baptized into the Church, Christ's Body, in order to participate in his mediatorial role and continue his work on this earth until the day that God becomes 'all in all.'"

Intimately connected to the Profession of Faith—signaled by the maintenance of the posture of attentive and reverent standing—is the Prayer of the Faithful, or what the GIRM calls the "Universal Prayer." Like the Creed, these intercessions are meant to be a response to the Word of God but are also a participation in Christ's priestly ministry by "representing Christ to the world and the world to God."[75] The GIRM states: "In the Universal Prayer or Prayer of the Faithful, the people respond in some sense to the Word of God which they have received in faith and, exercising the office of their baptismal priesthood, offer prayers to God for the salvation of all."[76] Regarding this ritual element that concludes the Liturgy of the Word, Searle writes:

> The *Prayers of Intercession* continue the movement of growing communion within the gathered congregation as they move us from common listening to common prayer. In this prayer we become aware of our identity over against the larger society, for it is on behalf of that society that we lift up our voice in common prayer. We exercise our vocation to be a priestly people, interceding for the world, in union with Christ our head, who lives to make intercession for ever.[77]

Therefore, the Prayer of the Faithful rehearses the Christian attitude of faith as the assembly claims its baptismal duty of attending to the public nature of prayer, for the assembled Church "is the place where the timeless intersects with time, heaven and earth meet, and God and humanity embrace."[78]

While liturgical history suggests that intercessory prayer was incorporated into the introductory portion of the Mass as a plea for God's

---

[75] Ibid., 30–31. See also Philippart, *Saving Signs, Wondrous Words*, 24–25. He writes: "The scripture readings in the liturgy proclaim and present the reign of God. So at Mass we hear that, with the coming of God, the blind will be able to watch the lame dance, the mute will sing and the deaf will hear the song, children will be safe from all harm, no one will be without life's necessities and joys, the earth will be tended with care, and creation itself will live in harmony. Then we stand before God and admit in concrete terms that this in not happening everywhere and for everyone. . . . We begin to see the world with Christ's eyes and hear it with Christ's ears. . . . So we speak up. We speak up for those whose pain is so great, whose struggle is so all-consuming that they might not even be able to speak up for themselves."

[76] GIRM 69.

[77] Searle, "Rites of Communion," 127.

[78] Searle, *Called to Participate*, 31.

mercy,[79] the placement of the prayer at the conclusion of the Liturgy of the Word suggests that it is a hopeful articulation of faith in what God has accomplished in the past, achieves in the present, and promises to fulfill in the future. The Prayer of the Faithful reinforces that the unity of the assembly is not separate from but one with the world, and it manifests the theological truth that wholeness is God's gift. Thus, the intercessions are fundamentally the prayer of Christ and his yearning for the coming of God's Just Kingdom.[80] The assembly looks beyond itself—in a very real sense abandons itself—and thereby articulates its faith by taking part in Christ's prayer. In his 1974 piece, "The Church Celebrates Her Faith," Searle makes it clear that such self-abandonment is what faith is all about:

> Thus faith is man's *total* response to God's self-revelation in history. It seizes a man in his entirety: it claims every fiber of his being, every area of his life. Consequently it cannot remain a purely internal assent: a man must express this surrender to God and his reliance upon him in what he says and what he does. So we can distinguish, without separating, two forms of external expression for this internal assent and submission to God: a man must give his faith living expression in what he says and in his moral behavior.[81]

After having just been confronted by the Word of God, it could be a tempting response to reorder one's life and relationships according to one's own will and design, but a faith response demands that all attempts at constructing a more just and loving world, of healing and restoring relationships, be done according to dependence on God's will, thereby "making us aware that our lives only have meaning insofar as they are lived in dependence on the Father and in union with

[79] See my article "The History, Theology, and Practice of the Prayer of the Faithful," *Pastoral Liturgy* 41, no. 6 (2010): 4–8 (Reprinted in *The Order of Mass: A Roman Missal Study Edition and Workbook*, ed. Michael S. Driscoll and J. Michael Joncas, 327–39 [Chicago, IL: Liturgy Training Publications, 2011]).

[80] See Don Saliers "Pastoral Liturgy and Character Ethics: As We Worship So We Shall Be," in *Source and Summit: Commemorating Josef A. Jungmann, S.J.*, ed. Joanne M. Pierce and Michael Downey (Collegeville, MN: Liturgical Press, 1999), 190. He writes: "Liturgical participation thus requires learning to 'pray with' Christ's on-going intercession, and to be attentive to the Holy Spirit's 'sighing in us and through us' when we do not know how to pray for ourselves as we ought."

[81] Searle, "The Church Celebrates Her Faith," 4.

Christ, whose life we share through the gift of his Spirit poured out into our hearts."[82]

CONCLUSION

Learning how to "listen" as the Body of Christ, rather than as a collection of disparate individuals, is no easy task. However, if Christians are to identify and to participate in ushering in God's Just Kingdom, it is necessary that they master obedience to God's will—as did Christ—in order to assess the best response to the needs of a waiting world. This is precisely the point of the Liturgy of the Word, which does not simply tell the story of God's reign as events accomplished in the past but confronts the gathered Body of Christ with God's living and active voice. The liturgical proclamation of Scripture is more than a simple rendering of the blueprint of what God desires for creation, it is real encounter with divine life.[83]

Thus, as the liturgical assembly grows deeper in its recognition and celebration of unity in Christ, it can be said to be learning the way of "listening" to God's word. This ritual "listening" begins with the rehearsal of an attitude of *trusting imagination*, in which the assembly is not engaged in the project of accumulating information but rather attempts to discover insight into the working of God in the world. Searle devoted a large part of his academic career to furthering the understanding that the liturgy, and most specifically the liturgical word, is metaphorical in nature and is meant to expand the horizons of the Christian imagination. In his words, "It is not explanation we need, but contemplation; not ideas but disclosures."[84] Thus, after the assembly discovers its life in the midst of the story of God's Word, it then proceeds to practice the attitude of *faith*. It does so, first, by making a

---

[82] Ibid., 7.

[83] See Janowiak, *Standing Together in the Community of God*, 87. He writes: "God loves (takes in), speaks that Word (lets go), which is the expression of that generative Love, and then listens to the Son's obedient answer of self-emptying surrender to it (takes in), whose life Christ shares with the world in the same rhythm and power of the Spirit (lets go). . . . *Bodiliness* provides the necessary arena of encounter for this hearing and responding in Love. . . . The *vulnerability of such a connection*, which God shares with us in the *kenotic* (self-emptying) offer of the Word-made-flesh, opens for us the way for our active participation in this redemptive event to real communion and complete surrender in union with the Trinity."

[84] Searle, "Liturgy as Metaphor," 116.

confident claim to identity as Christ's Body, baptized into his mission, and secondly, by articulating utter dependence on God for the direction and the strength to participate in this work.

All in all, the celebration of the Liturgy of the Word makes Christ's presence alive in his gathered Church, as it makes its response one of submission to God's will. It is this self-sacrifice which takes on a visible manifestation in the celebration of the Liturgy of the Eucharist that follows. It is here that the Church declares that its "listening" must bear real fruit: union with divine life and communion with all that exists in God's Just Kingdom. Having practiced the way of listening, the Body is now ready to rehearse the attitude of sacrifice, as it utters its great prayer of thanksgiving.

Chapter 5

The Rehearsal of Sacrificing

What does it mean to call the Eucharist a "sacrifice"? This question has long been debated, as exhibited in the controversy between the medieval monks Paschasius and Ratramnus at the Abbey of Corbie in Northern France in the mid-ninth century,[1] through Luther and the Protestant Reformation in the mid-sixteenth century,[2] and even in the writings of contemporary scholars such as Jesuit theologians Edward Kilmartin and Robert Daly.[3] Furthermore, at the outset of chapter 2 of *Sacrosanctum Concilium*, "The Sacred Mystery of the Eucharist," the Fathers of the Second Vatican Council took the opportunity to define the eucharistic celebration in terms of a "sacrifice." They write:

> At the last supper, on the night he was betrayed, our Savior instituted the Eucharistic sacrifice of his body and blood. This he did in order to perpetuate the sacrifice of the cross throughout the ages until he should come again, and so to entrust to his beloved spouse, the church, a memorial of his death and resurrection: a sacrament of love, a sign of unity, a bond of charity, "a paschal banquet in which Christ is received, the mind is filled with grace, and a pledge of future glory is given to us."[4]

---

[1] See Nathan Mitchell, *Cult and Controversy: The Worship of the Eucharist outside Mass* (New York: Pueblo Publishing Company, 1982), 73–86.

[2] See David N. Power, *The Sacrifice We Offer: The Tridentine Dogma and Its Reinterpretation* (New York: Crossroad Publishing Company, 1987).

[3] See Edward J. Kilmartin, *The Eucharist in the West: History and Theology* (Collegeville, MN: Liturgical Press, 1998) and "The Catholic Tradition of Eucharistic Theology: Towards the Third Millennium," *Theological Studies* 55 (1994): 405–57. See also Robert J. Daly, *Sacrifice Unveiled: The True Meaning of Christian Sacrifice* (New York: Continuum Books, 2009); and "Sacrifice Unveiled or Sacrifice Revisited: Trinitarian and Liturgical Perspectives," *Theological Studies* 64 (2003): 24–42. See also Joris Geldhof, "The Eucharist and the Logic of Christian Sacrifice: A Discussion with Robert J. Daly," *Worship* 87 (2013): 292–308.

[4] *Sacrosanctum Concilium* 47 in Flannery, *The Basic Sixteen Documents*.

Thus, the Council reaffirms that the Eucharist is both a "sacrifice" and a "banquet"; it sacramentalizes both the obedience of the Cross and the joy of a celebratory meal. Yet, it is difficult to grasp both concepts at once. If "sacrifice" conjures up ideas of "self-deprivation, inconvenience, endurance, even suffering,"[5] then how can the Eucharist be simultaneously a celebration of fulfillment and endless joy?[6] The answer is rooted solely in Christ's sacrifice itself. "To speak of Christ's death as a sacrifice," writes Mark Searle in a 1984 editorial, "is to speak of it as his supreme testimony to God and God's supreme testimony to him, for the ultimate happiness of all humanity."[7]

While acknowledging that "sacrifice" eludes a singular definition, Searle continues in the same editorial to argue that "what makes something a sacrifice is the Godwardness of the intent: undertaken in pursuit of the ultimate happiness of oneself and others."[8] Given this understanding of the term, the sacrifice of the Cross is centered in the Lord's intention of directing his suffering Godward, trusting that union with God would be the fruit of his obedience. Thus, Searle contends that we must attend to the rehearsal of sacrifice in the Eucharist:

[5] Kevin W. Irwin, *Models of the Eucharist* (New York: Paulist Press, 2005), 217. Irwin's eighth model is titled "Sacramental Sacrifice." He concludes the chapter with the following: "We began this chapter by referring to the many ways we use the word 'sacrifice' in daily life and in the liturgy. One of the most challenging ways of understanding this term is to allow it to be a constant reminder of the total self-surrender of Jesus for us and for our salvation. He acted in humility and obedience. These are characteristic ways that we should reflect our faith in him and as celebrated in the Mass. An integral liturgical theology of the Mass as sacrifice must always be framed in a sacramental context. Similarly, a mainstay of any act of liturgy or sacrament, but especially that of the Eucharist, is that it is born from and returns us back to the one sacrifice of Christ. In effect, the celebration of the Eucharist is both sacramental sacrifice and a sacrificial sacrament" (236–37).

[6] See Matthew Levering, *Sacrifice and Community: Jewish Offering and Christian Eucharist* (Malden, MA: Blackwell Publishing, 2005). Levering writes: "The full context of sacrifice, in other words envisions expiation, purification, restitution, complete self-gift, and thankful communion. . . . Sacrifice is completed in feasting; far from being simply renunciatory, sacrifice is profoundly fulfilling" (64–65).

[7] Mark Searle, "Sacrifice" (Editorial), *Assembly* 10, no. 4 (1984): 241.

[8] Ibid.

Perhaps one of the most striking contrasts between preconciliar and postconciliar Catholicism is to be found in the role of the term "sacrifice." For those of us who grew up before the Council, the image of sacrifice was central to our vocabulary and pervasive of our religious ethos: the Mass was ever the holy Sacrifice; the spiritual life ran on personal acts of sacrifice; Christ, whose image, always portraying him in the agony of his sacrificial death, was everywhere to be seen. Since the Council, so much of this has been swept away and talk about sacrifice has become awkward and apologetic. Nevertheless, sacrifice will not go away. . . . *It is central to Christianity and, if it dies, our faith dies with it, for it is the concept or image which serves to link together the death of Christ, the celebration of the Eucharist, and the Christian life as a whole.*[9]

While the Mass in its entirety is intended to school the Church in the embodiment of Christ's sacrifice, it is the movement from the ritual act of "listening" to God's Word to responding with the prayer of thanksgiving that practices sacrifice as a Christian attitude. Just as Christ himself listened attentively to discern the will of the Father prior to his death, as founded in his prayer at Gethsemane—"Father, if it is possible, let this cup pass me by. Nevertheless, let it be as you, not I, would have it" (Matthew 26:39; Mark 14:36; Luke 22:42)—so too the Church, in Christ, discerns God's will and proceeds to enact a prayer of faith and total trust. The Church does not repeat the Lord's sacrifice, it learns how to live it.

AN ATTITUDE OF COLLECTING

The instructions provided by the GIRM to govern the Liturgy of Eucharist begin by acknowledging the pattern of four-fold action that will serve to seal the Church's response to the proclaimed Word. The GIRM states:

> For Christ *took* the bread and the chalice, *gave thanks*, *broke* the bread and *gave* it to his disciples, saying: Take, eat and drink: this is my Body; this is the chalice of my Blood. Do this in memory of me. Hence, the Church has arranged the entire celebration of the Liturgy of the Eucharist in parts corresponding to precisely these words and actions of Christ.[10]

[9] Ibid. Emphasis mine.

[10] GIRM 72. Emphasis mine. For a description of Eucharistic theology based on the four action words of the Institution Narrative see Gregory Dix, *The Shape of the Liturgy* (New York: Seabury Press, 1982). Dix first published this work in 1945.

The very first action that occurs in this description of the Last Supper is *taking*, which begins in the gathering together of the gifts offered by the members of the assembly. No verbal explanation accompanies either the collection of gifts or their presentation, and yet these liturgical gestures ought to be powerful symbols to the community of the sacrificial nature of the Eucharist. "Even though the faithful no longer bring from their own possessions the bread and wine intended for the liturgy as was once the case," states the GIRM, "nevertheless the rite of carrying up the offerings still keeps its spiritual efficacy and significance."[11]

However, what about the ritual gesture of collecting that precedes the rite of presenting? The GIRM makes no concrete suggestions as to how the collection should be conducted, other than to say that "money or other gifts for the poor or for the Church . . . are to be put in a suitable place away from the Eucharistic table."[12] Yet Searle believed that this component of the liturgy is in need of serious reform, precisely because, in its present enactment, it is not a real redistribution of wealth as seen in the early Church (see, for example, Acts 2:44-45). In his 1979 piece, "Contributing to the Collection," Searle writes:

> The history of word-usage is a curious and fascinating study, for the history of a word's meaning often reveals unsuspected relationships. The word "collection" is a case in point. *Colectio* in Latin meant originally a gathering together of people or things; in liturgical Latin it, or its related form *Colecta*, could also refer to an assembly of the Christian community or to the prayer offered by the celebrant to "gather up" the prayer of the whole people, (a usage retained in our word "collect"). But its roots would indicate rather the sense of tying or fastening together, a making into one. The collected dollars make one lump sum: but are the donors, too, "gathered together"? Or does the alienation of earning pass over into the alienation of giving?[13]

In this article, Searle goes on to suggest that the action of contributing to the collection needs to be seen as a true embodiment of the attitude of the Magnificat (Luke 1:52-53), in which the Lord deposes the mighty and raises up the lowly, feeds the starving and sends the rich away empty. The collection ought to be a real reversal of one's status in the

[11] GIRM 73.
[12] Ibid.
[13] Mark Searle, "Contributing to the Collection," *Assembly* 6, no. 1 (1979): 62.

world. One contributes to the collection as "living proof of the reality of reconciliation,"[14] whereby there exists a oneness in creation—those who have been blessed with wealth realize their poverty, while those who endure deprivation recognize their fulfillment.

Thus, Searle places the words "collection" and "recollection" in juxtaposition with one another and ruminates on whether or not "collected dollars" are more a sign of alienated giving than a truth gathering together of the community's substantial and sacrificial gifts. He suggests that a restored understanding of the historic purpose of the collection in the liturgy may assist in reuniting the intimate relationship between giver and gift, laborer and product:

> Perhaps it is too much to dream of a day when we might all bring to the assembly loaves of bread and bottles of wine, and witness for ourselves the sacramental transformation of gifts which are the fruit of land we ourselves have worked and the work of our own careful hands. Perhaps we now live in too complicated a society and too remote an economy for the Sunday offertory ever again to be the occasion for a regular redistribution of wealth. . . . We are alienated from our work, for most of us have little or no responsibility for the products we are hired to manufacture, or for the goods we sell, or for the services we provide. We are alienated in our giving, for it does not cut deeply enough into our lives to make us really aware of our mutual dependence. We are alienated from the recipients of our gifts, for not only do we rarely meet the poor and see their needs, but we often have no idea what the money is used for, or if it even reaches the poor.[15]

Searle suggests here that the collection as it is now most often executed in parishes underscores three types of alienation: alienation from our work, alienation from our giving, and perhaps most importantly, alienation from the receiver of our gift. A gift is not a gift until it is duly received, and the liturgical gestures that accompany the collection do not reveal a real relationship with the recipient. Searle himself offers no remedy for the alienation he describes other than to demand that the collection of gifts must awaken in people's hearts and minds the inherent connection between worship and a Christian worldview. Although still only "a vestigial reminder of what used to be," the collection "may yet serve as a clue to rediscovering the meaning of

---

[14] Ibid., 64.
[15] Ibid.

Christian community and to rediscovering the lost connection between liturgy and life."[16] In short, a contemplative perspective on the collection may view it as a ritual rehearsal of the assembly striving to be attentive to every part of the whole, thereby realizing that the Body is dependent on all of its parts for sustenance and survival.[17]

While the collection and the presentation of the gifts is to be accompanied by an Offertory Chant (see GIRM, 74), greater meaning is to be placed on the action of exchange. In other words, the sacrificial aspect of the Presentation of the Gifts stands out when a tangible relationship is established between the assembly and the gifts. In an editorial for *Assembly* titled simply "Liturgical Objects," Searle contends that the material gifts of liturgy "become extensions of ourselves, mirrors of our souls, symbols of our relationships."[18] Besides the sprinkling

[16] Ibid., 63. See also Searle, "Grant Us Peace . . . Do We Hear What We Are Saying?," 9. He writes: "One of the earliest and most indispensable parts of the Mass is the collection. Originally, it was a taking up of all sorts of gifts: not only bread, wine and money, but other foodstuffs, as well as clothing, oil for lighting and cooking, and candles. These gifts were collected by the president or the deacons. Some was set aside for the immediate use of the community in the Eucharistic meal; the rest was distributed by the presider and the deacons to the sick, the imprisoned, the orphans and the widows, that is to say, to the members of the community who could not provide for themselves. What we have here is nothing less than a redistribution of the wealth of the community. . . . The collection is intimately connected with the communion. Traditionally, excommunication meant that a person was barred not only from taking part in the act of communion, but also from being able to offer their gifts at the altar. They had cut themselves off by serious sin from the order of justice."

[17] See Searle, *Liturgy Made Simple*, 59. He writes: "People brought corn and oil and eggs and cheese and spare clothing—whatever they had that they didn't need for themselves. It was the moment of redistributing the wealth of the community, so that no one grew fat while another starved, and no one kept coats in the wardrobe while others shivered in the cold. They could not celebrate the memory of Jesus' gift of himself without themselves being generous with one another." He goes on to offer the following recommendation for the collection: "Today what we often refer to by its old name as 'The Offertory' is properly called 'The Preparation of the Gifts.' By this we mean God's gifts to us and our gifts to God. But really we cannot give anything to God himself unless it be by way of giving to his people. We therefore need to restore the sense of the collection as a realistic distribution of wealth."

[18] Mark Searle, "Liturgical Objects," *Assembly* 8, no. 1 (1981): 137.

of water and the incensation of the altar (both rarely executed) at the opening of the Mass, the Presentation of the Gifts serves as an intense isolation of the symbolic nature of gifts given and received. The collection, the bread and the wine—as objects of creation mixed with human ingenuity—may be seen as fulfilling a destiny, achieving "the role of glorifying him by whom and for whom they were created."[19] For this very reason, the liturgical objects used during the Presentation of the Gifts must be approached through the attitudes of "respect" and "reverence." Searle writes:

> "Respect" and "reverence" are terms we habitually associate with liturgy as also with life. Interestingly enough, they both derive from roots connected with the act of seeing. Both of them refer to a kind of looking which regards not only the thing-as-thing, but the thing as medium of mystery. . . . To look upon something with reverence, then, would not so much be a matter of "seeing through" it as of seeing how it connects with us and we with it. Reverence and respect thus imply a disciplined kind of looking, a properly focused visual attention which is quite different from the attitude of the casual onlooker or the curious spectator. They refer not so much to the way the eye is captured by the novel or the unusual, as to the contemplative fixing of the eye upon what is already familiar and loved and can only yield to the look of love. Then looking cedes to seeing. *Respect and reverence are the attitude of those who look, knowing there is something there to see.*[20]

"Respect" and "reverence" as attitudes, or ways of approaching the world, entail deep concentration. Searle suggests that they are not ways of looking "through" or beyond the object or act, but rather, "respect" and "reverence" are ways of peering into mystery, ways of making intimate connections that establish commitment to the larger reality that is being celebrated. He writes: "Seeing requires an emptying of the self, a refusal of judgment, even of thought—the suspension of all evaluation in favor of being receptive to communication: 'Look it in the eye until you feel it looking back at you.'"[21]

---

[19] Ibid. See also Irwin, "A Sacramental World—Sacramentality as the Primary Language for Sacraments."

[20] Searle, "Liturgical Objects," 144. Emphasis mine.

[21] Ibid. Shortly before, Searle quotes the work of Frederick Franck, *The Zen of Seeing*, and says much the same thing: "To see with the heart is to see without prejudice or passion, without evaluation or hope of profit. It is a matter of being empty so that one may be filled with the gift of that to which one is

From the action of taking up the collection, to the connections made in the bread and wine carried gracefully in procession, this isolated moment of liturgical prayer offers the assembly an opportunity to "see"—to understand that in seeing the gifts presented, we are seeing ourselves received.[22] So, what of the "respect" and "reverence" rehearsed with the bread and wine themselves; what is the assembly to "see" and behold? Searle offers a poetic description of the bread and wine that demonstrates their nature: their very purpose for being is sacrificial. In other words, bread and wine exist in order to become life for others. He writes:

> It is of the nature of food that it should be eaten.
> It is of the nature of food that it should be consumed.
>
> Food exists only that it may be devoured.
> Drink exists only to be poured out.
>
> Food is food, not for its own sake,
>   but to give life to the hungry.
>
> Drink is drink, not for its own sake,
>   but to give joy to the drinker.
>
> Food and drink are creatures which achieve fulfillment
> in being put at the disposal of others:

---

attending. Frederick Frank, in his book *The Zen of Seeing*, puts it as follows: 'Look it in the eye until you feel it looking back at you. Feel that you are alone with it on earth! That it is the most important thing in the universe, that it contains all the riddles of life and death. It does! You are no longer looking, you are seeing. . .'" Searle continues by applying this way of seeing to the liturgy: "Liturgical objects are there to be looked at, touched, smelled. All these actions may be done perfunctorily or they may, if done with respect, be three ways of seeing. . . . Such a way of relating begins to break down the distance between object and subject, establishes communion. Am I entering the church or is the church embracing me. Am I looking at the icon or is the icon looking at me? Am I receiving the ashes or are the ashes receiving me?"

[22] Ibid. Searle suggests that the "paradox of looking and seeing and the basic paradoxes of the Christian life" are intertwined, and he looks to the words of St. Francis: 'For it is in seeing that we are seen, it is in touching that we are touched, it is in receiving that we are received, it is in emptying ourselves that we are filled and it is in dying that we are born to eternal life.'"

they exist to serve the needs of others;
their destiny is met in their destruction.

When the Lord Jesus, shortly before he was betrayed,
took bread and wine as symbols of himself
and gave them to his disciples
he expressed himself perfectly:
bread that we might have life,
wine that we might be glad;
one bread, broken and shared in friendship,
one cup, pledge of a common destiny.

This bread is my body, which is for you;
this cup is my blood, poured out for you.

He is for us.
It is the story of his life.[23]

"Food and drink are creatures which achieve fulfillment in being put at the disposal of others." However, the way in which food and drink are disposed is either a sign of justice or injustice—they can either be used to build up relationships, or they can be used to create division.[24] In his "Serving the Lord with Justice," Searle contends that the bread and wine offered as gifts in the Eucharist are marked with the words of Jesus so as to achieve their true, God-given purpose again, to be given and shared:

> When Jesus took the bread, said the blessing, broke the bread and
> shared it, he demonstrated, unforgettably, the proper use of all mate-
> rial things. The early Christians realized this: they "eucharistized"

[23] Mark Searle, "Bread and Wine," *Assembly* 8, no. 1 (1981): 143. See also John Baldovin, *Bread of Life, Cup of Salvation: Understanding the Mass* (Lanham, MD: Rowman & Littlefield Publishers, Inc., 2003), 1–11. In his first chapter titled "Food, Glorious Food," Baldovin suggests that food and drink used improperly (the way they are most often used) represent the sin of "grasping," while food and drink used properly (or food and drink redeemed) symbolize self-emptying. He writes: "If sin is grasping, then redemption is letting go. If sin means symbolically grabbing at food, then redemption means sharing it and giving it away. Jesus accepted his creaturehood with open hands as a gift. Ironically, being divine for Jesus meant accepting humanity to the fullest . . . the reality that the Mass manifests is the process of divine self-emptying in a ritual nutshell" (6–7).
[24] See Searle, "Liturgical Objects," 137 and 144.

their lives by blessing God in all things and by making their possessions available to one another. And when Jesus took the cup and gave
thanks to God and passed it among his disciples, he rediscovered for
the human race the joy of not claiming anything for one's own—not
even life itself. . . . Creation, groaning to be redeemed from the homi-
cidal perversions to which our sinful use has subjected it, finds its lib-
eration when it is used as it is used in the liturgy: to acknowledge and
express the justice of God in the midst of his people, who are being
bonded into a community by their common and respectful use of material things.[25]

It may at first seem better suited to talk about the bread and wine
achieving their fulfillment in the context of the Eucharistic Prayer,
when, in the midst of the community's prayer, the Spirit is invoked
upon them and the words of the Lord at the Last Supper are spoken
over them; however, such reversal of "sinful use" begins in the preparation of the gifts themselves. It is not simply the fruits of creation that
are participating in a just reversal, but it is the human ingenuity and
labor necessary to make bread and wine that are redeemed as well.[26]
"Respect" and "reverence" call the assembly to see the sacrifices of the
earth and of human hands that have produced such great gifts and to
see their sacrifices received in the exchange of the gifts.

Is the sacrificial nature of the bread and wine, in and of themselves,
truly comprehended by our worshiping communities today? Most
likely the answer is "no." The bread and wine presented at the altar
usually neither come from the fields of those assembled, nor does the
assembly have any sense of the work that is invested in producing
bread out of wheat and wine out of crushed grapes.[27] When we "see"

[25] Searle, "Serving the Lord with Justice," 27–28.
[26] See Catherine Vincie, "The Preparation of the Gifts: The Mystagogical
Implications," in *A Commentary on the Order of Mass of* The Roman Missal,
ed. Edward Foley, et al. (Collegeville, MN: Liturgical Press, 2011), 222. Vincie
writes: "We do not bring God's gifts of grain and grapes in their natural state.
We transform them into bread and wine, adding our own efforts of labor and
culture to the sacrifice. This proclaims not only that nature is good but that
human effort and all manner of culture are also good and worthy to be used
for praise. The fruit of our work also will be taken up by God and transformed
into gifts of eternal life."
[27] See Daniel Groody, "Fruit of the Vine and Work of Human Hands: Immigration and the Eucharist," *Worship* 80 (2006): 386–402. As the title suggests,

the bread and wine processed gracefully and lovingly to the altar, held carefully and with dignity in the hands of the priest, and placed gently upon the table, do we "see" the struggle that is paradigmatic of our own struggle to "eucharistize" all of life, giving so that others might live? Searle writes:

> Today, men and women will talk of their struggle to support their families as a struggle to put bread on the table. But here is no ordinary table. It is the table prepared by God for his people in the person of his Son. As it becomes a paradigm for all tables everywhere, making us recognize in all food and drink the fruit of the earth and the work of human hands: the gift of God and of his human co-workers. It makes us see that all human labor is cooperative venture. We dig and plant, but God gives the growth. We transform the world by our technology, but God gives the raw materials and the skill.[28]

David Power echoes the necessity of the bread and wine to visibly represent a sacrifice that comes from the assembly itself: "If the food and drink do not come from the people who gather, if they do not represent their lives, then the meaning of their transformation into the body and blood of Christ is lessened."[29] Celebrating the liturgy should train us to see that creation bestowed as gift, and gift cherished, transformed and returned is the pattern of living justly. "The simplest celebration of the Eucharist," writes Searle, "cries out against the normalization and rationalization of injustice in the use of material goods,

---

Groody believes that the bread and wine used in the Eucharist offers immigrants a way of viewing their struggles for survival and provides a critique regarding the just production of goods in this country. He writes: "When we think of the Eucharist, we think of bread, we think of wine. We reflect on the words, 'this is my body, this is my blood.' But less often do we reflect on the words in the Order of Mass, less frequently do we think of the Eucharist in terms of 'the fruit of the vine and the work of human hands.' Given that the agricultural industry in the United States is sustained largely through immigrant labor, the bread and wine that come to the table is very often the result of immigrant labor. And in many parts of the country, this kind of labor is a modern-day slavery. And such slavery brings us face to face not only with the immigrant story but the Passover story all over again" (399).

[28] Searle, *Liturgy Made Simple*, 58.

[29] David N. Power, *The Eucharistic Mystery: Revitalizing the Tradition* (New York: Crossroad Publishing Company, 1993), 343.

and against the way we turn the creation committed to our care into weapons of power and destruction."[30]

In placing the gifts of bread and wine upon the altar, the presider quietly recites the blessing prayers. As a gesture of reverence and as a sign of exchange, the priest may incense the gifts, the entire altar, and likewise the assembly. "The incensing signifies that the church's prayer and offering rise to God as the incense itself rises upward."[31] The presider then washes his hands as a moment of personal preparedness for the prayer that follows. Finally, he begins to engage the assembly in dialogue as he invites them to pray: "Pray, brethren (brothers and sisters), that my sacrifice and yours may be acceptable to God, the almighty Father." The people reply: "May the Lord accept the sacrifice at your hands for the praise and glory of his name, for our good and the good of all his holy Church." Thus, the gifts of the Church are to be sacrificed both for God's glory and our good.[32] In a 1981 edition of *Assembly*, Searle provides the following rumination on the meaning of this dialogue and the intricate and multifaceted nature of "sacrifice":

> Pray that our sacrifice might be acceptable to God,
> the almighty Father.
>
> Sacrifice: a chilling word for the grief of the world,
>   a blood-stained word of irretrievable loss,
>   reeking of slaughtered animals;
>   a euphemism to cover incompetence
>   haunted by the blood of young men gone to war
>   *o quam dulcis, quam gloriosus pro patria mori.*
>
> May the Lord accept the sacrifice. . . .
>
> Sacrifice: an angry word flung by parents
>   ("I've slaved and sacrificed for you . . . ")
>   which is truest when unuttered

[30] Searle, "Serving the Lord with Justice," 28.

[31] Vincie, "The Preparation of the Gifts: The Mystagogical Implications," 225.

[32] Ibid. Vincie writes: "The Eucharist weaves a rhythm of offering and receiving again and again; each time we offer the gifts they are transformed and given back to us in greater measure. In this holy exchange of gifts, we always receive more than we can ever give" (226).

through the loving, unconditioned care of many years
unthinking expenditure of life and energy.

May the Lord accept the sacrifice. . . .

Sacrifice: the cruel end of gaunt, tortured souls
upon the altars of Dachau, Bremen, My Lai
and a thousand other cathedrals built by
demonic priests of racial pride
shepherded to death
a sacrifice acceptable to the Fatherland.

Sacrifice: Jesus, the Christ, the Son of God
torn, bleeding piece of earth offered up to heaven
on the pole of the Cross
mockery of the God who made us by self-made men
"We had hoped he was the salvation of Israel."
Those who had high hopes found no hope in him
only for the hopeless was his hopeless cause yet hopeful
only for the victim was this victim a cause of benediction.
Messy business of a God who messes in messy lives.

May the Lord accept the sacrifice at your hands. . . .

How is this sacrifice ours that we should offer it?
we of the clean hands and homely comforts
we decent, tidy people
we ordinary people of ordinary lives.
May the Lord accept it at your hands
(Keep it at arm's length, lest it redound upon us,
for our good and that of mother Church,
splatter its blood upon our clean cloths
turn decency to ignominy and shame. . .
and save us.)[33]

As the many images of this poetic piece suggest, when the presider utters the command: "Pray, brethren (brothers and sisters), that my sacrifice and yours may be acceptable to God, the almighty Father," the word sacrifice is meant to be ambiguous with "a richness which both permits it to function as a root metaphor for the whole Christian thing, but which also allows for particular aspects or insights into its

---

[33] Mark Searle, "May the Lord Accept the Sacrifice . . . ," *Assembly* 7, no. 3 (1981): 16.

meaning to be cultivated at different times."[34] And yet there is an objectivity to the sacrifice, and thus, Searle employs the definition of St. Augustine: "A true sacrifice is every work which is done that we may be united to God in a holy fellowship, and which has a reference to that supreme good and end in which alone we can be truly blessed."[35] In what has taken place at the altar thus far, the assembly should "see" with "reverence" and "respect" that the Church is "collected" by what it has given up in self-surrender and received by God's willingness to accept. The action begun in the gathering together of the assembly's gifts concludes now in a prayer that collects its hopes for a "holy exchange": "Receive our oblation, O Lord, by which is brought about a glorious exchange that, by offering what you have given, we may merit to receive your very self."[36]

AN ATTITUDE OF SELF-SACRIFICE

According to the GIRM, the Eucharistic Prayer that follows the initial presentation of the gifts upon the altar is "the center and high point of the entire celebration."[37] This prayer enacts the unity of the whole Church—the Church on earth together with the Church in heaven. It is a rehearsal of the oneness of relationships that exist in "thanksgiving and sanctification" before God—perfect doxology.[38] The GIRM continues its description of the Eucharistic Prayer as follows:

> The Priest calls upon the people to lift up their hearts towards the Lord in prayer and thanksgiving; he associates the people with himself in

[34] Searle, "Sacrifice," 241.

[35] Ibid. Searle continues the quote of Augustine later in the editorial: "This is the sacrifice of Christians: we being many are one in Christ. And this also is the sacrifice which the Church continually celebrates in the sacrament of the altar . . . in which she teaches that she herself is offered in the sacrifice she makes to God."

[36] *Roman Missal*, Prayer over the Offerings for the Thursday after January 2.

[37] GIRM 78.

[38] Ibid. See also Geoffrey Wainwright, *Doxology: The Praise of God in Worship, Doctrine, and Life* (New York: Oxford University Press, 1980). He writes: "I see Christian worship, doctrine and life as conjoined in a common 'upwards' and 'forwards' direction towards God and the achievement of his purpose, which includes human salvation. They intend God's praise. His glory is that he is already present and within to enable our transformation into his likeness, which means participation in himself and his kingdom" (10).

the Prayer that he addresses in the name of the entire community to God the Father through Jesus Christ in the Holy Spirit. Furthermore, the meaning of this Prayer is that the whole congregation of the faithful joins with Christ in confessing the great deeds of God and in the offering of Sacrifice. The Eucharistic Prayer requires that everybody listens to it with reverence and in silence.[39]

The kind of "listening" that the Eucharistic Prayer demands is the contemplation of its dialogical nature. It is not a monologue uttered by the presider. Instead, it is the prayer of Christ, Head and Body, to the Father. In his article "Rites of Communion," Searle describes the act of praying the Eucharistic Prayer in this way:

> It begins with a dialogue, calling the body to common prayer, to a concerted lifting up of hearts, to a common act of praise and acknowledgement of God, offered through our high priest, Jesus Christ. It rehearses our common history, renews our common hope of eschatological unity with God, the saints, the departed, in the kingdom of his glory. The prayer is offered in the name of the community by a priest who represents the *totus Christus*: Christ *and* his people. But the solitary spokesman is persistently interrupted by the acclamations of the people and finally and ringingly affirmed in the Great Amen. The Eucharistic Prayer is not the priest's part; it is the prayer of the whole priestly Church, the prayer of Jesus the high priest, together with his body, offering self-sacrifice to the Father.[40]

For this exchange to be recognized, the assembly must learn to truly see itself participating in a dialogue with the priest and, through this dialogue, participating in the priestly work of Christ. Nevertheless, many people in the pew (and many priests at the altar!) continue to

---

[39] GIRM 78. See also Mark Searle, "The Eucharistic Prayers," *The Way* (Supp. N. 11, 1970), 91. Here Searle expresses a certain hope for the day when each local community is to confess the "great deeds of God" according to their own history: "Today, as in the past, the liturgy will express the faith of the community celebrating it and reflect that community's attitude to the world in which it lives. The great merit of the constitution on the liturgy lies in its having put an end to the period of rigid fixity and having set the Church free to celebrate the *mirabilia Dei* in a way which will 'allow for the legitimate variations and adaptations to different groups, regions and peoples' (*Sacrosanctum Concilium*, 38)."

[40] Searle, "Rites of Communion," 127.

suffer from the preconciliar attitude that the Eucharistic Prayer is the priest's domain into which the assembly is merely invited to peer.

Proper understanding of ritual dialogue was crucial to Searle's understanding of liturgical prayer in general. Searle believed that it is something very much undervalued in our culture, and in fact is looked upon with great contempt, believed to lead participants into a conditioned, rote behavior, which fails to communicate both meaning and feeling.[41] He writes:

> It is an axiom of folk-morality in our culture that one shouldn't say anything one doesn't mean—or, in pop psychology, that one shouldn't say anything one doesn't feel. There is a distrust of formalities, as if formalities were necessarily mere formalism. The virtues commonly applauded (perhaps because so uncommonly practiced) are honesty, sincerity and openness. . . . The oldest liturgical formulae are those on the lips of the congregation. But, if they are put on our lips, how can they be meaningful? How can they ever be more than an unthinking, automated response to a given cue? A conditioned reflex void of any human intentionality?[42]

Therefore, when the opening dialogue of the Eucharistic Prayer's preface unfolds between the presider and the people—"The Lord be with you." / "And with your spirit." "Lift up your hearts." / "We lift them up to the Lord." "Let us give thanks to the Lord our God." / "It is right and just."—how can this be anything more than "a conditioned reflex void of any human intentionality?" Is it possible to understand personal investment in such a routine pattern of exchange?

Searle takes these questions very seriously and suggests that suspicion regarding ritual dialogue is ultimately rooted in the attitude of fear, fear of losing one's identity, of becoming just another face in the crowd. He employs the evidence of the ritual dialogue used in football games and political rallies to substantiate his point that the very purpose of the dialogue is what people actually fear the most: "a deep sense of solidarity" and the sacrifice of self:

> What is immediately remarkable about all these rehearsed responses and acclamations, of course, is that they are cries and shouts repeated

---

[41] See Searle, "Ritual Dialogue," 113.
[42] Ibid.

over and over again. It would be an entirely odd experience to find picketers or football fans reading words off a program, saying them only once, or having someone at the microphone saying, 'Our next vituperation will be #3 on your sheets. . . . One of the most frightening aspects of such mass rallies, of course, is the way in which people who are otherwise reserved, gentle human beings get swept up into the common mood, whether angry or euphoric, and are carried away, losing their individual identities to the movement of the crowd. For this, the responses are largely responsible. *This, in turn, suggests that the role of such shouts and cries is not merely to express the feelings and thoughts of individuals but to arouse them and fill them with new attitudes and new intensity.* In the mob, this process is often quite demonic. In the congregation, could the same process not also happen, if in more angelic fashion?[43]

Thus, in an "angelic fashion," the ritual dialogue at the outset of the Eucharistic Prayer, as well as through the prayer as a whole, attempts to create the attitude of self-sacrifice that is both "right" and "just" and that opens the heart to genuine thanksgiving. In turn, this attitude is formed as solidarity is created and individuality is suspended. Searle calls this experience "a transient experience of being caught up with others in an exhilarating moment of togetherness. It is ecstasy, the transcendence of one's lonely individuality in a moment of communion."[44]

Therefore, to underscore what this implies for the opening dialogue of the Eucharistic Prayer, the point of the exchange between priest and people is to acknowledge the newly fashioned identity of the Body of Christ as "lifted up to the Lord," as being recreated in a "deep sense of solidarity and belonging."[45] Likewise, Searle concludes:

[43] Ibid., 120. Emphasis mine.

[44] Ibid. He continues: "And lest this be too quickly dismissed as alienation, let us add that the enjoyment of our common humanity, however momentary, is an important counterweight to the solitary individualism which our culture fosters."

[45] See Mark Searle, "Semiotic Analysis of Roman Eucharistic Prayer II," in *Gratias Agamus: Studien zum Eucharistichen Hochgebet für Balthasar Fischer*, ed. Andreas Heinz and Heinrich Rennings (Freiburg, Germany: Herder, 1990), 474–76. Using the language of semiotics, Searle calls the Opening Dialogue an *"enunciative performance,"* in which "mutual urging and empowerment occur in the very act of engaging in the dialogue." He continues: "The two parties (priest and people) wish each other the presence of the Lord, find that

They (the responses and acclamations of the liturgy) are formalities
that form those who engage in them. They do not express a solidarity
that already exists so much as constitute an invitation to solidarity. At
worst, and too often, they degenerate to the level of mindless rote, but
they have the potential to arouse a new awareness of who we are and
who we have been and who we might yet become. They invite us to
take up a position vis-à-vis ourselves, our God and one another, offering us the opportunity together to confront, concur, confess, acclaim,
assent, convert and, not least, connect.[46]

Nothing makes the "invitation to solidarity" clearer than the singing
of the *Sanctus* that concludes the Preface, for it enacts the contemplative "seeing" of the earthly Church united with the hosts of heaven,
"the meeting of this world with the world to come."[47] "Holy, holy,
holy . . . heaven and earth are filled with your glory." These words
place us on the edge of the great abyss, where our imaginations lift
the veil between the things of this earth and the things of heaven, so
that only thanksgiving for the wonders of God's desire to unite together all things overwhelms any claim to self-centeredness or isolated
individuality.

It is necessary to comment on the gesture of kneeling, which the
assembly enacts immediately following the singing of the *Sanctus*. A
posture mandated by the bishops of the United States,[48] what are we to
make of kneeling within the context of the Church's great prayer
of thanksgiving? Is it meant to be a gesture of surrender in utter

---

presence realized, and then express the duty and the willingness to thank the
Lord who is *their* God for unspecified past actions. Thus, while the opening
dialogue is oriented towards what follows, it is unintelligible without a commonly acknowledged past. It is on the basis of this past that a certain mutual
understanding ('fiduciary contract') is evoked in the dialogue which will serve
as the motivator and enabler of the joint act of thanksgiving."

[46] Searle, "Ritual Dialogue," 120.

[47] Mark Searle, "The Saints in the Liturgy," *Assembly* 8:2 (1981): 151.

[48] See GIRM 43. "In the dioceses of the United States of America, they
should kneel beginning after the singing or recitation of the *Sanctus* (*Holy,
Holy, Holy*) until after the *Amen* of the Eucharistic Prayer, except when prevented on occasion by ill health, or for reasons of lack of space, of the large
number of people present, or for another reasonable cause. . . . The faithful
kneel after the *Agnus Dei* (*Lamb of God*) unless the Diocesan Bishop determines
otherwise."

gratitude or a gesture of penance and contrition? Searle, for his own part, interpreted kneeling in a variety of ways. First of all, in 1979, he offered the following brief, poetic reflection which substantiates a plethora of meanings for the gesture:

> The wrestler, forced to his knees . . .
> The lover, proposing on his knees . . .
> The plaintiff, going down on his knees . . .
> The victim, flinging himself to his knees . . .
> The visionary, dropping to his knees . . .
> The beggar, groveling on his knees . . .
> The loyal subject, falling to his knees . . .
> The loser, brought to his knees . . .
> The worshipper, taking to his knees . . .
>
> . . . before our God, we are all of these.[49]

What is common in all these embodiments of kneeling is the expression of powerlessness on the part of the one on "his knees."[50] The lover proposes on the knees with uncertainty, taking the chance that he or she might be refused. The visionary drops to the knees in awe, recognizing something so much greater than the self. The worshiper takes to the knees with humility, believing that God alone is the almighty One. The actual placing of one's weight on the knees entails a physical sacrifice; a person is vulnerable when kneeling.

Nevertheless, is the attitude of powerlessness appropriate within the context of the Eucharistic Prayer? In his early writing, Searle suggests that standing together is the best expression of reverence before God in this supreme act of corporate prayer. For instance, in his 1981 book *Liturgy Made Simple*, he writes:

> It is also helpful when a congregation has developed the custom of standing for the Eucharistic Prayer. Of course, kneeling is a good

---

[49] Mark Searle, "Kneeling," *Assembly* 6, no. 3 (1979): 74.

[50] See Mark Searle, "Genuflecting," *Assembly* 6, no. 3 (1979): 74. Here he specifically spells out the powerlessness involved in the act of going down on one knee: "Have you noticed how many people wobble as they go down on one knee? Those who stand on their own two feet may think themselves strong, in charge of their own lives. Genuflecting, we surrender our illusions and admit: we are vulnerable, unsteady, defenseless. We falter in the presence of the living God."

attitude for prayer, too, but it is a posture which suggests abasement and penance and, while there is a lot of room for that in Christian life, it is questionable whether it best expresses what we are about at Eucharist. At the Eucharist we are praying less in our own name than as the Body of Christ. We identify ourselves with the one whom the book of Revelation sees as slain yet standing before the throne of God, and there seems something appropriate in our adopting, even now, this posture of resurrection and victory and confidence as we proclaim the works of God and urge him to bring them to completion.[51]

One of the key aspects about kneeling that clearly bothers Searle is that it is better suited for individual prayer rather than communal liturgy; it is a gesture that best articulates the response of an individual who is powerless before God. However, in an article that appeared the next year (1982) titled "On the Art of Lifting Up the Heart: Liturgical Prayer Today," Searle offers a more positive assessment of kneeling within liturgical prayer: "It should be clear that we do not kneel because we feel humble or abject before God. We kneel in order to express our creaturehood in the presence of our creator. If we are not particularly conscious of our creaturehood and dependence, it may be that in following the prescribed ritual of kneeling we shall discover what it means to be a creature."[52] Thus, he begins to suggest that there is a positive sign value in a corporate gesture of kneeling—not so much that we *feel* a sense of abasement as that we *recognize* our oneness with all things in God's care.

Therefore, Searle promotes kneeling as a demonstration of our creaturely dependence on God. In his later writings, his thinking continues to display a growing development, as he provides an even stronger rendition of the positive value of kneeling within the Eucharist. It may be seen as an "epiphany" of Christ's own humble obedience.[53] For

[51] Searle, *Liturgy Made Simple*, 66.

[52] Searle, "On the Art of Lifting Up the Heart: Liturgical Prayer Today," 408.

[53] See, for example, Searle, *Called to Participate*, 58–62. He writes: "But if the whole liturgy is in principle an act of Christ, an exercise in visible form of his invisible, heavenly mediation, then we ought to be able to undertake the same exploration in regard to the humbler gestures of the rite, such as walking, standing, genuflecting, or kneeling. How do these become epiphanies? Such a question is not addressed only to liturgy planners, but to every worshipper in the assembly" (59). See also my article, "Gesturing for an Epiphany: Renewing the Unspoken Language of Worship," *Pastoral Liturgy* 42, no. 5 (2011): 4–8. Regarding the "epiphany" of kneeling, I offer the following critique: "Is it too

Searle, the real issue is what is being communicated by the gesture as a *corporate* act; does the posture of the assembly (kneeling or standing) best express Christ's confidence (even pride?) before God, or is it about his humility? Certainly, it is the latter, and he writes in "On Gestures":

> To people who take pride in standing on their own two feet, kneeling comes as something of a surprise. On one knee you are off balance. On two knees you are defenseless, at the mercy of the one who stands over you. This is the posture of the plaintiff and the lover, the captive and the slave. We many not easily identify with any of these roles; we may even reject them. But our tradition teaches us that this is an appropriate posture in the presence of God. *We do not kneel because we* feel *plaintive or loving or defenseless or servile. We kneel* to discover *who we are.* We kneel to be delivered from our illusions of independence. We kneel to find that we are creatures before our Creator, sinners before the one who loves us. Kneeling, we are clearly dependent upon the one who gives us life and sustains us, who may take away our breath and return us to the dust from which we came.[54]

Once again, the objective nature of the liturgy as the prayer of Christ suggests that the gesture of kneeling is praiseworthy precisely because it disciplines the Body of Christ in a much different way than does the act of standing. We contemplatively see the assembly, composed of the rich and the poor, those who experience tremendous suffering and those who appear to never be phased by life's calamities, kneeling together in self-sacrifice, making sacramental the humility perfectly manifested in life and in death by Christ.

Returning to the spoken prayer, after the singing of the *Sanctus*, the Church continues its dialogue in Christ and encounters words of *epiclesis*, whereby "the Church implores the power of the Holy Spirit that the gifts offered by human hands be consecrated, that is, become Christ's Body and Blood, and that the unblemished sacrificial Victim to be consumed in Communion may be for the salvation of those

---

harsh to critique our kneeling during the Eucharistic Prayer as casual, perhaps almost lazy? Almost universally, our corporate kneeling takes on the attitude of individual choice—we can choose whether to kneel with rigid form or to take the ever popular half-kneeling/half-sitting position. We have lost sight of the act of kneeling gracefully as a disciplining of our bodies in the ways of obedience and reverence" (7).

[54] Mark Searle, "On Gestures," 6. Emphasis mine.

who will partake of it."[55] Searle sees an intimate connection between the previously acclaimed *Sanctus* and the prayer of *epiclesis*: "This acknowledgement of God's holiness serves, in turn, as ground for "manipulating" God, i.e., for trying to persuade God to undertake some further activity: 'Hæc ergo dona, *quæsumus*, spiritus tui rore sanctifica.'"[56] In other words, the acknowledgment of God's unconditional holiness—sung by all of creation—is immediately followed by a request for God's holiness in the form of the Spirit's power to dwell in the gifts of the Church and to become a mark of the Church's lasting identity—i.e., to "become one body, one spirit in Christ."[57]

Therefore, what is the attitude the Church rehearses in the epiclesis? Quite simply, this prayer expresses the belief that the Church is never self-sufficient; it must always depend on God's blessing in the confident hope that God listens and responds to its prayer.[58] Searle himself understands the epiclesis in terms of unity: "We ask to send his Spirit upon us and upon our gifts that we may be drawn more and more

[55] GIRM 79.

[56] Searle, "Semiotic Analysis of Roman Eucharistic Prayer II," 476. Note that the word "manipulation" comes from the so-called "canonical schema" of Semiotic Theory, which is based on four necessary phases: "Manipulation" (someone looks for someone else to perform a task), "Competence" (the one performing the task must have whatever is needed to do so), "Performance" (the actual carrying out of the desired intention), and "Sanction" (the performer must be recognized for having accomplished the task).

[57] Eucharistic Prayer III. See also Yves Congar, *I Believe in the Holy Spirit*, trans. David Smith, vol. 3 (New York: Crossroad Publishing Company, 2001). Congar's final chapter is titled "The Life of the Church as One Long Epiclesis," and he writes: "The Church can be sure that God works in it, but, the Church has to pray earnestly for his intervention as a grace" (271). This, quite simply, is what it means to say that the Church lives as an epiclesis.

[58] See Jeremy Driscoll, "Anamnesis, Epiclesis and Fundamental Theology," *Ecclesia Orans* 15 (1998): 230. Driscoll defines "epiclesis" as follows: "By the action of the Holy Spirit in the transformation of the gifts of bread and wine—gifts which represent at one and the same time the specific history of Christ and the specific history of the community which brings the gifts—the life and death that Christ underwent in history is brought into profound accord with the life in history that I am living. His particular life from a moment in history far different from my own is meant to function as the norm and the only meaning of my time in history. Only the Spirit could bridge this otherwise impossible gap."

into unity with him and one another."[59] The epiclesis is the reminder that true unity is not something that we construct, rather, it is rooted in baptism into Christ and renewed by the gift of the Spirit, "for the Spirit creates in our hearts the real sense of solidarity with our fellow human beings and with the mystery of God-in-Christ."[60] Thus, at the outset of the Eucharistic Prayer proper is the expression of the yearning for unity, which cannot be accomplished by human resources alone, but rather is utterly dependent on the action of God for its realization. Lukas Vischer appropriately designates the *epiclesis* "an expression of the impatient waiting for the coming of the kingdom. . . . It is a *maranatha*, prayer that this Spirit will complete his work and bring everything under Christ."[61]

Immediately following the *epiclesis*—which the presider symbolizes through the gesture of hands extended over the bread and wine—the words of the *Institution Narrative and Consecration* are spoken "by which, by means of the words and actions of Christ, that Sacrifice is effected which Christ himself instituted during the Last Supper."[62] The element in this Eucharistic Prayer component considered by Searle as most important is *obedience*: the memorial of the Last Supper action is done in *obedience* to the Lord's command. "We remind God and ourselves," Searle writes, "that we are doing this because Jesus himself told us to do it in his memory."[63] Therefore, the *Institution Narrative* is first and foremost an enactment of the Church's attitude of obedience, an attitude that simply cannot be rehearsed if participants resist in sacrificing the self. Searle poetically describes this fundamental act of obedience:

> His to command, ours to obey
> He obedient unto death, we obeying unto life
> His to lead, ours to follow
> His to suffer, ours to find hope in suffering
> His to hunger and thirst, ours to feast in his kingdom
> His to die, ours to trample on death
> His to descend into hell, ours to exult with his saints

[59] Searle, *Liturgy Made Simple*, 62.

[60] Searle, *Called to Participate*, 42.

[61] Lukas Vischer, "The Epiclesis: Sign of Unity and Renewal," *Studia Liturgica* 6 (1969): 36.

[62] GIRM 79.

[63] Searle, *Liturgy Made Simple*, 62.

His to yield up his spirit, ours to receive it
His to be sown in the cold earth, ours to reap the harvest of salvation
His to glorify the Father, ours to bear witness to his glory
His to redeem, ours to give thanks for redemption
His to command, ours to obey.[64]

"His to command, ours to obey" somewhat encapsulates the sense of the entire Eucharistic Prayer—we are called to "do this" in his memory. Therefore, while the physical "showing"[65] of the bread and wine in the midst of the *Institution Narrative* signals a deeper manifestation of Christ's presence in the gathered Church, it is not celebrating a working of God from without—as though divine presence suddenly appears from nowhere—but rather is a moment that rehearses the Church's abiding response to Christ's call. It is an act of the Lord saying "Stay here, and keep watch with me," and the Church responding "Here I am, Lord." This is the Church's greatest expression of obedience! Here the Church is to "see" everything anew; its worldview has been recreated in this act of obedience; it discovers, or glimpses into the mystery, of Christ's own perfect obedience.

What becomes of the Church's attitude? Obedience, with its attendant discovery, turns into a bold proclamation of faith—the mystery that is celebrated becomes the utter certainty of the praying community. The assembly not only provides its own acclamation that heralds "the mystery of faith," the *anamnesis* that follows is the fulfillment of "the command that she [the Church] received from Christ" and recalls "especially his blessed Passion, glorious Resurrection, and Ascension into heaven."[66] The Church celebrates new insight; Searle sums this up as real knowledge of true love:

[64] Mark Searle, " . . . At Whose Command We Celebrate This Eucharist . . . ," *Assembly* 11, no. 4 (1985): 284. The phrase "at whose command we celebrate this Eucharist" is found in Eucharistic Prayer III.

[65] The rubrics that govern the execution of the gestures surrounding the bread and the chalice during the Institution Narrative state that the priest "shows" the bread and the chalice to the people. Some distinction must be acknowledged between what it means to "show" and what it means to "elevate."

[66] GIRM 79. See also Mark Searle, "Growing through Celebration," *Music and Liturgy* 12, no. 4 (1986): 114. On the paschal mystery, Searle writes: "We never spoke of the paschal mystery in the old Church, but it became a catchword of the new. Everything was somehow part of the paschal mystery. But

All love that ever was, that ever shall be
finds its root, its wellspring, here:
for love is of God
and God is love.
Look upon the broken bread,
the cup of bitterness and joy,
and know your God.
Know the depth of God
in the wounded side
in the pierced heart
of Christ.
Knowing the depths of God beyond all knowing,
slake your thirst of his fullness.[67]

The proclamation of the commitment to remember the death, resurrection, and future coming of the Lord on the part of the assembly (the acclamation) and its echo or its ratification in the subsequent words of the Eucharistic Prayer serve as the mark of the Church's participation in the one sacrifice of Christ and therefore in the relationship of love that is divine life.[68] As Kevin Irwin writes: "What occurs is that the paschal mystery is *perpetuated* for our sakes, and in experiencing it ever new in our need we experience a new act of God's saving power for our salvation. . . . What 'we remember' is what God did in Christ; what we do in the eucharist is to allow our lives to be reshaped and reformed in that image and likeness."[69]

---

we did not understand what we were saying. The emphasis was on paschal, as in paschaltide and paschal candle, and 'paschal' meant 'Easter' and thus joy, sunshine, resurrection, new life. And that, of course, was what we seemed to be enjoying. But the term paschal does not refer to resurrection, at least to resurrection alone. . . . The paschal mystery is not sunshine and sanitized smiles. It is the awful mystery of human sin, violence and death into which God himself has entered in the person of Jesus, to free us and to lead us out into the new world of the kingdom. . . . And this is the paschal mystery: that growth comes about, not through celebration, but through death."

[67] Mark Searle, " . . . He showed the depth of his love . . . ," *Assembly* 11, no. 4 (1985): 285. The phrase "he showed the depth of his love" is found in Eucharistic Prayer IV.

[68] See Searle, *Called to Participate*, 56.

[69] Kevin Irwin, "Models of the Eucharist," *Origins* 31 (May 31, 2001): 40. Emphasis mine. See also Searle, "The Church Celebrates Her Faith," 7. Searle writes: "And this is how the faith of the Church has been kept alive through

Furthermore, because our remembrance is "a new act of God's saving power for our salvation," the Church is able to lift up "the Bread of life and the Chalice of salvation"[70] as an offering pleasing to God. Thus, in the Eucharistic Prayer, *anamnesis* is tied into the words of *oblation*—offering is inseparable from the Church's memory and its overall giving of thanks. The GIRM states:

> The *oblation*, by which, in this very memorial, the Church, in particular that gathered here and now, offers the unblemished sacrificial Victim in the Holy Spirit to the Father. The Church's intention, indeed, is that the faithful not only offer this unblemished sacrificial Victim but also learn to offer their very selves, and so day by day to be brought through the mediation of Christ, into unity with God and with each other, so that God may at last be all in all.[71]

While the sacrifice of Christ in unrepeatable, the Church's experience of it and participation in it is renewed every time the Eucharist is celebrated, precisely because the experience of sacrifice in the life of the Church—in the members of the Body—is daily reshaped. Thus, to remember all that Christ did for us in his death, resurrection, and glorification is to celebrate the saving activity of God in the life of the Church as it lives in the image and likeness of Christ *today*. "We joyfully and thankfully accept the sacrifice which Christ has achieved and offered for us," writes R. P. C. Hanson, "and which is a gift, the gift, of God to man, and try to live worthy of this gift. Sacrifice therefore becomes something which God graciously gives (us), not something which (we) anxiously offer God."[72] Or as Searle maintains: "Fulfilling this mandate (to remember the death and resurrection of the Lord

---

the centuries and has come to us: not in doctrinal definitions alone, but in a whole community life-style, and above all in the community celebrations where that same faith finds lyrical expression in prayer, praise and symbolic gesture: in short, in remembrance-with-thanksgiving. But just as faith is more than intellectual assent, so remembrance is more than a casual recollection of past events. The God who is remembered is the God who acted in the past, in certain specific historical events which form the foundation of our faith, but he is also involved in the very texture of history itself and continues to operate in our world in our own day."

[70] Eucharistic Prayer II.

[71] GIRM 79.

[72] R. P. C. Hanson, *Eucharistic Offering in the Early Church*, Grove Liturgical Study No. 19 (Bramcote: Grove Books, 1979), 29.

until he comes again) is understood to necessitate a symbolic action of offering: an offering symbolizing the gratitude of a people who deemed themselves chosen by God for the divine service."[73]

What follows this holy exchange of gifts (God's expression of love in Christ's acts and the Church's gratitude and fidelity) is the *epiclesis* for a fruitful communion and *intercessions* for unity. Here the Church recognizes for itself a new identity; if God accepts the Church in Christ's offering, then it expresses a new outlook toward all its relationships. According to the GIRM, the intercessions demonstrate that "the Eucharist is celebrated in communion with the whole Church, of both heaven and earth, and that the oblation is made for her and for all her members, living and dead, who are called to participate in the redemption and salvation purchased by the Body and Blood of Christ."[74] The Church's identity rests upon looking to the future with the attitude of hope: hope that "we may be gathered into one by the Holy Spirit," hope that the Church through its ministry may be brought "to the fullness of charity," hope that all the dead may be welcomed "into the light of your (God's) face," and finally, hope that, with all the saints, "we may merit to be coheirs to eternal life" for the praise and glory of God's name.[75] Once again, the Church manifests its epicletic outlook, whereby it recognizes that none of this is possible without God's grace. Searle writes:

> We pray God to bring to fulfillment what he has already begun in history and in our lives. We look forward to the end of history when God's plan will be complete and when we shall be joined in one great, joyful community with all the dead, with Mary and all the saints, and with Christ himself as our head, so that through him and with him and in him God will have praise and thanksgiving from all his creation for ever and ever. . . . We pray for the Holy Spirit of God to enter anew into our history and into our lives through this celebration, so that God's work of salvation may be experienced now and, through our sanctified lives, be brought closer to its completion.[76]

---

[73] Searle, "Semiotic Analysis of Roman Eucharistic Prayer II," 479. Searle continues: "What is remembered then, is not just the death and resurrection of Christ, but the death and resurrection of Christ *for us*, by which we were acquired for God as a holy people, called to minister before God" (479–80).

[74] GIRM 79.

[75] Eucharistic Prayer II.

[76] Searle, *Liturgy Made Simple*, 62–63.

As Searle writes elsewhere, the *intercessions* "express the Church's desire that God's work in Christ for the unity of humankind be brought to its proper conclusion."[77] However, as mentioned previously in the discussion of the *epiclesis*, the *intercessions* not only acknowledge God's work in the world, drawing all things together as one, they simultaneously rehearse the Church's participation in Christ's priestly ministry "of representing God to the world and the world to God."[78] Quite simply, the vision of the future that is yearned for in the *intercessions* at the end of the Eucharistic Prayer makes present the inclusivity of God, as the Body of Christ "prays for the unity of the whole Church and of the whole world, and for the unity of the living with the dead in that one kingdom which is God's goal and end for the world."[79]

The dialogical nature of the Eucharistic Prayer is expressed supremely in the acclamation of Amen that brings it to a conclusion. Just as we said that the Liturgy of the Word provides more than a mere blueprint of God's Just Kingdom but rather enacts a real living into relationships that are reconciled and renewed, so too is the Eucharistic Prayer a living encounter with the presence of the Kingdom. Participation in divine life is a living reality as the Church prays in the Spirit and declares its reclaiming of Christ's worldview in the Great Amen. The "Amen" cried aloud at the end of the Eucharistic Prayer is the ultimate "YES" to all that has been sacrificed in order to graciously accept all that is to be received. In his 1982 article, "On the Art of Lifting Up the Heart: Liturgical Prayer Today," Searle writes:

> We are invited . . . to step back from our community building activities and to discover the community we already are. We are invited to discover the level at which we are already one—far beyond the level of liking the liturgy or being excited about the same kind of music, or sharing the same theology, or bathing in the successes achieved in our parish. To cease identifying community with shared activities and values, especially with shared success, is more easily said than done, not in the least because it goes against the grain of our culture. . . . The liturgy, like the Gospel, requires a loss of self, a repudiation of the claim to be unique and different. It requires community, not as its goal, as something to be striven for, but as something already given as the basis and precondition for community prayer. *The prayer of the liturgy,*

---

[77] Searle, "Semiotic Analysis of Roman Eucharistic Prayer II," 483.
[78] Searle, *Called to Participate*, 42.
[79] Ibid., 84.

invariably expressed in the collective form and always requiring the 'Amen'
of the assembled faithful, assumes that they speak with but one voice and from
one heart.[80]

The praying of the Eucharistic Prayer affirms for the Body of Christ
that our oneness is real, that our oneness is a result of all God accom-
plishes for us, and that our oneness is meant to permeate all our life's
decisions and goals. Thus, the "Amen" that concludes our Eucharistic
Prayer is a corporate declaration that our true identity comes not from
specializing in our differences but from our common life in Christ.
God accepts the sacrifice of our "self" in order to deepen our union in
his Son.

CONCLUSION
Learning how to "sacrifice" in a world that promotes perfecting
the art of accumulation is no easy feat. From material possessions to
personal achievements, "massification" is the mark of success in our
society. The Christian celebration of the Mass, and particularly the
Liturgy of the Eucharist, is designed to rehearse the way of sacrifice,
which becomes not simply a ritual performance, but a "life" performance. In other words, the worldview of the Eucharistic Prayer is
meant to be the every-day pattern of life for the Christian community.
As Searle writes:

> The sacrifice offered by the Christian community is not a ritual act, but
> rather the self-abandonment of men to God in faith. Faith itself is the
> sacrifice of the Church. To come to faith is to be converted, to undergo a
> radical change of values, to adopt a new life-style. The term "sacrifice"
> is used of Christians, then, in relation to such matters as dedication to
> the apostolate, prayers, fastings, collections for the relief of the poor, the
> care of orphans and widows, and conversion itself.[81]

If faith is the real sacrifice of the Church, then the project of the Eucharist is about being freely drawn into a deeper level of participation in
Christ. It is about gradual abandonment of self-oriented ways of seeing the world in order to behold the Kingdom in Christ "in which all

---

[80] Searle, "On the Art of Lifting Up the Heart: Liturgical Prayer Today," 403.
Emphasis mine.

[81] Searle, "The Church Celebrates Her Faith," 5.

created things are called to fulfill their rightful purpose and destiny under God."[82]

In the context of "thanksgiving," the Liturgy of the Eucharist first rehearses the way of *collecting* so that it may proceed to embody *self-sacrifice*. Bringing together into one the fruits of creation that have been engineered into life-giving food and drink is inseparable from the action of God's filling these same gifts with the sacrifice of his Son. "Sacrifice" is the God-given end of "collecting," as opposed to the sinful, human end which is hoarding. Therefore, the entire Liturgy of the Eucharist is an act of deep remembrance that sacrifice is the way to true communion and the way to the realization of God's Just Kingdom. "Remembering the death of Jesus," Searle contends, "is not something that can be done simply by thinking about it. To remember Jesus is to live as he lived, to think as he thought, to act as he acted."[83]

Far from being the personal prayer of the presider, the Eucharistic Prayer is best understood as the prayer of Christ to the Father which the Church overhears. In its enactment, it is not just a dialogue between the presider and the assembly but a prayer between the Church and God as well—"Prayer is at once humanity's response to God and at the very same time God's own word and act in us."[84] Searle writes:

> On the face of it, a Eucharistic Prayer is a faith narrative, a confession or acknowledgement of God. It is a remembering of the story of God, a story glimpsed in the episodes recalled from creation to the end of time. The past, only ever recalled in fragments, such as an episode or two from the history of Israel or the life of Jesus, is not over and done with. It continues to work itself out now and into the future ordained by God, a future already partially realized in the present. . . . This is not then just the story of God. Because we are living in it, it is our story also. Best of all we could say that it is a common story: the story of God and us, the story of God's appeal to human freedom. . . . It is a prayer that the story we are living *in* may also be the story we are living *out*: that the story of God and the story of our lives may become one story.[85]

[82] Searle, "Serving the Lord with Justice," 21.
[83] Searle, *Liturgy Made Simple*, 63.
[84] Searle, *Called to Participate*, 56.
[85] Ibid., 56–57.

148

However, even when the assembly acclaims the "Great Amen" to this story of God and us, the story does not end. This is precisely because this story is a story of communion. It is not simply a story about sacrifice for its own sake, but sacrifice in order to bring all things into the fullness of God's life. Thus, while this story has been told upon ambo and altar alike, it must continue in us, in an act of real reception. For this, we turn now to the ritual actions of eating and drinking and thus the rehearsal of the attitude of "communing."

Chapter 6

The Rehearsal of Communing

While the nature of Christ's sacrifice and the physicality of Christ's Body and Blood began to be a theological controversy in the mid-ninth century—as characterized in the exchange between the monks Paschasius and Ratramnus mentioned at the outset of the previous chapter[1]—the Medieval Church witnessed fewer and fewer of the faithful participating in communion. As masterful theologians worked to clarify the link between "matter" and "form," as well as sacramental "cause" and "effect," those in the pews grew increasingly terrified of partaking in such a great mystery.[2] "Ocular" communion, whereby the act of communion was extended through gazing upon the elevated host, became popular participation at Mass as early as the twelfth century.[3] Miri Rubin summarizes the situation of the late Medieval Church as follows:

> As the elevation was built up in practice and in meaning, it came to be seen as possessing some sacramental efficacy. The enhancement of the power of the eucharist, as it was formulated to be the very body of Christ, had made access to it more problematical, and communion less easy and simple. Elevation offered a sort of substitute "sacramental viewing," which like communion was taught to affect one markedly. As the significance of the elevation was stressed, and the benefits of the

---

[1] See footnote 1 of the previous chapter.

[2] See Power, *The Eucharistic Mystery: Revitalizing the Tradition*, 241–65.

[3] See Miri Rubin, *Corpus Christi: The Eucharist in Late Medieval Culture* (Cambridge, UK: Cambridge University Press, 1991), 55. Rubin suggest that the earliest text that governs elevation of the consecrated bread for the purpose of allowing the members of the congregation to see it is from the statutes of the synod of Paris (1198–203): "It is ordained to priests that, when they begin the canon of the mass, at *Qui pridie*, holding the host, they should not immediately raise it too high so that it can be seen by the people; rather, only keep it in front of their chests while they say *hoc est corpus meum* and then they should elevate it so that it can be seen by all."

elevation seemed so great that questions were posed as to how differ-ent it was from spiritual communion.[4]

Theology went hand in hand with practice: emphasis on the awesome wonder of consecration translated into a growing attitude of unwor-thiness on the part of congregants. Furthermore, as the Mass became increasingly understood as the work of the priest, his communion was seen to be sufficient for its valid enactment.

It was not until the Council of Trent, in 1562, that the issue of fre-quent reception of communion became a matter for the deliberation of the universal Church. During the twenty-second session of this council, the Fathers declared: "The Holy Council wishes indeed that at each Mass the faithful who are present should communicate, not only in spiritual desire, but sacramentally, by the actual reception of the Eucharist."[5] In fact, the final rendering of this decree saw the words *aliqui fideles* (some of the faithful) changed to *fideles adstantes* (the faith-ful who are present), thereby suggesting that physical presence at Mass necessitated the reception of communion.[6] Nevertheless, the tendency toward private devotions during the Eucharist rather than communicating proved to be a force to be reckoned with, a force so strong that Pius X would promulgate *Sacra Tridentina Synodus*, on December 20, 1905, reviving the Council of Trent's norm: "Frequent and daily Communion, as a practice most earnestly desired by Christ our Lord and by the Catholic Church, should be open to all the faith-ful, of whatever rank and condition of life."[7]

Interestingly enough, the attempt by Pius X to actualize frequent communion coincided with the powers of the world at war and econo-mies on the brink of disaster, meaning that it would prove difficult to move the faithful out of the comfort that devotional prayer provided. For Pius, and for the reformers of the blossoming Liturgical Move-ment, this inconsistency would result in disaster. "A Church whose membership lived on forms of piety that were themselves deeply im-bued with the spirit and tastes of the age was ill-equipped to reassert

---

[4] Ibid., 63.

[5] Session XXII, chapter 6. See also James F. White, *Roman Catholic Worship: Trent to Today* (New York: Paulist Press, 1995): 16–17.

[6] See Power, *The Sacrifice We Offer: The Tridentine Dogma and Its Reinterpretation*, 123–24.

[7] *Sacra Tridentina Synodus* 1. See Yzermans, *All Things in Christ*, 217.

its own identity in a secularized and secularizing world."[8] Whether lack of participation could be laid squarely on the shoulders of those in the pews or whether it could be attributed to the Tridentine liturgy itself (designed more for the priest than for the people), the mandate of the Second Vatican Council's *Sacrosanctum Concilium*, article 55, seeks to address the issue directly:

> The more perfect form of participation in the Mass whereby the faithful, after the priest's communion, receive the Lord's body from the same sacrifice, is warmly recommended. The dogmatic principles about communion of the faithful which were laid down by the Council of Trent are confirmed, yet communion under both kinds may be granted when the bishops think fit, not only to clerics and religious but also to the laity.[9]

In 1985, twenty years after the close of the Second Vatican Council, the Notre Dame Study of Catholic Parish Life, in which Mark Searle played a major role, reported that "the long campaign in favor of more frequent Communion has paid off handsomely in American parishes."[10] However, while the frequency of Communion may no longer be a major concern in American parishes, the more important issue is the meaning of this "more perfect form of participation." In other words, what does the action of eating and drinking the Lord's Body and Blood really mean to those participating in this ritual performance? Is it an individual exercise between the communicant and the Lord, or does it entail a deeper level of engagement with the Body of Christ?

This was a particularly relevant question for Searle, as he saw a creeping sense of individualism spreading through American parishes

[8] Searle, *Called to Participate*, 5.

[9] *Sacrosanctum Concilium* 55 in Flannery, *The Basic Sixteen Documents*.

[10] Mark Searle and David C. Leege, *The Celebration of Liturgy in the Parishes*, Notre Dame Study of Catholic Parish Life, n. 5 (Notre Dame, IN: The University of Notre Dame, 1985), 6. The study reports: "In 90% of the Masses observed, more than three-quarters of the congregation received Communion, with no significant differences from one Mass to another. Where Communion from the cup is concerned, however, the picture is not so uniform. It was available at only 47% of the Masses: at 44% of secondary Masses and 51% of principal Masses. Even when the cup was available, a majority of the congregation drank from it only in one-third of the cases."

in the mid-1980s.[11] From his perspective, parish liturgy demonstrated "a growing alienation from precisely that sense of collective identity and collective responsibility which the liturgy might be thought to rehearse."[12] Nowhere in the liturgy is this rehearsal more pronounced than in the physical act of participating in communion, and Searle rooted the problem in the very definition of "communion" itself. He writes in *Liturgy Made Simple*:

> We have various phrases for expressing what goes on here. We talk about "going to Communion," or "receiving Communion," or "administering" or "giving out Holy Communion." These phrases sound strange when we reflect on them. What does the word "Communion" mean? Some people talk about "communicating." But communications theory tells us that it takes two to communicate and they must both be involved, whereas "giving out Communion" suggests distributing something that people can take away with them. Perhaps we should talk about the "act of Communion," for Christ cannot enter into communion with us unless we communicate with him.[13]

In this brief depiction of the issue, Searle makes clear that the action of eating and drinking the Lord's Body and Blood is a *Communion* with Christ that involves the real effort of *communication* on the part of the receiver. In other words, "communion" can never be a passive activity, whereby communicants receive without any real investment of the heart. "Communion" requires commitment on the part of all participants, and it is the commitment to the ongoing unity of the Body of Christ that comprises the final portion of the eucharistic celebration. And thus, Searle contends: "We have to find ways of celebrating the Communion Rite in such a way that people realize they are communicating with one another in Christ."[14]

AN ATTITUDE OF "PEACE"

It is surely not well understood among those in the assembly (and perhaps even among many presiders) that the final segment of the Mass begins immediately after the "Great Amen" of the Eucharistic

---

[11] See Searle, "The Notre Dame Study of Catholic Parish Life," 312–33.
[12] Ibid., 333.
[13] Searle, *Liturgy Made Simple*, 69.
[14] Ibid., 71.

Prayer, as the gathered Church is invited to pray the Lord's Prayer. Although the most visible cue for the transition to the Communion Rite is the assembly's shift in posture from kneeling to standing, the purpose of the Lord's Prayer is uncertain to most: is it a prayer that sums up all that has been recited in the Eucharistic Prayer, or is it a prayer that looks forward to, or anticipates, the act of communion? The GIRM provides clear evidence that the latter is intended in the structure of the Mass: "In the Lord's Prayer a petition is made for daily bread, which for Christians means principally the Eucharistic Bread, and entreating also purification from sin, so that what is holy may in truth be given to the holy."[15] If the concluding doxology of the Eucharistic Prayer lifts up the community and the entirety of creation before the throne of God for reconciliation and oneness, then the Lord's Prayer may be understood as the blueprint for sustaining such reconciliation through the seal of communion and beyond.

Attention should be given to the words of the presider's invitation to the prayer: "At the Savior's command and formed by divine teaching, we dare to say." There is something to be said for the literal translation of the word *audémus* ("we dare"). The sense of the assembly being "daring" in its response to the "Savior's command" is important as it now knows the unity that has been reestablished in the Church through the hearing of the word and the lifting up of the heart, so much so that it wishes to make communication with the Lord a tangible reality at the table. Patricia Gallagher focuses on the "authority" felt by those who stand in God's presence, seeking to deepen the commitment to making divine mercy a mark of the Body of Christ: "In teaching this prayer to his disciples, Jesus gave to them and to each of us the authority (by which we *dare*) to pray to God as *Abba*."[16] The point to be underscored here is that the confident stance of the community, at this point in the liturgy, is decidedly greater than when the Body was formed in the Gathering Rite. For the assembly to deny what God has done in the course of "listening" and "sacrificing," for the assembly to be ensnarled in division rather than to be utterly overcome by renewed unity in Christ, would be to lack the confidence of disciples "formed by divine teaching."

Therefore, having been trained by the Lord, the community stands together and boldly prays directly to the Father. The Lord's Prayer is

[15] GIRM 81.

[16] Patricia A. Gallagher, "The Communion Rite," *Worship* 63 (1989): 318.

really the prayer of the Christian heart: the prayer that is given over to the newly baptized, the prayer that is memorized at a young age, the prayer that is turned to most often in times of crisis or need. It is the prayer of comfort precisely because it is a prayer shared by all, with familiar words and a rhythmic cadence. Searle denotes the Lord's Prayer as the "teaching" prayer:

> The Our Father is the prayer Christ taught us, the prayer we have to learn to say wholeheartedly if we are to have a part with him. It teaches us to speak of God as our common Father, thereby making it impossible to treat anyone as if he or she were not part of our family. It teaches us to pray for our daily bread—the bread, the support of life—that comes from God, the giver of life, of which the Eucharist is a symbol. But then it reverts to the theme of reconciliation and unity: "Forgive us our trespasses as we forgive those who trespass against us." Another way of putting this would be: accept us unconditionally, and we will try to do the same for one another. *The meaningfulness of the breaking of bread depends upon our realization of our oneness under God and upon our willingness to actualize it in our relationships with one another.*[17]

The movement of the prayer, as portrayed by Searle is significant, for its opening words put on the lips of disciples the Kingdom "vision" that Christ has taught them—"Our Father, who art in heaven, hallowed be thy name; thy kingdom come; thy will be done on earth as it is in heaven"—turns to the petition to "give" and "forgive." In other words, recognition of the Kingdom (the Kingdom as taught by Christ) is inseparable from the commission to give and forgive. To reiterate what Searle states above, the meaning of the breaking of the bread will be lost on the community if there is not a real openness to the giving and forgiving that is demanded in relationships with others.

In "Rites of Communion," a piece quoted frequently throughout this work, Searle suggests that the sign value of the Lord's Prayer is found in its articulation of right relationship—those who "dare" to utter the prayer claim to have a "deep identification" with God, with others, and with every aspect of creation. He writes:

> The plural form (*our* Father, give *us*) supposes deep identification between those who pray. The petition for forgiveness acknowledges that

---

[17] Searle, *Liturgy Made Simple*, 68. Emphasis mine.

reconciliation with God means forgiveness of one another. The prayer concludes with the prayer for deliverance from evil, i.e. from the Evil One, the Father of Lies, the sower of dissension and disunity. The interpretation of "evil" as the evil of final separation from the unity of the body of Christ is affirmed by patristic commentary and by the "embolism" that follows: "Deliver us, Lord, from every evil and grant us peace in our day . . . " The peace which Christ gives is more than undisturbed tranquility. It is the peace of one who has triumphed over sin and death. It is shared by those who share his death and resurrection in baptism.[18]

Therefore, the word "evil," as found in the context of the Lord's Prayer, may be understood as destructive "separation," in which "deep identification" with God, others, and creation is hampered. Once again, the prayer is a "daring" act to address God with the hope that relationships which have been formed and built up in Christ contradict separation (the lack of right relationship) within the Body. We would be fools to utter words in Christ's name without recognizing the oneness he provides in setting before us the work of God's Just Kingdom with relationships healed and restored.

Thus, as the presider prays the embolism that concludes the Lord's Prayer, the Church articulates in very clear language the attitude of "peace," which entails ongoing unity ("Deliver us, Lord, we pray, from every evil"), the extension of mercy, freedom from sin, safety from distress, and ultimately a commitment to hope. In a very real sense, it is the way of living in the Kingdom:

> Deliver us, Lord, we pray, from every evil,
> graciously grant peace in our days,
> that, by the help of your mercy,
> we may be always free from sin
> and safe from all distress,
> as we await the blessed hope
> and the coming of our Savior, Jesus Christ.

In the form of a doxology (praise of God's name), the assembly acclaims: "For the kingdom, the power and the glory are yours now and forever." This is a statement of surrender made by those who see that the Kingdom of God is at hand; these are the disciples who have been

[18] Searle, "Rites of Communion," 127.

trained to behold the dawning of God's Just Kingdom as relationships are lived righteously, in "peace" through the actions of "giving" and "forgiving."

The Lord's Prayer, the concluding embolism, and the doxological acclamation by the assembly flow seamlessly into the Sign of Peace.[19] While there is no distinct ritual break here, the presider noticeably addresses the prayer of the community to the "Lord Jesus Christ" instead of "Our Father." Furthermore, the imagery of the prayer is that of the Upper Room encounter between Christ and his disciples after his Resurrection.[20] The words of the prayer follow:

> Lord Jesus Christ,
> who said to your Apostles:
> Peace I leave you, my peace I give you,
> look not on our sins,
> but on the faith of your Church,
> and graciously grant her peace and unity
> in accordance with your will.
> Who live and reign for ever and ever.

Being drawn ever more deeply into mystery, the Church is transported from the broad vision of the Kingdom restored and redeemed to the Church's witness of Christ's triumph over the grave. It is the hope that Christ will see the faith of the Church who recognizes his presence, and, who like the doubting Thomas, is able to cry out: "My Lord and my God!" (John 20:28). In other words, the daring confidence of the disciples trained by the Lord to recognize the presence of the Kingdom is displayed yet again, as with awe and wonder the disciples understand themselves to be in the presence of the Risen One, with their doubt overturned by faith. To recognize the Risen One is to be embraced by true peace. Repeating Searle's earlier comment on the Our Father, "The meaningfulness of the breaking of bread depends upon

[19] See Joyce Ann Zimmerman, ""The Communion Rite: The Mystagogical Implications," in *A Commentary on the Order of Mass of* The Roman Missal, ed. Edward Foley, et al. (Collegeville, MN: Liturgical Press, 2011), 616.

[20] Ibid. Zimmerman writes: "The prayer for peace links peace and forgiveness ('look not on our sins,' no. 126, line 5) and strongly suggests Jesus' postresurrection appearance to the disciples in the Upper Room (see John 20:19, 21, 23)."

our realization of our oneness under God and upon our willingness to actualize it in our relations with one another."[21]

This leads precisely to the ritual gesture that Searle found quite problematic in the Roman Rite—namely, the execution of the Sign of Peace. The GIRM defines this gesture simply as the way "by which the Church entreats peace and unity for herself and for the whole human family, and the faithful express to each other their ecclesial communion and mutual charity before communicating in the Sacrament."[22] Therefore, the Sign of Peace has both an eschatological significance, whereby the Church lives in the peace that will exist when "all will be one" in God, and it has an immediate ecclesial significance whereby the act of communion is the consequence, or the sign, of relationships that have been healed and restored. The question must be how to prevent such a serious and mysterious symbol from becoming "just a how-d' ya-do or a chance to say 'good morning.'"[23] Searle underscores the forgotten eschatological nature of the Sign of Peace in the following reflection:

THE PEACE OF THE LORD BE ALWAYS WITH YOU.

Peace, salaam, shalom alaikum!
Ancient greeting heavy with future promise
a word worn with the interchange of centuries
of meeting and parting and passing on the road,
stranger to stranger, friend to friend.
A word transmuted in the crucible of Golgotha:
"Peace"—uttered from beyond the grave,
from the other side of suffering,
from the one who has travelled the road we too must travel,
from a place we too must visit.
"Peace is my gift to you,
my own peace I give to you,

[21] Searle, *Liturgy Made Simple*, 68.

[22] GIRM 82. Procedural instructions follow: "As for the actual sign of peace to be given, the manner is to be established by the Conferences of Bishops in accordance with the culture and customs of the peoples. However, it is appropriate that each person, in a sober manner, offer the sign of peace only to those who are nearest."

[23] Mark Searle, "The Kiss of Peace: Ritual Act and Image of the Kingdom," *Assembly* 11, no. 3 (1985): 278.

not as the world gives
is my gift of peace to you."

May we meet again in that place, you and I;
may we make it through safely, you and I;
for we meet on the road to Jerusalem,
city of death, city of peace.[24]

While Searle poetically interprets the Sign of Peace as a gesture of "meeting and parting and passing on the road," this is no casual exchange because it is a greeting "from beyond the grave." When Christ's gift of peace is symbolized by a ritual gesture within the assembly, the attitude is to be one of resurrected life, of seeing life "from the other side of suffering." Is this even mildly comprehended by those who are invited to "offer each other the sign of peace"? For our contemporary assemblies, the execution of the Sign of Peace appears as a sort of momentary "time-out," when they are permitted to take a brief pause from the intensity of prayer.

Overtly critical of this modern-day decline in the seriousness of this gesture, Searle continues his call for the reform of the Sign of Peace in his 1985 article, "The Kiss of Peace: Ritual Act and Image of the Kingdom." The Sign of Peace "is less a 'time out,'" he writes, "than 'eternity in': an awesome moment when we realize (in both senses of that word) the presence of the mystery of eschatological peace."[25] Although he does not advocate a return to the actual imparting of an actual "kiss" as the ritual gesture of Christ's peace, Searle suggests that its enactment ought to contain the vulnerability involved in the action of kissing. He writes:

The kiss is a symbol of—quite literally—spiritual union. Lovers who kiss each yield their breath-spirit to the other and inhale the other's. It is thus an expression of the most profound union, of the conjoining not merely of bodies but of souls. *It is a symbol of deepest communion, of shared life at the deepest level.* . . . Thus, when Christ kisses his own in that closed room on the day of the resurrection he is effecting what his words promise: *shalom*, peace. In the biblical and liturgical tradition, *shalom* is all that the human spirit yearns for: tranquility, wholeness, completeness, perfection, ease. This in turn is the fruit of justice, of right relations with God, world, neighbor and self. If all our

[24] Mark Searle, "Peace Be With You," *Assembly* 7, no. 3 (1981): 118.
[25] Searle, "The Kiss of Peace: Ritual Act and Image of the Kingdom," 280.

relationships are all that they ought to be, all that they can be, then we are in a state of *shalom*, peace.[26]

In the context of the liturgy, a change occurs in the simple gesture of a handshake or an embrace: the assembly has been drawn deeper into the living Christ throughout the liturgy, and now the unity of the Body is declared and given by Christ and accepted and manifested by his members.[27] This is real communication. "The liturgical congregation is a *sacramentum futuri*," writes Searle, "a realized eschatological symbol of a divided, hostile and bloodstained humanity reconciled into the Body as a new humanity, a new Adam."[28] Elsewhere he states: "There is no union with Christ which can take place while excluding any other members of his Body. So the exchange of peace ought not to be a light interlude, but the final step before the actual breaking and sharing of the one bread which expresses our unity in Christ."[29]

AN ATTITUDE OF "LIFE TOGETHER"

The rubrics in the Order of Mass offer virtually no recognizable break in the action of offering the sign of peace and the breaking of the bread. The presider is instructed simply to "take" the host, "break" it over the paten, and "place" a particle in the chalice, as he utters this prayer "quietly": "May this mingling of the Body and Blood of our Lord Jesus Christ bring eternal life to us who receive it."[30] To accompany the gesture of breaking the bread, the assembly sings or recites the "Lamb of God." As with the prayer for peace that turned our attention to the presence of Christ in our midst, so the liturgy continues in this direction of recognizing that the Lord is before our eyes. Although the "Lamb of God" introduces words that appear penitential in nature—"have mercy on us"—the emphasis is on the Church's cry of recognition that the Risen One is in our midst—"Lamb of God"—

[26] Ibid., 277. Emphasis mine.

[27] Ibid., 280. Searle writes: "The gesture may look the same, as so many other things in the sacramental economy look much the same as their secular counterparts, but in the context of the Christian people, baptized into the one Body of Christ and animated by his Spirit, its meaning is transformed. It becomes an efficacious sign of the *shalom*, the peace within God, realized on earth in the Body of Christ."

[28] Ibid., 278.

[29] Searle, *Liturgy Made Simple*, 68–69.

[30] *Roman Missal*, 129.

and has come to grant peace by the oneness of our life. In his 1986 "Participation and Prayer," Searle writes:

> In the liturgy we occasionally step back, as it were, to acknowledge Christ, especially at those moments where we cease to worship the Father and instead receive the gifts of the Father from Christ, as at communion, when we sing the "Lamb of God." In such moments, the church ceases to be Body of Christ approaching the Father in and through him, and becomes the Bride of Christ, receiving the love of God at the hands of Christ. But even then, the same Spirit which prays in us to the Father is at work in us to open us to the gifts of God. And indeed, the gift of God is finally nothing other than the very Spirit itself, which transforms us into the likeness of Christ, the beloved of God.[31]

Searle suggests that there is a very important role change that takes place in the assembly at this moment of prayer: the Church moves from the position of praying in Christ to the Father to that of the "Bride of Christ," in order to be touched by Christ's love and receive the gift of presence. This change in posture is really very critical theologically, because what it suggests is that we ultimately have no responsibility for the building and strengthening of communion in Christ; that is a gift from God. Therefore, as the praying Church experiences the touch of Christ's presence in the Sign of Peace and verbally acknowledges that presence by echoing the words of John the Baptist ("look, there is the lamb of God that takes away the sin of the world"; John 1:29), it practices an attitude of being awestruck at the greatness of the gift of the living God, namely, the life of his Son in our midst.

Although the GIRM states that the "fraction" of the bread "signifies that the many faithful are made one body (1 Cor 10:17) by receiving communion from the one Bread of Life," it mandates that gestures of reverence in breaking the bread "should not be unnecessarily prolonged or accorded exaggerated importance."[32] One could argue that this ritual gesture has diminished in symbolic importance precisely because what is generally broken in contemporary celebrations hardly looks like a common loaf of bread. Regarding the fraction, Searle writes:

---

[31] Searle, "Participation and Prayer," 151.
[32] GIRM 83.

Centuries of using individual hosts have led us to identify each piece of bread with the body of Christ, without thought of the other pieces. But the sacrament is not just in the bread: it is in the bread broken and shared, which "aptly reflects the figure of the Church," the body of Christ, composed of many, forming a single whole. "This bread which we *break*, is it not the body of Christ?" The possibility of our all being able to share one loaf is the sacrament of our being able to share the life of a single body. So with the cup: it is not only his blood, it is our blood—"you receive your own mystery." It is our common life poured out, mingled, transfused, consumed. We live no longer for ourselves but for him who lives for us all.[33]

Therefore, while the breaking of the bread need not be "prolonged" or "exaggerated," it has deep symbolic meaning that sparks the imagination of the assembly that is called upon to recognize the Lord. John Baldovin places great importance on the breaking of the bread, as he writes: "The very act of breaking bread, necessary so that food not be hoarded but shared, is the action that reveals the identity of Christ."[34] Once again the "Bride of Christ" is invited to see in the action of breaking the gift of self-offering and faithful love. The gifts of peace, mercy, and the totality of Christ's self are not signs of what the Church has accomplished, but rather gifts of who and what it continues to become: "life together."

Understanding precisely what "life together" looks like was an issue of paramount concern for Searle, and it is necessary to reiterate his belief that community (and therefore "communion") is *recognized*, it is not *constructed*.[35] The Church celebrates the Eucharist as a weekly, and even daily, event in order to share and represent "life together,"

[33] Searle, "Rites of Communion," 127.

[34] Baldovin, *Bread of Life, Cup of Salvation*, 143. Baldovin continues: "The breaking of the bread thus communicates in a symbolic way the fact that as Christians we only have life through free self-sacrifice—the brokenness of the Lord" (145).

[35] See, for example, Mark Searle, "The Liturgy and Catholic Social Doctrine," in *The Future of the Catholic Church in America: Major Papers of the Virgil Michel Symposium*, ed. John Roach, et al. (Collegeville, MN: Liturgical Press, 1991), 68–69. Searle writes: "What needs to be recognized above all, especially in the Church, is that this unity is not something we are working to achieve, as if it were some new and original creation, but a God-given reality, already in existence, to which we must be true. In society and in the world, we must practice solidarity not to achieve a unity that would somehow be added to

a concept he attributes to the writing of Dietrich Bonhoeffer.[36] Searle believed that the liturgy often falls victim to attempts to create "make-believe community" that fails to recognize the seriousness of the Spirit's work to do that without our feeble efforts.[37] He argues: "The real question—one that has profound pastoral implications—is, how can we give appropriate expression in this place and at this time to the community we already are in Christ?"[38] He continues:

> All sorts of organizations try to build community on the basis of friendship, common interests, shared tastes, and so forth. Whenever the Church tries to do the same, we get into trouble. The pastor decides to build a social club to foster community in the parish, but then has additional financial, staffing, and management problems, and still has to figure out a way of keeping up attendance in order to justify the investment. And the social club may or may not lead people into the church building. It is well meant but beside the point. The same is true of attempts to develop a community spirit in and through the liturgy: they invariably serve simply to obscure the real basis of our identifica-tion with each other—which is not ethnic, or socio-economic, or

---

what we are already, but because mutuality and reciprocity are constitutive of who we are as human beings, made that way by God."

[36] See Dietrich Bonhoeffer, *Life Together: A Discussion of Christian Fellowship*, trans. John W. Doberstein (New York: Harper & Row, 1954). The following quote, found on page 26, was particularly influential for Searle: "Just at this point Christian brotherhood is threatened most often at the very start by the greatest danger of all, the danger of being poisoned at its very root, the danger of confusing Christian brotherhood with some wishful idea of religious fel-lowship, of confounding the natural desire of the devout heart for community with the spiritual reality of Christian brotherhood. In Christian brotherhood everything depends upon its being clear right from the beginning, first, that Christian brotherhood is not an ideal, but a divine reality. Second, that Chris-tian brotherhood is a spiritual and not a psychic reality."

[37] See Searle, *Called to Participate*, 73. He writes: "Very often, our liturgies are used in awkward attempts to create pseudo-communities. The presider tells the assembly to turn and introduce themselves to one another; the preacher speaks of the parish as a 'family'; hands are held at the Our Father. But all this seems to be playing make-believe community, pretending to be a community that can never be. It can ultimately be alienating, for it invites all the partici-pants to see reality other than it actually is."

[38] Ibid.

affective, or a matter of institutional pride or loyalty, but our common life in Christ.[39]

Therefore, as the presider shows to the assembly the host, raised slightly above the paten or chalice, with the accompanying invitation to Communion—"Behold the Lamb of God, behold him who takes away the sins of the world. Blessed are those called to the supper of the Lamb"—the Church is invited to make a verbal response to pure gift. That response is the expression of the lived attitude of "life together," meaning that divisions in our world based on economics and race continue to exist even while Communion, as gift of divine love, heals those who humble themselves to receive. Thus, the assembly proclaims from a kneeling position the humble faith of the Centurion: "Lord, I am not worthy that you should enter under my roof, but only say the word and my soul shall be healed."

However, nothing rehearses the attitude of "life together" better than the procession to Communion and the physical actions of eating and drinking the Lord's Body and Blood. It is clearly in this moment when the human condition becomes universally witnessed on the part of the Body: mothers mourning at the recent death of a child, fathers searching for employment, little children reaching out for a host, newly married couples filled with joy and hope, countless numbers with aches and pains, and some too with life-threatening illnesses— vulnerability witnessed as a "life together." It is this mixture of people that process as one, yearning to respond one at a time to the encounter

---

[39] Ibid. Searle goes on to describe the Church as a "company of strangers," who "have little in common beyond our common humanity and the Spirit poured into our hearts in baptism. This Body of Christ, in which there is neither Jew nor Greek, male nor female, slave nor free (Gal 3:28), cannot be true to itself if its unity is predicated on ethnic heritage, male bonding, socio-economic status, or the intimacy of first-name friendships. Indeed, the Body is more clearly visible for what it is when its members are most aware of their social divisions (male vs. female, rich vs. poor, black vs. white), and at the same time committed to not letting those divisions stand between them and not letting the solidarity within those divisions supplant the primary unity created by baptism. . . . *This then is the paradox: the parish is at its best, its most Catholic, when it is a real mix, a real company of strangers*" (75; emphasis mine). Searle borrows the term "company of strangers" from Parker J. Palmer. See his *Company of Strangers: Christians and the Renewal of America's Public Life* (New York: Crossroad, 1983).

with Christ, communicating a sign of love—"Amen"—to Christ's gift of himself. While extremely personal, there is nothing private about the Communion we celebrate. The following reflection that appeared in a 1979 issue of *Assembly*, a piece titled simply "Communing," represents Searle's depiction of this encounter:

1. I have stood in line at
    check-out counters
    box offices
    U.S. Customs
    bargain sales
    buffets
    cafeterias
    bus stops
    . . . wearily waiting my turn.
   Is this any different?

   "Then I heard what sounded like the shouts of a great crowd, or the roaring of the deep, or mighty peals of thunder, as they cried:
   'Alleluia!'
   The Lord is king. . . .
   Let us rejoice and be glad and give him glory!
   For this is the wedding day of the Lamb;
       his bride has made herself ready. . .'
   The angel then said to me:
       'Write this down: Happy are they who have been invited to the wedding feast of the Lamb.'"

2. Life together is a matter of give and take:
    giving and taking
    express and shape our common life.
   Bread and cup, given and taken,
    express and shape the Body of Christ
    for we are his Body:
    One for all,
    all for one.

3. In eating and drinking,
    food and drink pass into our bodies,
    become part of us
    to build us up.
   In this eating and this drinking
    we become what we eat;
    become part of the Body we receive,

to build it up
into the fullness of Christ
that God may be all in all.

4. Returning to my place,
    conscious of the Gift within,
    the sweetness of the Lord still in my mouth.
Do I know what I have done?
    Did I feel the burning coals upon my lips?
Shuffling to my place,
    people squeezing by,
    settling down,
    a child cries,
    a couple share a whisper and a smile,
    the shuffling of feet and papers,
    the Word is made very flesh
    and dwells among us
    in hidden silence
    holding us all
    in hidden unity.[40]

Searle writes here that "life together" is all about "give and take," and the Communion procession embodies just that; communication is silently manifested in the giving and taking of both the bread and the cup. Furthermore, he reveals four distinct moments for the assembly in the action of Communion: standing in line, "taking" the bread and the cup, eating and drinking, and returning to one's place. Each of these contains a component of the attitude of "life together" that is to be rehearsed at this point in the Mass.

First, Searle makes it clear that there is something significant about forming a procession to the altar for participating in Communion. The examples of standing at check-out lanes, box offices, customs, bargain sales, buffets, cafeterias, and bus stops are all instances of waiting as an individual. The Communion line is something very different. According to the contemplative vision of Searle, the act of standing in line is the joining of oneself to the great throng of guests "who have been invited to the wedding feast" and who come with immense joy and a sense of triumph. In his very first contribution to *Assembly*, in a piece titled "The Act of Communion: A Commentary," Searle notes the sign-value of standing:

[40] Mark Searle, "Communing," *Assembly* 6, no. 3 (1979): 79.

166

The person who stands is the one who is ready to serve, alert and attentive—like the Israelites who ate the Passover meal standing in readiness, awaiting the summons of the Lord who was to call them out of slavery and adopt them as his own free people. *We give you thanks that you have counted us worthy to stand before you and serve you.* And the victor stands, stunned perhaps to know that he has survived the struggle, but on his feet and alive. . . . The Risen Christ stands triumphant over death, and his disciples rise to their feet to share his victory and to acclaim his triumph: *And I saw a huge number . . . standing in front of the throne and in front of the lamb.*[41]

Quite simply, the formation of a procession in line for Communion provides a visible, tangible sign of attentiveness and recognition of being caught up in Christ's humble giving of self. This is precisely why singing accompanies the procession: "in order to express the spiritual union of the communicants by means of the unity of their voices, to show gladness of heart, and to bring out more clearly the 'communitarian' character of the procession to receive the Eucharist."[42] Those who stand in line waiting to approach the table move as one body, and participation in the ritual music makes waiting as an individual impossible, as voices form a distinct, inseparable whole. On this role of music, Searle writes:

Liturgical song . . . is ritual singing, in which, as in our bodily acting and congregating, it is not we who are the agents, but Christ who moves, acts and sings in and through us by the power of his Spirit in which we submit. Thus the role of music is not just to get everyone to join in, (what, after all, are we joining in?), but to draw us into contemplative awareness of the one prayer, the one heavenly song, that rises up from the depths of the Spirit in the midst of the community before the throne of God. Far from "expressing" ourselves in the songs of the liturgy, therefore, we were rehearsed to sing in such a way as to "overhear" the song singing itself through us.[43]

Can the act of standing in line become an act of prayer in which the Body learns to hear "the song singing itself through us," the song

[41] Mark Searle, "The Act of Communion: A Commentary," *Assembly* 4, no. 4 (1978): 7. Emphasis original.

[42] GIRM 86.

[43] Mark Searle, "The Spirit of the Liturgy: A Workshop," *Assembly* 13, no. 5 (1987): 373.

which is that of the whole Christ, the *totus Christus*, that celebrates the Kingdom's banquet feast? Is it possible that our Communion procession can be that kind of epiphany?[44] It can if we abide by the liturgy, which at this moment seeks to rehearse in us the self-emptiedness by which we selflessly receive that which is selflessly given.

Another way of approaching the dynamic of standing in line and entering into the communion hymn is to examine it as an act of communication. In the examples of waiting in line that Searle describes above, the primary objective is to receive something—a movie ticket, a meal, or a ride—but in the act of the liturgical procession, the objective is to "become"; what is communicated is identity.[45] However, often times liturgical singing during the communion procession can appear to be more about imparting information rather than promoting self-forgetfulness, unity of the Body, and ultimately a sense of what we are becoming.[46] Music that rehearses the Body of Christ as it is realizing anew the bonds of relationship in the seal of Communion must resist novelty and seek what can be sung "from the bones."[47] "We must ask,"

---

[44] See Searle, *Liturgy Made Simple*, 88. Here he offers the following commentary on the need for planning the Communion procession: "The Communion Rite is not something that has to be planned anew every weekend, but it is something that needs serious thought in the early days of a planning committee's life . . . [I]n the long-term we should be thinking about how this procession to Communion can become a community act, an eating and drinking together in affirmation of our common life in Christ. Too often it is simply a matter of lining up and awaiting one's turn."

[45] See Searle, "Renewing the Liturgy—Again. 'A' for the Council, 'C' for the Church," 620. Here Searle defines the discovery of identity as the goal of all liturgical participation: "Thus, liturgical participation is more than just 'joining in': it is first and foremost a conscious and willed participation in the acting out of the relationship of Christ to the Father, expressed in worship of God and the sanctification of human beings, both of which are inseparable dimensions of the Paschal mystery of self-sacrificial submission to the will of God. It is for this reason that the council encouraged all the faithful to take part by means of acclamations, responses, psalmody, antiphons, and songs, as well as by actions, gestures, and bodily attitudes.'"

[46] Searle, "Ritual and Music: A Theory of Liturgy and Implications for Music," 317.

[47] See Thomas Day, *Why Catholics Can't Sing: The Culture of Catholicism and the Triumph of Bad Taste*, 85–86. Here he describes success stories of liturgical music that flowed forth "from the bones" of the assembly. He provides the following analysis: "The common ingredients in these two 'success stories' are

writes Searle, "what kind of music could sacrifice the immediate gang-appeal of the sing-along or the aesthetic peak-experience of the concert hall, for the sake of a more humble, contemplative service of the liturgical act?"[48]

The second component of the act of communion, outlined in Searle's reflection on "communing," is "taking" the bread and the cup which are "given" by Christ. The simultaneous "taking" of what is being "given" reveals a central truth about Christianity. "Life together," writes Searle, "is a matter of give and take: giving and taking express and shape our common life."[49] To say that Christians "give and take" means that they pay attention to others; one who does not "give and take" is one who is considered selfish, unable to look out with openness toward the world. Searle writes:

> The Eucharist is the sacrament of giving and taking in the community of Christ's Body, which is the Church. The community shares, in giving and taking, what Christ has given and told us to take: his body broken for us, his blood poured out for us. This is the substance of that giving and taking which we call communion. He gave to us that we might take and we learn to take that we might learn to give. One bread broken and shared; one cup poured out and passed around; one people giving and taking. Not eating in private, not self-service, but feasting in common: hand to hand, person to person, all for one and one for all, given and taken.[50]

Searle suggests that the "giving" and "taking" that is enacted in Communion is noticeably different from the way in which we normally approach food and drink. Other than when we are infants or are on

---

subtle: This music—special, distinctive—evoked a sense of *pride in ownership*. The singing had an *effortless quality*; without displaying any hint of being self-conscious, the music flowed easily into and out of the ceremony. The music seemed to be *part of the ritual* and not something irrelevant added just to keep everyone busy. There was *no coercion* ("now we are all going to sing this hymn and you better participate"). The melodies *sounded important*, as if they had existed forever. They were *familiar* tunes which had been *memorized*. Perhaps the inner secret of this 'success' was that the music just seemed to *take place*; it did not sound like something presented to the congregation" (86).

[48] Searle, "Ritual and Music: A Theory of Liturgy and Implications for Music," 317.

[49] Searle, "Communing," 79.

[50] Searle, "The Act of Communion," 6.

our deathbeds or experience some kind of debilitation, we generally feed ourselves. But not so with the Body and Blood of Christ; here we must extend our hands and cooperate with the generosity provided. Our hands, therefore, become a sign of welcome. "Open-handedly, gently," writes Searle, "the Gift is given and received, from hand to hand: not the perfunctory, hurried snatch of greed, but the reverent, two-handed welcome of gratitude; not the anxious gesture of a hand-to-mouth existence, but the warm cupped hands of those who know the treasure they hold."[51] Therefore, is it not too much to ask members of the assembly to reflect on the way in which they extend their hands to receive Communion?

Perhaps this question extends beyond how we "take" what we are "given" to the manner in which we "eat" and "drink"—the third moment of our communing. Beyond the sign-value of receiving the elements of communion, the actions of "eating" and "drinking" reveal the seal of participation in the covenant—they are a visible "Amen" to our willingness to sacrifice ourselves in becoming more fully members of Christ. For Searle, the restoration of the cup to the assembly was an important aspect of Vatican II liturgical renewal, for here "we are once again encouraged to lift the cup of salvation to our lips, and to taste and see for ourselves how good the Lord is (Ps. 34:18)."[52] Sadly, the Notre Dame Study of Catholic Parish Life suggested to Searle that the action of drinking from the cup was viewed "ambivalently," with almost half of the respondents claiming to be indifferent to the cup or desirous that it be withdrawn once again.[53] It would seem that drinking from the cup was not readily perceived as a fundamental liturgical gesture for the assembly to perform. However, the GIRM states: "It is most desirable that the faithful, just as the priest himself is bound to do . . . partake of the chalice (cf, no. 283), so that even by means of the signs Communion may stand out more clearly as a participation in the sacrifice actually being celebrated."[54]

---

[51] Ibid.

[52] Mark Searle, "The Tradition We Have Received," *Assembly* 5, no. 3 (1978): 40.

[53] Mark Searle, "Observations on Parish Liturgy," *New Catholic World* (November/December 1985): 260.

[54] GIRM 85. See also John M. Huels, "The Sign Value of the Chalice: Can It Be Negated for the People?" *Worship* 85 (2012): 403–19. Huels argues that even if a considerable number abstain from drinking from the chalice, it should be offered: "The distribution of Communion under both kinds at every Mass,

It could very well be the case that many in our assemblies refrain from the cup due to the very thought of drinking blood—eating flesh is one thing, but drinking blood is quite another. Yet Searle suggests that our participation in "drinking" is a testimony to our willingness to be plunged into discomfort and ambivalence. He writes, "This is a mystery which can only elude our rational minds with its evangelical paradoxes: the paradox of life-which-is-death and death-which-is-life, of salvation by crucifixion, of suffering which is bliss, of poverty which is riches, of past and future which are nonetheless present, of wine which is blood and blood which is heady wine, and so on *ad finitum*."[55] Ultimately, the action of "drinking" makes visible the assembly's willingness to embrace the will of the Father, to take on the lot of suffering rather than to reject it:

> The restoration of the cup of his blood, as a sacramental sign in which all the faithful can now share, is particularly significant for helping us see what is involved in communion with Christ. On the one hand, wine has associations of joy and festivity, so that drinking from the cup is a sacramental anticipation of our participation in the banquet in the Kingdom of God. It looks forward to the joy of everlasting life with God and his saints, which the Scriptures so often describe in terms of a feast. But there is another, not unconnected, set of associations: the cup as cup of destiny and cup of suffering. In the agony of facing his imminent passion and death, Jesus prayed that, if it could be his Father's will, this 'cup' might pass him by. When James and John asked for prominent places in the eternal Kingdom, Jesus asked them if they could drink of the cup that he himself would have to drink (Mark 10:38). All these associations come crowding back as we lift to our lips the cup of his blood, impressing upon us the fact that we are called to share in the likeness of his death if we are to have any share in the likeness of his resurrection (Rom 6:5).[56]

---

even if a notable part of the faithful lawfully exercises their freedom not to drink from the chalice, nevertheless always remains a strong witness of the Church's fidelity to the Lord's command" (418–19).

[55] Mark Searle, "The Cup of His Blood," *Assembly* 5, no. 3 (1978): 33.

[56] Searle, *Liturgy Made Simple*, 70. See also Searle, "The Act of Communion," 7. He states: "Take this all of you and drink from it: this is the cup of my blood which is poured out for you. Even today it is permitted in the liturgy to sip through a tube, or to communicate by intinction. These are convenient, but they are not drinking. There is always the silver spoon to carry the life-blood of Christ to the lips of his little ones. But the challenge is to drink of the cup

Therefore, the actions of "eating" and "drinking," while certainly a seal of our identity in Christ, are fundamentally about our *destiny*, a destiny that is the passing through death to life.[57] Communion in the Body and Blood of Christ is not a temporary comfort but rather a commitment to oneness with Christ in his brokenness for the good of others.[58] Communion is always an indictment against attachment to self and a false sense of peace that is not born of real forgiveness. Thus, in poetic language, Searle alludes to drinking from the cup as protection from our selfish selves:

> At peace with God?
>
> Through the blood of Christ
> the messenger of peace
> whom we slay for our own protection?
>
> Protection and peace of mind
>   protection against forgiveness
>   protection against peace
>   protection against the love that overcomes
>   even the death of the heart.
>
> His murder shall haunt us into peace
>   his blood crying to heaven
>   soaking into our sodden earth
>   into hate-hardened hearts
>   into fear-ridden ghettos
> for us and for all
>   so that sins may be forgiven.

---

of destiny: *Can you drink of the cup of which I am to drink?* This is the cup which would not pass by him and we must take it and put it to our lips, for the servant is not greater than his master. *Father, if it is your will, take this cup from me; yet not my will but yours be done.* The Blood of Christ: Amen—so be it."

[57] See Searle, "The Act of Communion," 7. He writes: "For we become what we eat. To take the broken bread is to become one with the broken Body of the Crucified and to grasp the cup is to share his destiny."

[58] See Searle, "Participation and Prayer," 151. Searle writes: "One of the consequences of such participation in the life and prayer of Christ is an increased sensitivity to the needs of other people. There are of course plenty of ways in which the spiritual life can become an ego trip, a process of self-delusion, and an escape from the responsibilities of life."

Forgive us our crucifixion
as we forgive those who crucify us
as we forgive those whom we crucify.[59]

Searle suggests here that participation in the blood of Christ is a "haunting" experience, in that it serves as a reminder that we are partly to blame for instances where forgiveness and peace do not reign. When "hate-hardened hearts" and "fear-ridden ghettos" lead to crucifixion, when these places stifle the flourishing of life, we can easily turn aside from drinking the cup that reflects our culpability. Once again, the actions of "eating" and "drinking," even in the joy and fulfillment they bring, contain a willing readiness for conversion.[60]

The fourth ritual action of Communion, which Searle isolates in the above mentioned 1979 piece "Communing," is the act of returning. Something as simple as returning to the same place one left in order to communicate with the Body of Christ as it eats and drinks its destiny is a moment of contemplation for Searle. It is a time for thanks, "conscious of the Gift within, the sweetness of the Lord still in my mouth," as well as a moment of arraignment: "Do I know what I have done? Did I feel the burning coals upon my lips?"[61] Over all of this, there is a return to the silence out of which came our first moments of prayer, "a time for reflecting on the Communion of which we are part—one with others in Christ."[62] But even more than this, the "return" is all about a change in vision, of seeing the world not as individuals but as the restored Body of Christ.

In his 1980 article, "The Journey of Conversion," Searle highlights the immense importance of the "return" in the process of conversion, which for him, is an awakening to a new worldview. He writes: "It is not that external circumstances change—simply waiting for things to

[59] Mark Searle, ". . . Lord, May This Sacrifice Advance the Peace of the Whole World . . . ," *Assembly* 11, no. 4 (1985): 287.
[60] See Mark Searle, "The Journey of Conversion," *Worship* 54 (1980): 50–51. While maintaining that every liturgical celebration is a "community rehearsal of the journey of the Body of Christ," and therefore is about conversion, he argues that ritual can be used to shirk commitment to change as well: "In protecting him from the terrors of chaos, it may insulate him against any very profound experience at all. In other words, ritual can end up actually helping the individual to bypass the experience of crisis which is thrust upon him."
[61] Searle, "Communing," 79.
[62] Searle, *Liturgy Made Simple*, 71.

get better is one of the ways of avoiding conversion—but our vision changes. We see things in a new light."[63] For Searle, words of T. S. Eliot have particular value and can easily be applied to the physical return to one's place in the act of communion:

> We shall not cease from exploration
> and the end of all our exploring
> will be to arrive where we started
> and to know the place for the first time.[64]

As communicants return to their places, singing together a song of praise, they witness all walks of life "eating" and "drinking" the resolve to be united in the Lord, and this is the greatest and most reliable sign of hope for the Christian community. In our Communion, we see where we have been, who we are, and where we hope to go.[65] "On the road to freedom," writes Searle, "we are sustained by the broken bread and the cup of blood. But these are symbols of sacrifice and death. When we eat this bread and drink this cup, we not only proclaimed the death of the Lord, but we commit ourselves to share it."[66] The change in vision demands a new sacrifice of ourselves in the Lord,

[63] Searle, "The Journey of Conversion," 43. He continues: "The question that tormented us, perhaps, is not so much answered as transcended or itself transformed into an answer. The dread of loneliness is converted into the quiet joy of solitude accepted. The fear of not being one of the crowd is converted into a deeper sense of one's own identity; or maybe the fear of losing oneself in the crowd gives way to a new and deeper compassion for one's fellows. Success and failure, which had so concerned one earlier, no longer seem important. *Unexpectedly, one becomes aware that a new vision has been given, a revelation has been granted, the grace of self-transcendence, of new life, of joy.*" Emphasis mine.

[64] T. S. Eliot, "Little Gidding," in *The Four Quartets*, as found in Searle, "The Journey of Conversion," 43.

[65] See Zimmermann, "The Communion Rite: The Mystagogical Implications," 615. She writes "Our 'Amen' as we receive the Host and the Precious Blood from the chalice is a faith affirmation of the Body and Blood of Christ being received as well as a faith affirmation of who we are and are becoming: more perfect members of the Body of Christ. It is as members of the Body of Christ that we are sent forth to live as Jesus lived, to serve as he did, to continue the saving ministry that makes present God's reign in the here and now."

[66] Searle, "The Journey of Conversion," 54.

with the accompanying hope that together we "look forward to the resurrection of the dead and the life of the world to come."

With this internal reordering of the corporate worldview of the Body of Christ, it is quite fitting that the Mass ends rather "abruptly"[67]—after the Prayer after Communion—with "brief announcements," the final blessing and dismissal, and the kissing of the altar.[68] In fact, the GIRM does not provide instruction on an exit procession or any other movement other than a "profound bow" to the altar. Even though the Eucharist concludes with swift brevity, the ritual elements of the conclusion are necessary to soften the blow of our transition back into the world; like a newborn infant, the reordered Body of Christ must be handled with care as it proceeds to live out its mission anew. Searle writes:

> With the post-Communion prayer, the Mass is essentially over. But we need some way of returning from the intensity of prayer and celebration to the ordinariness of our daily lives together. Just as at the beginning we need the Introductory Rites to get into the proper form of mind, so we need some sort of conclusion to send us on our way. . . . [T]he leader of the celebration greets the people anew and invokes God's blessing upon them as their return to their Christian lives in the larger world. Finally, the order is given to disperse: to go forth as bearers of Christ's peace and to be faithful to him in serving the Father in the world. . . . And so the work of God continues for the redemption of his world.[69]

With the final blessing that culminates in the common sign of our life—the cross—and the dismissal that provides a verbal command for the perpetuation of our "life together," the assembly that goes forth is to be a sacramental sign of what has been accomplished in prayer: we have sacrificed the "self" for Christ and his Body. In Searle's own

[67] See Searle, "*Semper Reformanda*: The Opening and Concluding Rites of the Roman Mass," 85.

[68] See GIRM 90.

[69] Searle, *Liturgy Made Simple*, 72–73. See also Searle, "*Semper Reformanda*: The Opening and Closing Rites of the Roman Mass," 88. Searle suggests here that leave-taking necessitates some form of ritual: "It appears that this rather informal exit was never queried or discussed at any time in the process of revising the Mass, which is rather extraordinary when the human dynamics of the situation are considered, for parting is usually found awkward unless adequately ritualized."

words: "So before there are seven sacraments there is the sacrament of the Christian people, the sign of a people who lived 'amazed' at the God who has shown himself to us in Jesus and 'amazed' at the vision of human life and destiny which he has opened up."[70] Thus, the Mass ends with the command in the singular given to Christ's Body: "Go in peace, glorifying the Lord by your life."[71]

CONCLUSION

The corporate rehearsal of "communing," which enacts a world in which broken relationships have been restored and union with the divine is a saving reality, ends as gift to be given. "*Peace*" is practiced as an attitude of recognizing the Risen Lord in our midst, and "*life together*" engrains in us the ability to "give" and "take." Our communing with one another in the Lord is a visible, tangible sacrament of our desire not to live for the self but to live for others.[72] Over and over again, we master the art of "communing" in order to become a priestly people, a people who offer themselves, in Christ, on behalf of the world.

If our corporate rehearsal of Communion is successful, it will hone our worldview to look past participation for personal needs and merit to the desire for the healing of this world's suffering. We will learn that Communion is not so much about anything *received* as much as it is about what we are *becoming*. In our "Amen," we say yes to life

[70] Mark Searle, "The Christian Community, Evangelized and Evangelizing," *Emmanuel* 86 (1980): 611. Searle reiterates this idea of "amazement" in the conclusion of his paper: "The liturgy is where our 'amazement' is sparked anew and pours forth in song and prayer, in praise and petition" (618).

[71] See Philippart, *Saving Signs, Wondrous Words*, 87. He writes: "We do not leave here a random group of strangers. We are sent out in the power of the Holy Spirit to be the body of Christ at work in the world. We are not sent out alone (the 'you' is not a bunch of me's, it's the second-person plural; it's us)."

[72] See Searle, "The Christian Community, Evangelized and Evangelizing," 616. He writes: "The notion of sacrament is much broader than that of liturgy: liturgy is rather the explicit, ritual celebration of the sacramentality of all Christian life. Liturgical celebrations do not stand apart from life any more— or any less—than other celebrations do. Like other forms of celebration, they make us aware and help us to affirm the things that underlie our ordinary lives and yet are most important to us. In the case of the liturgy, what we celebrate in word and action is the presence of the God of our lives who is the ultimate cause and meaning and salvation of our human existence."

together with all that God has formed, and we commit the pattern of our lives to the restoration of right relationship with others, God, and all creation. This means there is much work to be done. "The world cannot find justice," writes Searle, "until it is surrendered to God in Christ."[73] That is why we open the Scriptures and break the bread—to rehearse in our body and in *the* Body the surrender that calls the world to offer itself up—"so that from the rising of the sun to its setting a pure sacrifice may be offered in your name."[74] This is the promised perfection of God's Just Kingdom.

---

[73] Searle, "Serving the Lord with Justice," 34.
[74] Eucharistic Prayer III.

Chapter 7

Launching a New Liturgical Movement

The last four chapters have demonstrated Mark Searle's vision of the Eucharist as an enactment—a "rehearsal"—of God's Just Kingdom. The liturgy that is celebrated on a weekly, even daily, basis is composed of the attitudes of Christ, shaping in his Body a worldview of right relationship. It should be clear to the reader, however, that the actual performance of the liturgy often falls short of true "Kingdom" formation. In the last phase of his life, Searle himself labored arduously to address this topic by summoning the Church to contemplate anew the nature of its celebration. Furthermore, he provided an abrasive critique of culture in the United States, a culture embodying something far different from the "justice of God." Thus, he called for a new liturgical movement to assist assemblies in the skills of participation and to instill the attitudes of the liturgy in daily life. This last chapter explores both Searle's cultural critique and his summons for a new liturgical movement.

The indisputable cornerstone of postconciliar liturgical reform mandated by the Fathers of the Second Vatican Council is the participation of all the faithful gathered for the act of worship. This mandate is expressed with clarity in *Sacrosanctum Concilium* 14:

> It is very much the wish of the church that all the faithful should be led to take that full, conscious, and active part in liturgical celebrations which is demanded by the very nature of the liturgy, and to which the Christian people, "a chosen race, a royal priesthood, a holy nation, a redeemed people" (1 Pet 2:9, 4-5) have a right and to which they are bound by reason of their Baptism.
>
> *In the restoration and development of the sacred liturgy the full and active participation by all the people is the paramount concern, for it is the primary, indeed the indispensable source from which the faithful are to derive the true Christian spirit.*[1]

---

[1] *Sacrosanctum Concilium* 14 in Flannery, *The Basic Sixteen Documents*. Emphasis mine. This ideal is described further in number 30: "To develop active

While it is necessary to keep this ideal at the forefront of liturgical reform, there is no denying that the concept of "participation" is quite illusive.[2] What does "full, conscious, and active" participation really mean? From the perspective of a cantor, participation might mean to get each member of the worshiping community to sing, while from the viewpoint of the presider, concern for participation may entail proclaiming the Eucharistic Prayer in a way that is prayerful and conducive to the assembly's devotion. Furthermore, on a theological level, participation may be looked at from how the liturgy promotes an immediate experience of revelation or from how it leads to a developing sense of belonging in Christ.[3]

In promoting active participation as a major *leitmotiv* of liturgical reform, the Fathers of the Second Vatican Council certainly hoped that the liturgy itself would again become the indispensable pattern of life for the Christian community. The shift from "passive" to "active" liturgical involvement was not to be the goal in and of itself but rather was intended to foster greater Christian identity and communion with God. *Sacrosanctum Concilium* 48 makes clear this aim:

> The church, therefore, spares no effort in trying to ensure that, when present at this mystery of faith, Christian believers should not be there as strangers or silent spectators. On the contrary, having a good grasp of it through the rites and prayers, they should take part in the sacred action, actively, fully aware, and devoutly. They should be formed by God's word, and be nourished at the table of the Lord's Body. They should give thanks to God. Offering the immaculate victim, not only through the hands of the priest but also together with him, they should learn to offer themselves. Through Christ, the Mediator, they should be drawn day by day into ever more perfect union with God and each other, so that finally God may be all in all.[4]

---

participation, the people should be encouraged to take part by means of acclamations, responses, psalms, antiphons, hymns, as well as by actions, gestures and bodily attitudes. And at the proper time a reverent silence should be observed."

[2] See, for example, Frederick R. McManus, *Liturgical Participation: An Ongoing Assessment* (Washington, DC: The Pastoral Press, 1988).

[3] See Searle, "Active Participation," 72.

[4] *Sacrosanctum Concilium* 48 in Flannery, *The Basic Sixteen Documents*.

Clearly, liturgical action, both in its purpose and in its enactment, paves the way for a formative encounter with the divine. Therefore, at the very foundation of the Second Vatican Council's call for the participation of all the faithful in the celebration of the liturgy lies the challenge to learn how to pray as the Body of Christ, a challenge of not simply ceasing private devotion during the liturgy but also learning how to be absorbed into Christ's Body and infused with his Spirit.

By the mid-1980s, Mark Searle found himself in the circle of scholars and popular writers who were quite critical of the way in which liturgical reform was being implemented in the United States.[5] His fundamental concern hinged upon the display of a growing suspicion of ritual behavior in an ever increasingly secular society. Again and again, Searle touted the phrase that, for true reform to take place, we must learn to "trust" the liturgy.[6] "That we have lost faith in the efficacy of instituted rites," posits Searle, "is manifest in the way we commonly regard the liturgy as something that we do for God or ourselves, rather than as something that God (in Christ) does for us."[7]

---

[5] See, for example, M. Francis Mannion, "Liturgy and the Present Crisis of Culture," *Worship* 62 (1988): 98–123; Luis Maldonado, "The Church's Liturgy: Present and Future," in *Toward Vatican III: The Work That Needs to Be Done*, ed. David Tracy and Hans Küng (New York: The Seabury Press, 1978), 221–37; and John Garvey, "Let Liturgy Be Liturgy: Stop Trying to Put a New Spin on It," *Commonweal* (December 3, 1982): 648–49. In this rather inflammatory editorial, Garvey posits: "The solution is not a return to the old liturgy but rather an appreciation of the fact that we are called by our faith to transformation, something which liturgy ought to assist us in. That means not an affirmation of time, emotion, and language as we ordinarily perceive it, but help in seeing those common elements of our lives in depth, and this demands a radical shift in perspective. . . . The perfect church service would be one we were almost unaware of; our attention would have been on God" (649).

[6] For example, in 1984, Searle writes: "The only important thing is to trust the liturgy and the presence of the Spirit, allowing them to pray through one" (See Searle, "Images and Worship," 113). In 1991, Searle published an article that incorporated the phrase "trust the ritual." See Searle, "Trust the Ritual or Face 'The Triumph of Bad Taste,'" 21. He writes: "It is God's gift that evokes our response. *That, in the end, is why we have to put our trust in the efficacy of the instituted rites and the ineffable richness of our symbols.* To do otherwise can only be to trivialize them and turn them into human performances. Now *that* is what I would call the triumph of bad taste!" Emphasis mine.

[7] Searle, "Trust the Ritual or Face 'The Triumph of Bad Taste,'" 19. See also Mary Douglas, *Natural Symbols: Explorations in Cosmology* (New York: Vintage

In his 1988 *Commonweal* article titled "Renewing the Liturgy—Again: 'A' for the Council, 'C' for the Church," Searle states that, twenty-five years after its promulgation, the vision of *Sacrosanctum Concilium* "is still not widely understood or fully implemented."[8] In this article, he returns to the wisdom of Romano Guardini and his assessment that true reform demands the resurrection of "lost attitudes." Searle writes:

> By this, Guardini meant recovering in the church at large a capacity for what he called "the liturgical act" or "liturgical-symbolic" actions: a capacity for uttering and understanding words and gestures in such a way as to recognize them as *corporal expressions of spiritual realities;* and above all, to recognize in them the reality of *Christ's presence among and to his people.* It is probably not unfair to say that, despite the enormous educational effort that accompanies the "new liturgy," it rarely achieved the depth which Guardini warned was necessary: that of relearning a forgotten way of doing things and recapturing lost attitudes. So the new rites came into use in a church whose people were not attuned to them and whose buildings and music were designed on the basis of a different theology and a different conception of church.[9]

In Searle's view, the liturgical movement prior to and during the Council, by and large, prepared Catholics for the fact that change was coming but did not pave the way for understanding how change should be implemented and thereby shape the attitudes of worshipers. As a result, Searle identifies a "crisis" for the Church: "Even now, the fundamental problems of the reform are still with us, and the renewal that the council hoped for remains elusive."[10]

Books, 1973). Regarding the mistrust of ritual, Douglas writes: "One of the gravest problems of our day is the lack of commitment to common symbols. If this were all, there would be little to say. If it were merely a matter of our fragmentation into small groups, each committed to its proper symbolic forms, the case would be simply to understand. But more mysterious is a wide-spread, explicit rejection of rituals as such. Ritual has become a bad word signifying empty conformity. We are witnessing a revolt against formalism, even against form" (19).

[8] Searle, "Renewing the Liturgy—Again: 'A' for the Council, 'C' for the Church," 617.

[9] Ibid., 618. Emphasis mine.

[10] Ibid.

Again, the failure here is one of misunderstanding the dynamics of liturgical participation, a failure to corporately contemplate the Paschal Mystery and the presence of Christ in the gathered Church. In fact, Searle argues that the liturgy ends up manifesting the triumph of culture (more precisely individualism) over the unity of the assembly that is being built up into Christ's Body.[11] He writes:

> Indeed, the freedom of choice built into the revised *Ordo missae* has meant that congregations have experienced an increase in the idiosyncrasies of the presider and whoever else may be in a position to impose their personal tastes on the style of the celebration. It was not the intention of the revisers of the *Ordo* to undermine what Guardini called the "objectivity" of the rite, but that is largely what has happened. *The revised liturgy has proved highly susceptible to the individualism of our culture, rather than becoming, as the promoters of the liturgical movement had hoped, a bulwark against it.*[12]

In light of this critique, Searle maintains that what is needed is not further manipulation of the liturgy to make it resilient against unwanted cultural forces but rather a widespread program of catechesis aimed at teaching the principles of reform: "The time has come, surely, to relaunch the liturgical movement."[13] While he acknowledges that a new liturgical movement would necessarily seek to solidify the understanding of the most basic principles of *Sacrosanctum Concilium*—principles such as participation, the nature of "sacrament," and the link between the Church and the world—Searle's fundamental concern is the universal comprehension of Guardini's concept of "the liturgical

[11] See Mark Searle, "A Place in the Tradition," *Assembly* 12, no. 1 (1985): 302. He writes: "[T]he real rift in American Catholicism is not between pre and post-conciliar attitudes, but between individualistic religion and communal religion." Searle continues on the following page: "The biggest threat to the Church in America today is not old-fashioned attitudes, but voluntarism: the belief that no one has the right to make demands upon you or teach you or require anything of you that you would rather not do. Its opposite is not blind obedience but a sense of vocation to serve the larger community and to be part of a faith community that serves the world by being obedient servants of Word and Sacrament."

[12] Searle, "Renewing the Liturgy—Again: 'A' for the Council, 'C' for the Church," 621. Emphasis mine.

[13] Ibid. See also Lawrence J. Madden, "A New Liturgical Movement," *America* 117 (September 10, 1994): 16–19.

act." "The primary task of a new liturgical movement," Searle posits, "would be the same as that of the old movement: to improve the quality of our common prayer, especially in parishes, so that our liturgies expose us to the transforming fire."[14]

LITURGY AS A SOCIAL CRITIQUE

While Searle's call to launch anew the liturgical movement is undoubtedly rooted in the reestablishment of a contemplative understanding of the nature of ritual (i.e., repetition, formality, patterned behavior), he also saw liturgy as providing a valuable critique on culture that would simultaneously challenge the Church. Thus, in 1990, Searle published "Private Religion, Individualistic Society, and Common Worship," which begins with a study of cultural forces and from there assesses their impact on liturgical practice.[15] Clearly, this essay represents his most concentrated effort to acknowledge the destructive influence that certain prevalent cultural attitudes have on the performance of the liturgy in the United States. He offers his theory without apology:

> We tend to think too much of what the Church might bring to society and too little of what society is already bringing to the Church. We enthuse about what new prayers and new liturgical music might do to shape the liturgical assembly, overlooking the fact that culture has gotten there before us, unconsciously shaping the attitudes and language of both the experts and the participants.[16]

Commenting on this observation, theologian Mark Francis writes: "Once the liturgy has been opened to a relationship with local culture, the worship of the Church will be changed—not necessarily by Roman dicasteries, national bishops' conferences, liturgical experts or committees—but inevitably and often inadvertently by the cultural patterns or *Zeitgeist* of the human context in which it is celebrated."[17] Thus,

---

[14] Searle, "Renewing the Liturgy—Again: 'A' for the Council, 'C' for the Church," 621.

[15] See Mark Searle, "Private Religion, Individualistic Society, and Common Worship," in *Liturgy and Spirituality in Context: Perspectives on Prayer and Culture*, ed. Eleanor Bernstein (Collegeville, MN: Liturgical Press, 1990), 27–46.

[16] Ibid., 27.

[17] Mark R. Francis, "Introduction to 'Private Religion, Individualistic Society, and Common Worship,'" in Anne Koester and Barbara Searle, eds.,

Searle's objective here is to bring to light and to stimulate reflection on cultural characteristics that make "genuinely public worship" in America a near impossibility.

For example, as discussed throughout the chapters on the rehearsal of the Eucharist, Searle wrestled with the concept of "building" community. He writes that such an emphasis within the liturgy serves to disguise the community that is already built up in the Christian assembly by virtue of a common baptism in the Lord. Thus, he cautions against what he calls a nostalgic yearning to bring "a sense of old-fashioned community to modern life," for as he states: "We yearn for the homely togetherness and directness of an earlier and simpler age, but our attempts to restore it merely parody it. Behind the cheery informality of our celebrations and our 'ministers of hospitality,' the profoundly impersonal quality of our interactions remains untouched."[18] Furthermore, Searle identifies another adversary of the liturgy with the term "religious privatism," which he defines as the "tendency for Americans to belong to churches, but on their own terms. They come, not to submit to historical tradition and religious discipline in response to God's call, but for their own personal reasons and to meet their own personal needs."[19] Moreover, US capitalism and market values rival the living out of liturgical attitudes, for as Searle writes:

> Most generally and most importantly, the premium placed on cost-efficiency and profitability, on functional specialization and expertise

---

Vision: The Scholarly Contributions of Mark Searle to Liturgical Renewal, ed. Anne Koester and Barbara Searle (Collegeville, MN: Liturgical Press, 2004), 182. Francis continues: "While Church authorities and liturgical ministers may change texts and other ritual details, the way the liturgy is prepared and how it is experienced has more to do with the often unintended inculturation that comes about as a result of contact with the cultural context itself."

[18] Searle, "Private Religion, Individualistic Society, and Common Worship," 28–29. Searle bases his critique that nostalgia masks the pursuit for community on the work of British sociologist Bryan Wilson. See Bryan Wilson, *Religion in Secular Society* (Baltimore, MD: Penguin Books Inc., 1969), especially 115.

[19] Searle, "Private Religion, Individualistic Society, and Common Worship," 30. See also Martin Marty, *The Public Church* (New York: Crossroad, 1981), 25. Comparing the American Church to the free market, Marty writes: "The drift of religion today is, if anything, moving towards an utterly free market in which little trace of fate, election, or predestination remains." Searle quotes Marty on page 30 of his article.

creates a society where the dominant values are functional values and where matters of "ultimate concern" are relegated to the private realm. . . The effect, then, of massification is to reinforce the effects of pluralism, making the individual the sole arbiter of ultimate values and thereby undermining the bonds that create genuine community. *What holds us together as a society is not, as in most societies, a common world view, a "sacred cosmos," but the patterns of production and consumption into which we are socialized by secular education and the seductions of the mass media.*[20]

Likewise, Searle addresses the notion of individualism in the United States, revealing how contrary it is to the liturgical worldview: "Radical individualism celebrates the freedom that is now ours to select our own values and priorities without reference to any wider framework of common purpose or beliefs."[21] Within this narrow framework of individual priorities, liturgy is just another commodity that competes with a host of other social opportunities. Finally, Searle explores the dynamic of "civil religion"[22] as problematic for Christian worship, as he writes: "Church-going Americans fail to discriminate between the religion of nationalism and the Christianity they profess. . . . Instead of being resources for the recovery of genuine community, the churches and their liturgies end up peddling 'synthetic' community, designed to accommodate people's longing for community but finally incapable of actually engendering community."[23]

All of this makes "trusting" in the ritual counter-cultural indeed! Searle leaves no doubt that the liturgy in America has not only incorporated elements of the above cultural influences, but also has in many ways lost the ability to proclaim and manifest the soul of the

[20] Searle, "Private Religion, Individualistic Society, and Common Worship," 32. Emphasis mine. See also Thomas Luckmann, *The Invisible Religion* (New York: Macmillan Publishing Co., Inc., 1967), 58–61. Searle takes the notion of "sacred cosmos" from Luckmann, who writes: "The sacred cosmos is part of the world view. . . . The sacred cosmos determines directly the entire socialization of the individual and is relevant for the total individual biography" (61).

[21] Searle, "Private Religion, Individualistic Society, and Common Worship," 32.

[22] See Robert N. Bellah, *Beyond Belief: Essays on Religion in a Post-Traditional World* (New York: Harper & Row, 1970), 168–89.

[23] Searle, "Private Religion, Individualistic Society, and Common Worship," 34–35.

Christian story, the Paschal Mystery and our participation in it. Rather than being a corporate rehearsal of Christ's suffering, death, and resurrection, the liturgy in the United States often embodies the casual comfort of what Searle calls a "meaningful worship experience":

> . . . the smoothly orchestrated celebrations of suburbia with their choirs and folk-groups, their "easy-listening" music, their firm handshakes, and their abundance of lay ministers in bright dresses and sharp suits. But for the more radical reactions against the anonymity and impersonalism of our society, we should probably look outside the usual parish setting to Masses celebrated on the living-room floor in religious houses where "Father Mike" wears a stole and all join hands as he improves on the Eucharistic traditions of centuries with a sizable dose of earnest informality; or we might look to youth Masses where the Gospel is reduced to God wanting us to be ourselves and the last vestiges of ritual formality yield before a burning desire for authenticity. Better still, look to the culminating liturgy at experiences of encounter and renewal where deep and extensive sharing over twenty-four hours reaches climax and consummation in a "meaningful worship experience" oblivious both to history and to the future, celebrating the "now."[24]

The obvious link between these diverse settings for liturgical celebrations is that they all seem to make their primary goal the subjective contentment of the participants; when the liturgy makes the assembly "feel good," it is then deemed a "meaningful worship experience." The rather harsh reality is that this popular form of religious experience, while producing feelings of satisfaction, warmth, and solidarity does nothing to strengthen the attitudes that are essential for genuine Christian community. "It gives an evanescent experience of togetherness," writes Searle, "a passing *frisson* of religious excitement, but it doesn't impose the constraints of discipline and commitment."[25]

All of this points to Searle's overall critique, namely, that the pre–Vatican II private Mass has been replaced by what he calls "shared celebrations" rather than by true "public worship."[26] In other words,

---

[24] Ibid., 36.

[25] Ibid., 37.

[26] See Searle, *Called to Participate*, 70. He writes: "I would want to pose the challenge as followed: we have moved from *private* Mass (celebrated in public) to *community* celebrations, but how do we get from there to *public* worship? In other words, the pre–Vatican II Eucharistic was celebrated for private inten-

while the vision of the Second Vatican Council entailed the retrieval of the theological importance and the requisite role of the assembly, the aforementioned cultural attitudes would stand in the way of making this vision a reality. Searle writes:

> The full, active, and conscious participation of the assembled faithful was required; hence the vernacular, the prayers of the faithful, congregational singing, lay ministers, and the rest. All this was permitted, indeed demanded but no legislation or instruction could cure us overnight of our ingrained individualism and privatism. To the degree that liturgical celebrations have been suffused with individualism, they remain *shared celebrations* rather than common prayer. To the degree that we are there for our own private reasons, whether to express our faith or to enjoy singing and praying together, the liturgy is not yet that of a community, but merely an assembly of people all "doing their own thing." *However impressive or exhilarating it might be, it remains shared therapy; it is not yet public domain.*[27]

In this condemnatory observation, Searle identifies the key to the new liturgical movement, namely, the restoration of genuine "public worship." He contends that liturgy by its very nature "is more than shared celebration meeting private needs: it is an act of civic responsibility, of public duty."[28]

---

tions; the post–Vatican II Eucharist has tended to be celebrated for our shared intentions. But how can we learn to celebrate the Eucharist for public intentions?" Searle's point is that the celebration of the liturgy may be less "private" than before the Council, but our attitude about the nature of the liturgy and its purpose, largely due to American culture, continues to be private and individualistic. See also Mark Searle, "Culture," in *Liturgy: Active Participation in Divine Life*, ed. James P. Moroney (Collegeville, MN: Liturgical Press, 1991), 27–52.
[27] Searle, "Private Religion, Individualistic Society, and Common Worship," 37. Emphasis mine.
[28] Ibid., 38. Later, Searle describes what "public worship" might look like: "Liturgies celebrated as public worship will not be celebrated for the sake of togetherness nor for private intentions. They would be characterized by a certain fixity and solemnity, an objectivity which would constitute an invitation to us to enter in and be shaped by the ritual process. Congregations will not be whisked in and out in forty-five minutes and missalettes will probably be less in evidence. The proclamation of the scriptural Word would be taken more seriously than it presently is, being heard as a Word addressed more to

A LITURGY THAT IS BOTH "CONTEMPLATIVE" AND "PUBLIC"

In the early part of 1991, Searle began work on what would be his final manuscript and would serve as the *magnum opus* of his career as a scholar and liturgical reformer. In this work that he titled *The Evidence of Things Not Seen*, Searle stresses the formative value of ritualization as well as the need to promote the vocational (or obligatory) nature of celebration, thereby restoring the liturgy as a "public work."[29] Thus, for Searle, liturgical reform must always be focused outwardly, meaning that its goal is never ritual improvement or modification for the sake of the rite but for Christ's mission toward the world's salvation. He writes in *The Evidence of Things Not Seen*:

> It is our privilege and our duty; less a matter of choice than of vocation. We were quite right to speak about the Sunday mass obligation, for the worship of God and the vicarious representation of all humanity before God is an obligation incumbent upon us all in virtue of our baptism. The liturgy is the *opus dei*, the work of God; it is the *divinum officium*, or divine duty, an office to be carried out. It is a task laid upon us as members of the Church, a post we cannot forsake. *In the end, then, liturgy is not an option, but a duty; not a favor we do to God, but the work of God in which we are privileged to participate; not something we put on for the faithful, but something Christ has instituted for us to carry out in memory of him; not something we look to merely for our own spiritual advantage, but a work that God has initiated for the salvation of the world.*[30]

---

the community for the sake of the world than to individuals for their private consolation. In the homily, monologue will yield to dialogues as the Word of God establishes an agenda for the examination of social issues not only during but before and after the liturgy itself. Inspired by the Word, the congregation will become once again a 'community of memory,' remembering especially the things that our culture forgets: the radical equality of all human beings before God and the centrality in the Christian economy of those—like women and children, the unemployed, the handicapped, the sick, the dying, and the unsuccessful—whom society relegates to the margins" (42).

[29] Mark Searle, *The Evidence of Things Not Seen*, MSP, Folder "New Chapter IV," 24. Searle writes: "Finally, it seems to me important to recover an ancient conception of the liturgy as *leitourgia*, as a public work. *The liturgy is the work of our salvation undertaken by Christ to the glory of God.*" Emphasis mine.

[30] Ibid., 24–25. Emphasis mine.

In the end, Searle believes that the restoration of the liturgical movement points to reinstilling in the Catholic community the art of learning
"the obedient surrender of faith."[31] In other words, the liturgy sacramentalizes the obedience of Jesus Christ when its actions, words, and
song exhibit the attitude of surrender, when it becomes something that
participants live into rather than control. "No one can fruitfully participate in the liturgy," writes Searle, "without a minimum of faith or
trusting self-surrender and thus without some measure of Christ's self-
abandonment to the One who alone could save him out of death."[32]

While an important contribution of this text, published posthumously in 2006 under the title *Called to Participate: Theological, Ritual,
and Social Perspectives*, is Searle's succinct, theological portrayal of liturgical participation as a progressive movement from participation in
ritual to participation in Christ's priestly ministry to participation in
divine life,[33] what is unique here is his articulation of the "contemplative" and the "public" dimensions of liturgy as inseparably joined.[34]
With regard to the first dimension, Searle contends that liturgy is
"deep silence" and that corporate contemplation occurs when the
Body of Christ is formed by the attitudes it rehearses in the liturgical
celebration.[35] As demonstrated throughout this work, liturgical
contemplation entails surrender to the attitudes that are those of
Christ, not the expression of subjective feelings:

---

[31] Ibid., 25. Searle writes: "In the end it comes down to faith and faithfulness. Not to belief simply, but to the obedient surrender of faith; for it is in
that moment of surrender that the risk is validated and faith appears indeed
in actual form as the 'substance of things hoped for and the evidence of things
not seen.'"

[32] Searle, *Called to Participate*, 36.

[33] See Searle, *Called to Participate*, 15–45. See also Searle, "Culture," 45–47.

[34] See Peter E. Fink, "Public and Private Moments in Christian Prayer,"
Worship 58 (1984): 482–99. In this essay, Fink first lays out the classic tension
that exists between contemplative and public prayer and then seeks to demonstrate how the two are necessarily related. He writes: "Any thought that ritual
prayer precludes the possibility of personal space where people can dwell
with the needs and desires and deep realties of their own personal journeys
simply ignores the inner rhythms and dynamics of Christian ritual prayer, and
the needs of people who themselves make liturgy out of ritual text. Entrance
into liturgy to that extent is the fullness of the 'full and active participation'
called for by Vatican II" (496).

[35] See Searle, *Called to Participate*, 57.

Often it is hard to distinguish attitudes and feelings, especially since feelings are not infrequently tied to basic attitudes. But it is finally our attitudes that make us who we are. Our attitudes represent the way our lives are pointed, the more or less habitual ways of thinking, feeling, and acting that shape and color our lives and make us the persons we are. . . . Similarly with liturgy. If we only went to church when we felt like it, we would probably cease feeling like it rather soon. If we only knelt when everyone in the assembly felt humble, kneeling would never happen. If only those who felt connected to the rest of the assembly could exchange a gesture of peace, we would have a very different experience of the communion rite. *But liturgy is not an expression of emotions; it is a rehearsal of attitudes.* . . . Liturgy will not leave us on an emotional high because that is not its purpose. But regular, persevering participation and growing familiarity with liturgy's images and gestures will eventually shape our attitudes, our thoughts, and even our feelings.[36]

Thus, the liturgy makes present Christ's attitude of obedience; the liturgy makes present Christ's attitude of mercy; the liturgy makes present Christ's attitude of surrender.[37] "Through conforming to the constraints of the rite, we de-center ourselves, momentarily abandon our claim to autonomy, so that our bodies might become epiphanies of Christ in our midst."[38]

[36] Ibid., 61–62. Emphasis mine.

[37] See Theodore L. Westow, *The Variety of Catholic Attitudes* (New York: Herder and Herder, 1963), 10. Here, Westow provides an excellent portrayal of "attitudes"; he writes: "Attitudes are concrete things. They determine our actions, our outlook, not only personally but also communally. Individuals and whole societies derive their color and significance from the contemporary attitude. The attitude, that elusive, often subconscious, but vitally important element in the concrete human make-up, is therefore a historical thing. History is but the understanding of the phases of human evolution, of the moral and psychological attitudes of men and women toward other men and women, toward themselves, toward God, in any given period."

[38] Searle, *Called to Participate*, 62. Christian attitudes might be likened to the "mind of Christ." Earlier Searle writes: "But it is always the head that prays, its prayer welling up from the depths of the heart of Christ, which is the heart of all humanity. That 'welling-up' of prayer is what we call 'the Spirit,' the Spirit at work in us with Christ and through him, with God. That is why no prayer of ours can reach God unless we have that mind that was in Christ Jesus: unless our prayer is not only joined to his but is in fact *his* prayer welling up in us through our openness to his Spirit."

It is in the surrender to corporate contemplation that the assembly simultaneously moves to a second dimension of liturgy, namely, the "public" dimension and the ultimate goal toward which liturgical participation points—union with God.[39] The more participants in liturgy embrace Christ's outlook on the world, the more they come to understand their role in Christ's mission (liturgically and socially). Simply stated: the assembly sacramentalizes Christ's mission to the world and his offering to the Father, or in Searle's more erudite language:

> The assembly, as a realization of the mystery of communion, is an efficacious sign of union with God and of the unity of humankind, for it shares in the mediatorial work of Christ. In the liturgy we as a people represent all our fellow human beings before God, and invoke God's blessing upon the whole of humanity. *Thus, the liturgy of the Church cannot be separated from its social mission—at least as long as its liturgy is truly the act of a priestly people and as long as its social mission is rooted in its sacramental nature, i.e., in the Church's own attachment to Christ through submission to the Spirit.*[40]

Searle is essentially suggesting that we need to relearn why it is that we pray the liturgy. It is not primarily for ourselves; rather, "we must learn to pray the prayer of the liturgy with the voice of the whole Church" for the good of the world's salvation, for the fruition of God's

---

[39] Ibid., 68. On the inseparable link between the "contemplative" and the "public" dimensions of liturgy, Searle writes: "The premise of this work is that it is possible to develop a fuller, more conscious, and more active participation by moving in two directions at once: toward a more contemplative approach *and* toward greater social awareness. We need to develop the inwardness of our liturgy, as well as its outwardness. Both are important. If we develop only the inward and contemplative dimension of liturgy . . . there is the danger of not fully sounding its depths, in which case we may simply end up with an introverted, privatized style of liturgy. On the other hand, we have a healthy tradition of social activism in the Church that sometimes seems to offer an alternative to the contemplative tradition to liturgy. But if we let that alone shape our approach to liturgy, we run the risk of turning it into a platform for social and political issues, accentuating the verbal and communitarian aspects of the rite, and perhaps minimizing the more formal and deeper dimensions of the rituals that belong to the rite."

[40] Ibid., 81. Emphasis mine.

Just Kingdom.[41] For example, prescribed prayer and the psalms allow us "to pray beyond ourselves, on behalf of the stranger half a world away or in the county jail, on behalf of those who at this moment lie dying, suffering violence, or even leaping for joy."[42] The General Intercessions and the Eucharistic Prayer demonstrate that liturgy recalls not "tribal history but global history, the history of humanity as read as the history of God."[43]

As Searle ends his final reflection on liturgical participation, he reiterates his conviction that what is at stake is the very meaning of liturgy itself. Individualistic pursuits and preferences placed upon participation in liturgy, now ratified by the triumph of individualism within American culture, simply must be replaced by self-surrender lived as vocation.[44] Searle writes:

> Out of the sense of being a priestly people, a community of memory, a people who will not forget or escape into fantasy, arises a sense of solidarity with the rest of humanity, and especially with those who suffer,

[41] Ibid. Searle writes: "Whenever we celebrate the liturgy, therefore, it must not be for our own benefit so much as an exercise of our vocation to represent humanity before God."

[42] Ibid., 82. Searle goes on to suggest that prescribed prayer and the psalms may not express our present emotions but they shape our outlook (attitudes) in being connected to the larger world: "Which of us on any given day can be sure of being able to identify on the basis of our own personal experience or as an expression of our own current mood with many of the sentiments express is the psalms? Can we expect a concordance of words and personal feelings? Does that make the praying of the psalms unauthentic? Not at all—as long as we allow the words of the psalm to guide our minds and hearts into a prayer that is alien, the prayer of Another, in whom all the joys and griefs of all the ages are taken up as his prayer to the one who is God of heaven and earth, God of all the ages."

[43] Ibid., 83.

[44] Ibid., 84. Searle writes: "A priestly people. We do not stand around the altar simply for our own benefit but because it is our vocation to stand before God on behalf of the world. Over and over again, the liturgy confronts us with reminders of that wider connection and resists our desire to privatize, to control, to narrow the ambit of God's grace. By the very nature of its being symbolic, the liturgy is also ambivalent. It is so easy, so natural to think of the liturgy of the word as a service of instruction or edification and nothing more, to make the assembly an occasion of belongingness, to shut out the world and indulge in cozy self-delusion."

those who are powerless, and those who feel most keenly in their own flesh or their own spirit the terrible liturgy of the world. The liturgy requires of us a setting aside of the quest for personal satisfaction; it demands self-abnegation, self-emptying, self-forgetfulness, so that our emptiness may be filled with the memory of Christ and with the fullness of his Spirit, in whom we know we are one with God's people. Outside the liturgy, participation in the work of Christ continues in the form of solidarity with the suffering. . . . In the liturgy we join our prayers with theirs, put their prayers into words. A priestly people. A people who can offer in memory the sacrifice of the whole Christ, the passion of Jesus and the passion of the poor, the "little one's" of our generation.[45]

Thus, the "contemplative" dimension and the "public" dimension of Christian liturgical worship go hand in hand; there is no separating the epiphany of Christ in the midst of his assembly from the mission of Christ to heal the broken of this world. To participate in the "depth dimensions" of liturgical prayer is to participate in Christ's work to usher in God's Just Kingdom.[46]

CONCLUSION

In bringing his life's work and his heart's passion to a conclusion by summoning the Church to inaugurate a new liturgical movement focused on the skills of participation and the attitudes of Christ, Mark Searle suggests that we are at a "crossroads." For him, the present state of liturgical reform has undermined the very "authority" of the liturgy: "Instead of being an objective, communitarian rehearsal of our common identity, it becomes at times a stage for displays of individualism and subjectivism."[47] Thus, Searle believes the proper way to

---

[45] Ibid., 85.

[46] See Anne Koester, "Afterword," in *Called to Participate*, 88. Koester writes: "As Mark Searle points out, Christians have a responsibility to turn towards the world and to participate in the work of bringing about a more just, a more compassionate society. The Church's liturgy, according to Mark Searle, shapes attitudes intended to help us carry out this responsibility. Mark Searle had a remarkable ability to appropriate to present times what is core to Christian worship, and at the same time, he impels us into the future. The legacy he leaves to us is not to be underestimated, for it is nothing less than an exhortation to plumb the depth dimension of the Church's liturgy for the sake of ourselves and for the sake of the world."

[47] Searle, *Called to Participate*, 12. Searle continues: "As such it loses its authority and is there for us to make what we want of it."

negotiate this crossroads is to resurrect participation in the liturgy as an objective discipline rather than for subjective satisfaction. In his words:

> Perhaps instead of asking what will engage the assembly, we could begin to ask what the liturgy demands. Instead of asserting our ownership of the liturgy, we might ask how we can surrender to Christ's prayer and work. Instead of asking what we should choose to sing, perhaps we could start imaging how we might sing in such a way that it is no longer we who sing, but Christ who sings in us. We stand at a crossroads. We must decide which way to go. Shall we continue to think of the liturgy as something to be adapted to our needs and tastes? Or move toward a liturgy that in its objectivity and givenness transcends the individuals who participate in it, lifting them up to engage in something far beyond their ability to create or even imagine?[48]

While the Church's liturgy is less than perfect and must be open to adaptation, Searle believed that the enactment of the liturgy is neither the stage on which to experiment nor the platform on which to assert creativity.[49] For Searle, the liturgy is always about learning to surrender the self to the prayer of the Body; the mastery of this lesson requires committed discipline to and regular rehearsal of the Christian Eucharist.

Although the final works of Searle's academic career may exhibit a rather harsh (some would say "conservative") tone regarding the possibilities for ongoing reform of the liturgy, he believed his voice

---

[48] Ibid., 13–14.

[49] See Mary Collins, "Obstacles to Liturgical Creativity," in *Liturgy: A Creative Tradition*, Ed. Mary Collins and David Power (New York: The Seabury Press, 1983), 19–26. Here Collins lays out a theology for liturgical innovation based on *Sacrosanctum Concilium* 23. However, she also provides theological rationale for caution regarding personal creativity within the enactment of the liturgy: "All liturgy is the Church's symbolic enactment of the mystery of Christ and the Church. It is theologically sound to celebrate the mystery of salvation using forms which assert the dawning reign of God in human history in all its particularly. But a peculiar creativity, that of the Christian believer, is required to maintain evangelical tension within liturgical assemblies so that they are not merely mimetic of human achievement but a manifestation of what the reign of God promises (SC 2). Because the irruption of the reign of God in history is dangerous, genuine liturgical creativity cannot help but be potentially so" (23).

needed to take on a prophetic edge. His desire was to put into motion a liturgical movement that would get the liturgy into the bones of worshipers rather than one that would stimulate fleeting emotions and feelings. As Searle questions:

> Should we accommodate the liturgy to ourselves, encouraging a subjective approach to liturgy or engage in understanding the liturgy, regarding it in a more objective way? Perhaps we have had to work a number of things out of our systems to discover the shallowness of some of our earlier understandings and expectations, emerging with a real hunger for the life of the Spirit mediated by the liturgy, a life of the Spirit meant to change the face of the earth.[50]

Indeed, as the Church continues to struggle to "work a number of things out of [its] system," Searle's call to take the work of liturgical reform to a deeper level, beyond that of simply trying to get "everyone to join in," continues to ring loud and true. In the end, for Mark Searle, all of liturgy is the contemplative "seeing" of Christ present in the midst of his Body, yearning for all of creation to be one in God's Just Kingdom.

---

[50] Searle, *Called to Participate*, 13.

Conclusion

This study of Mark Searle and his corpus of writings has been organized according to two intertwined themes: first, liturgy defined as "rehearsal of Christian attitudes," through which liturgical celebration is understood as the Body of Christ learning how to live into Christ's worldview, and second, this rehearsal understood as making present (not just anticipating) God's Just kingdom. The celebration of the Eucharist is a particularly privileged venue in which the corporate Body at prayer enacts a worldview in which right relationships are established and renewed within the liturgical assembly, with God's good creation, and ultimately with divine life itself. For Searle, liturgical renewal hinges upon a deep understanding and respect for the ritual structure (the objective nature) of liturgy so that participants learn to surrender themselves wholeheartedly to a worship which forms and shapes the pattern of their entire lives according to the obedience and the sacrifice of Christ. "It is, then, chiefly by assembling together and celebrating its faith," writes Searle early on in his academic career, "that the Christian community retains its sense of identity, keeps its faith alive, continues to be a community of believers."[1]

Nevertheless, Searle would become more and more convinced throughout the remainder of his abbreviated professional life that the Christian community was in danger of losing its identity precisely because liturgical forms were being tampered with in a manner that did not respect the dynamics of corporate, ritual rehearsal. Thus, he believed that the very success of liturgical reform hinged upon the Church's ability to restore confidence in ritual practice in general.[2] The more assemblies are schooled in the execution of gestures and reverence for symbols, the more they would learn the art of giving themselves over to the liturgical event and participating in an "epiphany" of Christ. Liturgical renewal, for Searle, went beyond concern for external manifestations of beauty or togetherness to learning how to really pay attention: "Ritual words, songs, movements, and actions

---

[1] Searle, "The Church Celebrates Her Faith," 6.
[2] Searle, "Trust the Ritual or Face 'the Triumph of Bad Taste,'" 19.

direct attention away from themselves to that which they mean: Christ among us."[3]

However, attentive to the trappings and attraction of culture, Searle believed that the "rehearsal of Christian attitudes" would be especially challenging within a society that so prizes individualism as the "blood" that pumps through its veins.[4] Searle observed that many contemporary liturgical practices were failing to lead participants away from the attitude of individualism, as participation in the liturgy continued to be valued for personal and private gain rather than as the fulfillment of a vocation "to stand before God on behalf of the world."[5] This does not mean that liturgy has become irrelevant. In fact, for Searle, just the opposite is true; the liturgy, if approached contemplatively—knowing how to "move from the visible to the invisible, from the human to the divine, from the signifier to the signified"[6]—provides the community with the tools for living prophetic Christian lives in the midst of materialism, greed, and self-promotion. By relearning the skills of "full, conscious, and active" liturgical participation, we commit to memory that "we stand before God and that to do so is to stand before the Mystery, to stand on the edge of an abyss, on the edge of language, on the edge of knowing."[7]

A CORPUS OF BREADTH: FROM SCHOLARLY MEDIA TO SACRED MYSTAGOGIA

It is hoped that in reading this survey of Mark Searle's writings the reader will see the veritable breadth of his contribution to liturgical renewal and to the study of liturgy in general. Certainly, one of the most important aspects of Searle's academic career was his ability to write

---

[3] Ibid., 20.

[4] Searle, "Private Religion, Individualistic Society, and Common Worship," 27.

[5] See Searle, *Called to Participate*, 84.

[6] Ibid., 44.

[7] Ibid., 39. Searle continues to describe the contemplative nature of liturgical prayer in this fashion: "To pray is to hurl words into the vast infinity of the silent mystery of God, but often we rattle them off as if we were shelling peas, and they come pinging back to us, failing to penetrate beyond the sphere of our self-absorption. We know we have prayed only when we cannot remember what we were saying, when the nakedness of our exposure to God or the urgency of the spirit of prayer makes our spirit leap in God's Spirit and transcend what we can contain in words."

in ways both scholarly and pastoral. Furthermore, his writings demonstrate a profound interdisciplinary approach to the study of liturgy. He was not limited to one specialty in the field; rather, he was well-versed in a broad spectrum of scholarly interests and readily articulated them for both liturgical experts and those devoted to the pastoral implementation of liturgical reform. Barbara Searle testifies to the expansiveness of his approach in accepting the Michael Mathis award for her late husband in 1993:

> We desperately needed to hear what he had to say, to hear him speak of the tradition which ought not to be dispensed with lightly. We needed to hear him say that there were treasures in our heritage that could meet the needs of peoples searching for meaning in the contemporary world. We needed to see his brilliant intellect and his faithful heart and his concern for ordinary Christian experience interact, producing books and articles and tapes, innumerable lectures and classes and conversations. We needed his critical stance probing our cultural assumptions in liturgical practice. We needed his wit and his wisdom, his passion and his perseverance in the cause of liturgical renewal. *Mark's intellectual history of these years can be seen in his bibliography, how he moved easily between the rigors of the academy with its need to define a scope and methodology for this new science of pastoral liturgy, and the demands of an authentic contemporary mystagogia.*[8]

For her own part, Barbara Searle remains deeply edified by her husband's willingness to serve the Church not only through scholarly addresses delivered to liturgical academies but also through the medium of homilies delivered at parish retreats and editorials in *Assembly* directed to those in the "trenches" of liturgical reform. While Searle's unique and lasting niche in the liturgical world might well be his concern for the assembly and its participation, it is only too clear that this contribution flows from a well-rounded knowledge of the history and theology of Christian liturgy.

Simply stated, Mark Searle desired to help diverse audiences "see" what liturgy is all about. Perhaps this should not be surprising for a man who wrote his licentiate thesis on the great mystagogue, Cyril of Jerusalem. The following quote from Searle's *Liturgy Made Simple* sub-

---

[8] Barbara Searle, "Acceptance Speech Given in Response to the Presentation of the Michael Mathis Award to Mark Searle, Posthumously, June 17, 1993," 2. Emphasis mine.

stantiates the suggestion that his was a mystagogical approach aimed at leading worshipers to new insight and greater depth:

> Before discussing the details of specific rites, it might be helpful to establish a coherent picture of the liturgy of the Church. We hardly need to be told what the liturgy is, because we already know. It is rather like the man who was asked whether he believed in infant baptism. "No," he answered, "I've seen it." But the problem is this: when he saw baptism, what did he see? There is an old and familiar story about four blind men who were introduced to an elephant. Later, as they discussed their experience, they violently disagreed about what they had encountered. An elephant, claimed the first man, who had put his arms around the elephant's leg, is a kind of tree: a very large kind of tree is what an elephant is. No, argued the second man, an elephant is a kind of snake with a very coarse skin and a strange, soft mouth. He had, of course, grasped the elephant's trunk. The third man had felt the elephant's ear and swore black and blue that an elephant was a sail on a ship. The fourth man, who had grabbed the elephant's tail was utterly convinced that an elephant was a piece of old rope. . . . Similarly, people have very different and quite conflicting views on liturgy.[9]

Searle's study would expose him to different views on the meaning and the relevance of liturgy, but all along he held firm to his conviction that there is an objective reality that must be revered and to which the Church must submit. Thus, Searle's contribution as a modern-day mystagogue can be found in his conviction that liturgical formation does not begin by telling the assembly what it must believe about liturgy but rather by working to help the assembly "see" anew.[10]

[9] Searle, *Liturgy Made Simple*, 11.
[10] See Searle, "New Tasks, New Methods," 295. He writes: "The proper starting point for pastoral liturgical studies is the liturgical activity of the whole assembled community. It is concerned to study the various forms and degrees of engagement exemplified by all the participants, to analyze the claims made for such participation by the participants themselves as well as by the church's authorities and by theologians, and to identify whatever discrepancies may be occurring between what the rites and texts are supposed to communicate and what they may actually be communicating."

AN IMPERATIVE, PRESENT-DAY CONTRIBUTION:
THE FUTURE OF LITURGICAL PARTICIPATION

Mark Searle left his beloved homeland of England in the fall of 1975, chasing the dream that there was indeed a land out in the world that was ripe and eager for the implementation of the ideals of liturgical reform as envisioned by the Second Vatican Council. He certainly was not blind to the tremendous and potentially destructive influence that values of American culture played in relationship to communal worship. As early as ten years after the close of the Council, Searle would see the American Church in danger of falling into the error of equating "reform" with "experimentation." He believed the corrective for this temptation was in relearning the very nature of liturgical participation. As he wrote in 1979:

> Participation in the liturgy is not a matter of everyone doing the same things and singing the same songs: it is a matter of being able to transcend the superficial limitations of our narrow individualism in order to find our deeper and truer identity "in Christ" and in the Body of Christ, which is the Church. The meditative reading or hearing of the Scriptures, the encounter with Christ in prayer, the involvement with an actual congregation in a liturgical assembly not only require such contemplative self-emptying, but they actually promote it. *After centuries of individualism, and after a decade or more of liturgical experimentation, perhaps we are now at the point where the contemplative character of the Church's common prayer and celebration can once again be recognized. If so, the liturgy might once again be able to help us learn what it is to live and pray "in Christ."*[11]

Searle's recognition of "centuries of individualism" addresses the individualistic nature of the Roman liturgy before the work of the Council, but he would quickly learn of a further layer of entrenched individualism that is imprinted upon the celebration of the liturgy through the influence of American culture. As Searle observed in his interpretation of the empirical data from the Notre Dame Study of Catholic Parish Life, "American Catholics are in the process of becoming more characteristically American than characteristically Catholic."[12]

Therefore, Searle believed the Church to be at a crossroads whereby individual worshipers would simply be free to determine the parame-

---

[11] Searle, "Prayer: Alone or with Others?," 20. Emphasis mine.
[12] Searle, "The Notre Dame Study of Catholic Parish Life," 333.

ters of participation or they would embrace a form of participation more demanding, one requiring the surrender of ego and will to the corporate work of the Body of Christ. He believed intensely in the potentiality of the latter direction to lead the Church to a renewed understanding of liturgy as a contemplative exercise of being caught up in the love between the Father and the Son.[13] Thus, Searle argued that the liturgy contains attitudes that are strong enough to counter culture. The attitudes of the liturgy, the attitudes of Christ himself (for example: obedience, surrender, reverence, humility), are to be learned and rehearsed with careful discipline over and over so that they form Christians anew. In fact, his entire vision for liturgical participation rests on the understanding of liturgical prayer as corporate rehearsal for the Body of Christ rather than on the individual quest for the accumulation of grace.[14]

A DEATH OF WILLING SURRENDER: SEARLE'S FINAL REHEARSAL

It is quite possible that Searle's best, and most convincing argument for demanding the rehearsal of the attitudes found in the liturgy came not so much in the form of his writing but in the way in which he lived out the final year of his life after being diagnosed with cancer in June of 1991. As Barbara Searle testifies, his last days were spent learning the art of Christian surrender. To an audience of liturgical scholars, she states:

---

[13] Searle, "Renewing the Liturgy—Again. 'A' for the Council, 'C' for the Church," 620. He writes: "[Liturgical participation] is first and foremost a conscious and willed participation in the acting out of the relationship of Christ to the Father, expressed in worship of God and the sanctification of human beings, both of which are inseparable dimensions of the Paschal mystery of self-sacrificial submission to the will of God. It is for this reason that the council encouraged all the faithful 'to take part by means of acclamations, responses, psalmody, antiphons, and songs, as well as by actions, gestures, and bodily attitudes.' Not that these things *of themselves* constitute the 'active participation' the council had in mind, but that they are intended to 'promote' it (par. 30) as effective signs of this inner mystery."

[14] Searle, *Called to Participate*, 39–40. Searle writes: "Assembling for the liturgy, celebrating the hours and sacraments of the Church, is a calculated act of self-exposure at the edge of abyss. *The role of the sacraments is not to deliver God to us, not to package the One whom the world cannot contain, not to 'confer' grace, but to deliver us to the place where God can be God for us.*" Emphasis mine.

Many of you are familiar with Mark's idea that liturgy is a rehearsal
for death, for the ultimate surrender to the living God. We witnessed
in Mark in the fourteen months of his illness a real connection between
what he had always said and how he lived. He spent time daily in contemplative prayer, but it was at the liturgy that he was most sustained
in his journey into the unknown.[15]

With diminished energy, an inability to control the body as he once
had, and a growing level of pain, Searle patterned his final days on
the Paschal Mystery and refused to succumb to despair or complaint;
instead, he seemed to embody a contemplative cheerfulness.[16] He came
to believe in his body the words he himself wrote near the outset of
his academic career: "The 'sting' and 'victory' of death lie in death's
ability to take our life against our will and hence to defeat us. If, on
the other hand, we were to learn from the celebration of the paschal
mystery to surrender our lives totally to God in Christ, the death of
the Christian would be but the further and final rehearsal of a pattern
learnt in life and practiced over and over again in a lifetime of liturgical
participation."[17] For his own part, Searle's attitude toward his impending death clearly bore witnesses to a real rehearsal of surrender (mod-
eled on the liturgy) and the accompanying movement into mystery.[18]

[15] Barbara Searle, "Acceptance Speech Given in Response to the Presentation
of the Michael Mathis Award to Mark Searle, Posthumously, June 17, 1993," 3.

[16] See Paul Searle, *Searle Family History*, 63–64. Searle's father, Paul, recounts
how his son took "delight" in his final day of sitting in the family flower
garden, looking over the cornfields, listening to him read the Passion of
St. Matthew's Gospel. Furthermore, he describes the scene of Searle's final
evening: "Barbara and her children, Mary and Helen, Mum and Dad, prayed
and sang hymns in the evening, and all were amazed to hear Mark joining in,
in good voice: 'Praise to the holiest in the height.' When Fr. Bob Kreig came
with Holy Communion, all received, and afterwards everyone, including the
children, had a small glass of wine. Mark relished a good Californian red, and
when he had finished said: 'I shall not drink wine again until I drink it in the
Kingdom,' clearly remembering the words of Our Lord at the Last Supper. To
his mother he reached out and said: 'You are wonderful'" (63).

[17] Mark Searle, "On Death and Dying" (Editorial), *Assembly* 5, no. 5 (1979):
49. Furthermore, he writes: "The liturgy does not instruct us about themes;
it rather shapes and disciplines us in a style of life, that of conformity to the
dead and risen Christ."

[18] See Searle, *Called to Participate*, 40. Here Searle speaks of liturgical participation in terms of rehearsing the attitude of "trust." He writes: "To know the

Mark Searle's body is buried at Riverview Cemetery in South Bend, Indiana. The headstone chosen by Barbara Searle is a three-foot stone spiral that culminates in a circular opening in the center. Inscribed in the monument are words from Searle's *Christening: The Making of Christians*:

> *The pilgrimage of faith is not a journey*
> *in a straight line, with death waiting at the end,*
> *but a kind of spiral through which progress is made only*
> *in successively deeper experiences of death and rebirth.*

What Searle asserts regarding the life of faith is true as well of the liturgical forms that animate and express this faith: the goal of all liturgy is communal surrender to the God who draws the world into union with himself. Participation in liturgy is an exercise in being "spiraled" into God, thereby rehearsing over and over again the skills of living in God's Just Kingdom both now and for all eternity.

Mark Searle's headstone in Riverview Cemetery, South Bend, Indiana. Sculpted by William Cooper.

---

holiness of God is to know our own unholiness as finite, guilty creatures, called ultimately to struggle, to suffer, and to die. Against this painful recognition, we protest our good intentions, our respectfulness, our good works, clinging to the tattered illusions of self-worth. But in the end there is death, the limit that shadows and underlines all other limitations: death, where we lose everything we have left to lose. *Liturgy would deliver us from this futile and self-defeating campaign of self-justification by offering us an alternative: that of dropping the illusions we cling to, rehearsing the trust that will enable us to let go in the end of life itself and to surrender ourselves one last time into the hands of the living God.*" Emphasis mine.

Mark Searle's Chronological Bibliography
(1966–2006)[1]

1966
"The Sacraments of Initiation in the Catechesis of St. Cyril of Je-
rusalem, *Thesina ad gradum licentiatus consequendum*," *Pontifical
Atchanaeum Antonianum, Facultas Sacrae Theologiae*, Rome.

1968
"An Alternative Order for the Holy Communion in the Church of
England (1967): *Arbeit zum Erwerb des Diploms am Liturgischen
Institut*," Trier.
"The Communion Service of the Church of England, with Particular
Reference to the Experimental Order for Holy Communion, 1967:
A Study in 'Comprehensive Liturgy.' A dissertation submitted to the
Theological Faculty of Trier for the Doctorate in Sacred Theology,"
Trier.

1969
Review of *The Church is Mission*, by Edna McDonagh et al. *Clergy Review*
54:12, 992–94.

1970
"The Eucharistic Prayers," *The Way* (supp. N. 11): 89–92.
Review of *We Who Serve: A Basic Council Theme and Its Biblical Founda-
tions*, by Augustine Cardinal Bea. *Clergy Review* 55:5, 405–7.

1972
"The Word and the World," *Life and Worship* 41:1, 1–8.
"Liturgy for Holidaymakers," *Christian Celebration* (Summer): 14–16.

---

[1] This bibliography appears in Koester and Searle, *Vision: The Scholarly Contributions of Mark Searle to Liturgical Renewal*, 259–67. It has been emended to
include the 2006 entry and the list of unpublished sources.

1973

"History of Penance." In *Three Talks on Liturgy*. Edited by Harold
    Winstone. London: Thomas More Center.
"What Is the Point of Liturgy?" *Christian Celebration* (Summer): 26–27.
"An End of Retreat Service," *Christian Celebration* (Autumn): 18–24.
"General Absolution," *Christian Celebration* (Winter): 27–29.

1974

Stations of the Cross. Bristol, England: Clifton Cathedral.
Eight Talks on Liturgy (Private circulation).
"The Church Celebrates Her Faith," *Life and Worship* 43:3, 3–12.

1975

"Penance." In *Pastoral Liturgy*. Edited by Harold Winstone, 189–213.
    London: Collins.
"Penance Today." In *Penance: A Pastoral Presentation*, 3–11. London:
    Catholic Truth Society.
"The New Rite of Penance: A Report by John Robson and Mark
    Searle." *Southwark Liturgy Bulletin*, no. 17, 11–18.

1977

"Eucharist and Renewal through History," *Liturgy* 1:3, 4–19.
"The Mass as a Living Tradition." *Southwark Liturgy Bulletin*, no. 24,
    15–23.

1978

Christening: The Making of Christians. Southend-on-Sea, England: Kevin
    Mahew.

In *Assembly*
    "The Act of Communion: A Commentary," 4:4, 6–7.
    "The Washing of the Feet," 4:5, 14–16.
    "Sunday: Noblesse Oblige" (Editorial), 5:2, 25.
    "The Day of Rest in a Changing Church," 5:2, 30–32.
    "The Cup of His Blood" (Editorial), 5:3, 33.
    "The Tradition We Have Received," 5:3, 38–40.

1979

"Prayer: Alone or with Others?" *Centerlines* 1:5, 19–20.

In *Assembly*
    "The Word of the Lord" (Editorial), 5:4, 41.
    "On Death and Dying" (Editorial), 5:5, 49.

"The Sacraments of Faith," 5:5, 54–55.
"Liturgy and Social Action" (Editorial), 6:1, 57.
"Contributing to the Collection," 6:1, 62–64.
"Active Participation" (Editorial), 6:2, 65, 72.
"Liturgical Gestures" (Editorial) 6:3, 73, 80.
"Genuflecting," 6:3, 74.
"Kneeling," 6:3, 74.
"Sign of the Cross," 6:3, 75.
"Keeping Silence," 6:3, 76.
"Communing," 6:3, 79.
"Bowing," 6:3, 79.

1980

"Serving the Lord with Justice." In *Liturgy and Social Justice*. Ed. Mark Searle, 13–35. Collegeville, MN: Liturgical Press.
Christening: The Making of Christians, rev. ed. Collegeville, MN: Liturgical Press.
Ministry and Celebration. La Crosse, WI: Diocesan Liturgical Office.
Basic Liturgy (Four Talks). Kansas City: NCR Cassettes (Oral version of *Liturgy Made Simple*. Collegeville, MN: Liturgical Press, 1981).
"The Journey of Conversion," *Worship* 54:1, 35–55.
"The Christian Community, Evangelized and Evangelizing," *Emmanuel* 86:10, 556–62; 86:11, 609–18.

In *Assembly*
"The Three Days of Easter" (Editorial), 6:4, 81.
"Holy Thursday: Opening of the Paschal Feast," 6:4, 82–83, 88.
"Parish: Place for Worship" (Editorial), 6:4, 89.
"Advent" (Editorial), 7:1, 97.
"The Spirit of Advent," 7:1, 100–101.
"The Homily" (Editorial), 7:2, 105.
"Below the Pulpit: The Lay Contribution to the Homily," 7:2, 110–12.

1981

Liturgy Made Simple. Collegeville, MN: Liturgical Press.
"Introduction," *Parish: A Place for Worship*. Edited by Mark Searle, 5–10. Collegeville, MN: Liturgical Press.
"Liturgy as Metaphor," *Worship* 55:2, 98–120. (Reprinted in *Notre Dame English Journal* 13:4, 185–206).
"The Pedagogical Function of the Liturgy," *Worship* 55:4, 332–59.

"Diaconate and Diakonia: Crisis in the Contemporary Church," *Diaconal Quarterly* 7:4, 16–31. (Reprinted in *A Diaconal Reader*. Washington, DC: National Conference of Catholic Bishops [1985] 93–107).

"Conversion and Initiation into Faith Growth," *Christian Initiation Resources*. Vol. 1. *Precatechumenate*, 65–74. New York: Sadlier.

"Attending [to] the Liturgy," *New Catholic World* 224:1342, 156–60.

In *Assembly*

"Ritual Dialogue" (Editorial), 7:3, 113, 120.

"Lord, Have Mercy," 7:3, 114.

"May the Lord Accept the Sacrifice . . . ," 7:3, 116.

"Peace Be With You," 7:3, 118.

"(Inter)communion," 7:4, 121–22, 128.

"Rites of Communion," 7:4, 126–27.

"Keeping Sunday" (Editorial), 7:5, 129.

"Sunday Observed: Vignettes from the Tradition," 7:5, 130–31, 136.

"Liturgical Objects" (Editorial), 8:1, 137, 144.

"Bell," 8:1, 138.

"Chair," 8:1, 139.

"Oil and Chrism," 8:1, 141.

"Bread and Wine," 8:1, 143.

"The Saints" (Editorial), 8:2, 145.

"The Saints in the Liturgy," 8:2, 150–52.

1982

"Introduction" and "The Shape of the Future: A Liturgist's Vision." In *Sunday Morning: A Time for Worship*. Ed. Mark Searle, 7–9 and 129–53. Collegeville, MN: Liturgical Press.

"Reflections on Liturgical Reform," *Worship* 56:5, 411–30.

"The Narrative Quality of Christian Liturgy," *Chicago Studies* 21:1, 73–84.

"On the Art of Lifting Up the Heart: Liturgical Prayer Today," *Studies in Formative Spirituality* 3:3, 399–410.

"On Gesture," *Liturgy 80*, 13:1, 3–7. (Reprinted in *Worship and Ministry* 82:2, 10–17 and *Liturgy* 7:2 [1985]: 49–59.

"Welcome Your Children Newborn of Water . . ." *Pastoral Music* 6:4, 16–19. (Reprinted in *Pastoral Music in Practice*, vol. 3, *Initiation and Its Seasons*. Ed. Virgil Funk, 3–9. Washington, D.C.: The Pastoral Press).

"The R.C.I.A. and Infant Baptism: A Response to Ray Kemp," *Worship* 56:4, 327–32.

In *Assembly*
  "The Joy of Lent" (Editorial), 8:3, 153.
  "The Spirit of Lent," 8:3, 158–59.
  "Mary" (Editorial), 8:4, 161.
  "Mary, Seat of Wisdom," 8:4, 166–68.
  "Households of Faith" (Editorial), 8:5, 169.
  "Silence" (Editorial), 9:1, 177, 184.
  "The Child and the Liturgy" (Editorial), 9:2, 185.
  "Childhood and the Reign of God: Reflections on Infant Baptism," 9:2, 186–87, 192.

1983
"Liturgy: Function and Goal in Christianity." In *Spirituality and Prayer: Jewish and Christian Understanding*. Ed. L. Klenicki and G. Huck, 82–105. New York: Paulist Press.
"Liturgy as a Pastoral Hermeneutic." In Theological Education Key Resources, vol. 4, *Pastoral Theology and Ministry*. Ed. D.F. Beisswenger and D.C. McCarthy, 140–50. Association for Theological Field Education.
"Symbol: A Bibliography." With John A. Melloh. In *Symbol: The Language of Liturgy*. Ed. John B. Ryan, 70–72. Washington, DC: Federation of Diocesan Liturgical Commissions.
"New Tasks, New Methods: The Emergence of Pastoral Liturgical Studies," *Worship* 57:4, 291–308.
"Confirmation: The State of the Question," *Hosanna* 1:2, 4–11. (Reprinted in *Church* 1:4 [1985]: 15–22).
"Assembly: Remembering the People of God," *Pastoral Music* 7:6, 14–19. (Reprinted in *Pastoral Music in Practice*, vol. 6, *The Singing Assembly*. Ed. Virgil Funk, 3–16. Washington, DC: The Pastoral Press).
"The Liturgy of the Cantor." *Liturgy 80* 14:3, 2–5; 14:4, 5–7.

In *Assembly*
  "The Days of Pentecost" (Editorial), 9:3, 193.
  "Mystagogy: Reflecting on the Easter Experience," 9:3, 196–98.
  "Of Pasch and Pentecost" 9:3, 199–200.
  "Marriage" (Editorial), 9:4, 201.
  "Marriage: Sacrament of Faith," 9:4, 202–3, 208.
  "Liturgical Renewal" (Editorial), 9:5, 209.
  "Reconciliation" (Editorial), 10:1, 217.
  "A Time for Repentance," 10:1, 222–24.

"Church Building" (Editorial), 10:2, 225.
"Sacred Places," 10:2, 226–28.

1984
"Sunday: The Heart of the Liturgical Year." In *The Church Gives Thanks and Praise*. Ed. L. J. Johnson. Collegeville, MN: Liturgical Press, 13–36.
"Faith and Sacraments in the Conversion Process: A Theological Approach." In *Conversion and the Catechumenate*. Ed. Robert D. Duggan. New York: Paulist Press, 64–84.
"Images and Worship," *The Way* 24:2, 103–14.
"The Ministry of the Word" (Parts I and II). In *Proceedings of the 1984 Clergy Convention* of the Archdiocese of Portland, Oregon, 3–14.
"The Uses of Liturgical Language," *Liturgy* 4:4, 15–19. (Reprinted in *The Landscape of Praise: Readings in Liturgical Renewal*. Ed. Blair Meeks. Harrisburg, PA: Trinity Press International, 1996).
"The RCIA in the United States," *Southwark Liturgy Bulletin*, no. 49, 11–18.
"A Sermon for Epiphany," *Worship* 58, 342–45.
"Christian Liturgy and Communications Theory," *Media Development* 31:3, 4–6.

In *Assembly*
    "The Rites of Death" (Editorial), 10:3, 233.
    "Sacrifice" (Editorial), 10:4, 241.
    "Liturgy and Religious Education" (Editorial), 10:5, 249.
    "Perspectives on Liturgy and Religious Education," 10:5, 250–52.
    "The Introductory Rites" (Editorial), 11:1, 258–59.
    "Collecting and Recollecting," 11:1, 258–59.
Review of *Nuptial Blessing: A Study of Christian Marriage Rites*, by Kenneth Stevenson. *Worship* 58:1, 72–75.
Review of *Unsearchable Riches: The Symbolic Nature of the Liturgy*, by David Power. *Worship* 58:5, 451–53.

1985
The Celebration of Liturgy in the Parishes. With David C. Leege. Notre Dame Study of Catholic Parish Life, n. 5. Notre Dame, IN: The University of Notre Dame.
Of Piety and Planning: Liturgy, the Parishioners and the Professionals. With David C. Leege. Notre Dame Study of Catholic Parish Life, n. 6. Notre Dame, IN: The University of Notre Dame.

"Observations on Parish Liturgy," *New Catholic World* (November/December) 258–63.

In *Assembly*
"The Kiss of Peace: Ritual Act and Image of the Kingdom," 11:3, 276–80.
". . . at whose command we celebrate this Eucharist . . ." 11:4, 284.
". . . He showed the depth of his love . . ." 11:4, 285.
". . . Lord, may this sacrifice advance the peace of the whole world . . ." 11:4, 287.
"A Place in the Tradition," 12:1, 301–3.
"A Meditation on All Saints and All Souls," 12:2, 308–9.
"Ritual and Music: A Theory of Liturgy and Implications for Music," 12:3, 314–17. (Reprinted in *Church* 2:3 [1986]: 48–52; Reprinted in *Pastoral Music* 11:3 [1987]: 13–18).

1986

"The Parish at Worship." In *The Parish in Transition*. Ed. David Byers, 73–88; panel discussion, 88–96. Washington, DC: United States Catholic Conference.
"The Notre Dame Study of Catholic Parish Life," *Worship* 60:4, 312–33
"Issues in Christian Initiation: The Uses and Abuses of the R.C.I.A.," *Living Light* 22:3, 199–214.
"The Mass in the Parish," *The Furrow* 37:10, 615–22.
"Growing Through Celebration," *Music and Liturgy* 12:4, 110–18.
"Participation and Prayer," *Music and Liturgy* 12:5, 145–54.
"Not the Final Word," *Pastoral Music* 10:6, 44–45.

In *Assembly*
"Liturgical Language," 13:1, 337.
"The Feast of the Holy Family: Toward a Paschal Celebration," 13:2, 348–49.

1987

"Infant Baptism Reconsidered." In *Alternative Futures for Worship*, vol. 2, *Baptism and Confirmation*. Ed. Mark Searle, 15–54. Collegeville, MN: Liturgical Press, 192 pp. (Reprinted in *Living Water, Sealing Spirit: Readings on Christian Initiation*. Ed. Maxwell E. Johnson, 365–409. Collegeville, MN: Liturgical Press, 1995).
"Rites of Christian Initiation." In *Betwixt and Between. Masculine and Feminine Patters of Initiation*. Ed. Louise C. Mahdi et al., 457–70. LaSalle, IL: Open Court.

210

"Initiation and the Liturgical Year," *Catechumenate* 9:5, 13–19; 9:6, 13–19.
"Pastoral Liturgy," *Music and Liturgy* 13:1, 7–18.

In *Assembly*
    "The Spirit of the Liturgy: A Workshop," 13:5, 372–73.
    "Confirmation and the Church," 14:1, 377, 383–84.

Review of *Una liturgia per l'uomo: La liturgia pastorale e i suoi cómpiti*,
    edited by P. Visentin et al. *Worship* 61:6, 557–60.

1988

"Renewing the Liturgy—Again. 'A' for the Council, 'C' for the
    Church," *Commonweal* (November 18): 617–22.
"Forgotten Truths about Worship," *Celebration* 17:1, 5–10.
"For the Glory of God. The Scrutiny of the Fifth Sunday in Lent," *Cate-
    chumenate* 10:1, 40–47. (Reprinted in *Commentaries on the Rite for the
    Christian Initiation of Adults*. Ed. James W. Wilde, 61–72. Chicago:
    Liturgy Training Publications).
Review of *Beyond the Text: A Holistic Approach to Liturgy*, by Lawrence
    Hoffman. *Worship* 62:5, 472–75.

1990

"*Semper Reformanda*: The Opening and Concluding Rites of the Roman
    Mass." In *Shaping English Liturgy. Studies in Honor of Archbishop
    Denis Hurley*. Ed. Peter Finn and James Schellman, 53–92. Washing-
    ton, DC: The Pastoral Press.
*The Church Speaks About Sacraments With Children. Baptism, Confirma-
    tion, Eucharist, Penance*. With commentary by Mark Searle. Chicago:
    Liturgy Training Publications.
"Private Religion, Individualistic Society, and Common Worship." In
    Liturgy and Spirituality in Context. Perspectives on Prayer and Culture.
    Ed. Eleanor Bernstein, 27–46. Collegeville, MN: Liturgical Press.
"A Priestly People" (video). In *The Dynamic Parish Series* by the Insti-
    tute for Pastoral and Social Ministry. Notre Dame, IN: The Univer-
    sity of Notre Dame.
"The Effects of Baptism," *Catechumenate* 12:4, 15–22.
"God Writes Straight in Crooked Lines: Part I. The Inner Process: Con-
    version," *Catechumenate* 12:6, 2–9.

1991

"Culture." In *Liturgy: Active Participation in the Divine Life*. Ed. James P.
    Moroney, 27–52. Collegeville, MN: Liturgical Press.

"Tussen enonce en enonciatie: naar een semiotik van gebedsteksten."
In *'Gelukkig de mens' Opstellen over psalmen. Exegese en semiotik aange-*
boden aan Nico Tromp. Ed. P. Beentjes et al., 193–221. Kampen, The
Netherlands: J.H. Kok (Trans. from the English, "Between Utterance
and Enunciation: Toward a Semiotics of Prayer Texts," by Magda
Misset-van de Weg).

"*Fons Vitae*: A Case Study of the Use of Liturgy as a Theological
Source." In *Fountain of Life*. Ed. Gerard Austin, 217–42. Washington,
DC: The Pastoral Press.

"Liturgy and Catholic Social Doctrine." In *The Future of the Catholic*
Church in America. Major Papers of the Virgil Michel Symposium. Ed.
John Roach et al., 43–73. Collegeville, MN: Liturgical Press.

"Two Liturgical Traditions: Looking to the Future." In *The Chang-*
ing Face of Jewish and Christian Worship in North America. Ed. Paul
F. Bradshaw and Lawrence A. Hoffman, 221–43. Notre Dame, IN:
University of Notre Dame Press.

"Liturgy and Social Ethics: An Annotated Bibliography," *Studia Litur-*
gica 21:2, 220–35.

"God Writes Straight in Crooked Lines, Part II. The Social Process: Initiation," *Catechumenate* 13:1, 2–12.

"God Writes Straight in Crooked Lines, Part III. The Ritual Process:
Liturgies of the RCIA," *Catechumenate* 13:2, 11–20.

"Trust the Ritual or Face 'The Triumph of Bad Taste,'" *Pastoral Music*
15:6, 19–21.

Review of *Ritual Criticism*, by Ronald Grimes, *Worship* 65:4, 376–78.

1992

Documents of the Marriage Liturgy. With Kenneth W. Stevenson.
Collegeville, MN: Liturgical Press.

"Semiotic Analysis of Roman Eucharistic Prayer II." In *Gratias Agamus:*
Studien zum Eucharistichen Hochgebet für Balthasar Fischer. Ed. Andreas
Heinz and Heinrich Rennings, 469–87. Freiburg, Germany: Herder.

"Children in the Assembly of the Church." In *Children in the Assem-*
bly of the Church. Ed. Eleanor Bernstein and John Brooks-Leonard,
30–50. Chicago: Liturgy Training Publications.

"Preface: The Religious Potential of the Church." In *The Religious Po-*
tential of the Child. Ed. Sofia Cavalletti, 3–12. Chicago: Liturgy Training Publications.

"Ritual." In *The Study of Liturgy*, rev. ed. Ed. Cheslyn Jones et al., 51–58.
London: SPCK.

Foreword to *A Place for Baptism* by Regina Kuehn, iv–vi. Chicago: Liturgy Training Publications.

"An Imperfect Step Forward: A Response to Lectionary-Based Catechesis," *Church* (Summer): 48–49.

Review of *The Monk's Tale. A Biography of Godfrey Diekmann, OSB*, by H. Kathleen Hughes. *New Theology Review* 5:1, 112–14.

1993

Semioticis and Church Architecture. With Gerard Lukken. Kampen, The Netherlands: Kok Pharos Publishing House.

"From Gossips to Compadres: A Note on the Role of Godparents in the Roman Rite for the Baptism of Children," *Studia Anselmiana* 110, 473–84.

1995

"Benediction," "Cabrol, Fernand, OSB," "Communion Service," "Elevation," "High Church," "International Commission on English in the Liturgy," "Liturgical Movement," "Low Church," "Neophyte," "Paraliturgy," "Paschal Candle," "Prime," "Rogation Days," "Sanctorale," "Temporale" and "Terce." In *The HarperCollins Encyclopedia of Catholicism*. Ed. Richard P. McBrien. New York: HarperCollins.

2006

Called to Participate: Theological, Ritual, and Social Perspectives. Ed. Barbara Searle and Anne Y. Koester. Collegeville, MN: Liturgical Press, 2006.

Unpublished Sources

Searle, Barbara. "Acceptance Speech Given in Response to the Presentation of the Michael Mathis Award to Mark Searle, Posthumously, June 17, 1993."

Searle, Mark. "Christian Initiation." MSP: C38.

———. "Description of Proposed Study." MSP: C19.

———. *The Evidence of Things Not Seen*. MSP: "New Chapter IV."

———. "Grant Proposals: Lilly Endowment Faculty Open Fellowships 1988–1989 Application." MSP: "Matthew."

———. "Grant Us Peace. . . . Do We Hare What We Are Saying?" MSP: B16.

———. "The Hallowing of Life."

———. "Liturgy as Critical of Society." MSP: B16.

———. "Liturgy as Pedagogy." MSP: F28.

———. "Notes on an Educational Policy." MSP: F28.

————. "Semiotic Study of Liturgical Celebration: A Report Submitted to Lilly Endowment, Inc." MSP: "Matthew."

Searle, Paul. *Searle Family History.*

Grant Us Peace . . .
Do We Hear What We Are Saying?[1]

Mark Searle

It is almost two years now since I was invited to come and speak at this faith gathering, and the topic I was asked to speak on was liturgy and social justice. Having done this on a number of occasions before, I accepted without too much hesitation, but when the reprinted program appeared, I found that I had been assigned a title not of my own choosing: "Grant Us Peace . . . Do We Hear What We Are Saying?" Had they changed the topic on me? I began to think about it, and the more I thought about it, the more I began to see that the topic was the same but that the new title, echoing the *Agnus Dei* of the liturgy, offered a new and interesting focus for my convictions on the matter. Peace, I began to see, was another word for justice and, in some respects, a better one. So perhaps we should begin by reflecting on the term "justice" and the kind of "peace" the liturgy has in mind when it teaches us to pray for it.

"Justice," of course, means many things to many people. In a pluralistic society such as our own, it is hard to get any philosophical consensus on what might constitute justice in any absolute sense. The best we can hope for is a pragmatic definition; justice comes down to what the law defines as just or unjust. This is not always universally acceptable, which is why some people want to reelect Reagan, so he can pack the Supreme Court, and precisely why others don't want him reelected. Whoever appoints the Supreme Court justices tries to use the opportunity to pack the bench with people who share a particular kind of philosophy and who will therefore advance a corresponding kind of justice: human rights for fetuses, for example, or deregulation of industry. Thus, profound philosophical differences exist in our society over what constitutes justice, but the point is that, while we

---

[1] This unpublished talk by Mark Searle is found in MSP B16.

would all like to see people who think like us administering and interpreting the law, our society only holds together because the rule of law is respected and because we are more or less content to identify justice with legal justice, if not that of a particular piece of legislation, then at least that of the Constitution or the UN Bill of Rights.

This, however, is not what the Scriptures and the liturgy have in mind when they speak of the justice of God and when they summon us to act justly. The justice of God is the just-ness of God himself as revealed in history, recorded in the Scriptures, and proclaimed in the assembly of the Church. This is not the kind of justice that consists of arbitrating between conflicting claims or enforcing observance of legal codes. Not that these functions of justice are unimportant; it is just that the justice of God cannot be identified with the values of the Constitution or the Bill of Human Rights. The justice of God goes rather further, and it is a misunderstanding of the biblical meaning of justice to envisage God as a kind of high court judge who is exceptionally good at detecting and proving people's guilt and thinking up extraordinarily appropriate sentences. No, God's justice is identical with God himself, just as he is. It is a justice revealed in God's actions. In creation, the justice of God is revealed in things being just the way he made them and serving the purpose for which they were made. In history, God's justice is revealed in the people and events which fulfill and reveal God's will for the world. In other words, God's justice is realized when things conform to the purpose for which God made them: when they are what they are meant to be.

Human justice, it might be said, is at best a bridle on evil; divine justice is the flowering of the good. That is why legal justice, while it is indispensable and good as far as it goes, is not enough: "I tell you, if your justice goes no deeper than that of the scribes and Pharisees, you will never get into the Kingdom of Heaven" (Matthew 5:20). God's justice is done when arbitration is transformed into reconciliation: when people become more than objects of use, manipulation, and profit; when poverty is confronted by asking not how much the poor want but how much the rich need; when the goods of the earth are looked upon not at sources of private profit but as symbols and sacraments of divine and human communication. As and when such things are done, however fleetingly, then God's justice is done and the rule or Kingdom of God is there. The Kingdom of God is another word for the justice of God, and another word for both of them is peace, shalom.

Lamb of God, who takes away the sin of the world, grant us peace. The meaning of the word in the liturgy is derived, not from the usual con-

216

texts of that word in English, but from the Hebrew Bible and the New Testament. It is particularly in the prophet Isaiah that this word, peace/ shalom, finds its meaning, in some of those passages we are accustomed to hearing during Advent. To a people afflicted with a series of national disasters—invasions and the death, famine, and disruption which accompanied them—the book of Isaiah offers a series of visions of a time to come when all this would be changed. To a people overrun by heathens and feeling abandoned by God, crushed and worthless, it was said:

> It shall come to pass in the latter days
>> that the mountain of the house of the Lord
>> shall be established as the highest of the mountains,
>> and shall be raised above the hills;
>> and all the nations shall flow to it
>> and many people shall come and say:
>> "Come, let us go up to the mountain of the Lord
>> to the house of the God of Jacob
>> that he may teach us his ways
>> and that we may walk in his paths." (2:2-3)

In this vision, peace means the restoration of right relationships with God, but it also implies harmony and friendship among the peoples. Another passage from Isaiah emphasizes this aspect of peace:

> Then justice will dwell in the wilderness
> and righteousness abide in the fruitful field.
> And the effect of righteousness will be peace
> and the result of righteousness quietness and trust forever.
> My people will abide in peaceful habitation,
> in secure dwellings and in quiet resting places. (32:16-18)

This peace with God and one's fellow human beings flows over into a newfound relationship with nature, as a famous passage indicates:

> The wolf shall dwell with the lamb
> and the leopard shall lie down with the kid,
> and the calf and the lion and the fatling together,
> and a little child shall lead them.
> The cow and the bear shall feed;
> their young shall lie down together. . . .
> The suckling child shall play over the hole of the asp,
> and the weaned child shall put his hand on the adder's den.

They shall not hurt nor destroy in all my holy mountain;
for the earth shall be full of the knowledge of the Lord
   as the waters cover the sea. (11:6-9)

What each of these passages seems to suggest, through the richly poetic imagery they use, is that the justice or righteousness which we are promised and to which we are called is one that affects the whole human environment: our relationships to God, to ourselves, to our neighbors, to the natural world. These images speak of what God intends for the world, thus of the way things ought to be. Justice, we suggested, is realized when things conform to the end for which God made them. That is righteousness, right relations: "and the effect of righteousness will be peace."

Cardinal Bernardin has spoken of the seamless robe of pro-life issues, suggesting that opposition to abortion cannot be separated from opposition to capital punishment, nuclear war, and other threats to human life. In similar fashion we might speak of the seamless garment of justice: right relations with one another cannot be separated from right relations with God, and right relations with God and neighbor cannot be separated from right relations with nature. Justice is indivisible; it is a total way of being in the world. And its effect is peace. But peace is more than distributive justice, treating people according to their rights; peace is delight and enjoyment, the happiness of wholeness. It is often imaged in the Scriptures by reference to the conviviality of the banquet:

On this mountain the Lord of Hosts will make for all peoples
a feast of fat things, a feast of wine on the lees,
of fat things full of marrow, of wine on the lees well-refined.
And he will destroy in this mountain the covering
   that is cast over all peoples,
the veil that is spread over the nations.
He will swallow up death for ever
and the Lord will wipe away tears from all faces. (25:6-8)

Lamb of God, who takes away the sins of the world, grant us peace. This is the peace that is God's will for the world God has created: right relations with God, with one another, with the natural world—and a delight in all of these relationships. That is what is meant when Jews greet each other with "Shalom!" or Arabs with "Salaam!" It is what the angels announced at the birth of Christ: "Glory to God in the highest and peace/shalom to God's people on earth."

This is a wonderful vision of everything the human heart could hope for, but what are we to do about it? Are we merely to go on singing "grant us peace" literally until kingdom come? Is it purely a matter of passive eschatological hope, that after death we may rest in peace? Some might think so, but there are two things to be said.

It is true that the reign of justice in this sense—where love and faithfulness do meet and justice and peace embrace—is at best only intermittently realized in this world and that its full realization still awaits the parousia. But it is a matter of hope, not just of vague optimism, or of wishful thinking in the face of desperate injustice. It is a matter of hope because it has already happened. The justice and peace of God have been manifested at various points in human history, but above all they were realized in the person of Jesus. He was the Just One, of whom Zachariah said that he would "guide our feet into the way of peace." Through him, Peter claimed in a sermon in Acts, God was "preaching the good news of peace" to Israel; and the Letter to the Ephesians says of Christ that "he is our peace who has made both [Jews and Gentiles] one and has broken down the dividing wall of hostility" (Ephesians 2:14). He not only preached a Kingdom of peace and justice; he embodied it in his own person and extended its benefits to those with whom he came into contact—the sick, the blind, the crippled, the sinners. By living and dying in accordance with his Father's will, he achieved the end for which he was sent and indicated and promoted the purpose for which God had made us as human beings. He was just, not because he kept the Law, but because he lived out his vocation to be what God intended him to be. Not surprisingly, he ran into opposition, persecution, and eventual execution as he came into conflict with the legal systems of his own unjust society. But the fact of the matter is that divine justice was realized in his life and death. Consequently, the presence of God's rule and kingdom on earth is a matter of history. Henceforth, human longings for justice and for the peaceable kingdom are no longer a matter of day-dreaming, but of historically grounded hope.

And the second thing to note about this prayer for justice and peace is that it not only is founded in the event of Jesus but constitutes an agenda for us who pray for it. We are all children of God through Baptism into Christ, and the task of the children of God is clear: "Blessed are the peacemakers, for they shall be called the children of God.

Blessed are those who hunger and thirst for justice, for they shall be satisfied." In his farewell discourse according to John's Gospel, Jesus prayed that his disciples be given the same Spirit that animated him to do the works of God. And he promised: "Whoever believes in me will do the works that I do, and greater works than these." The task of the community of disciples we call Church is not merely to pray for peace but to work for it, not merely to pray for justice but to do the works of justice. Actually, the work is a dimension of the prayer. According to Evelyn Underhill, intercessory prayer "is offering your will and love that God may use them as channels whereby his spirit of mercy, healing, power and light may reach [those for whom you pray] and achieve His purpose in them." All true prayer is ultimately that God's kingdom, rule, justice, and peace may come, that God's will be done on earth as in heaven. Thus all true prayer is commitment to action for the kingdom, rule, justice, and peace of God on earth.

All this remains, however, wonderfully vague. How is the will of God to be done in the matter of nuclear arms, or massive poverty, or violations of human rights at home and abroad? Jesus lived out the exigencies of God's will to justice in the circumstances of first-century Palestine. He gave us less a theory than an example, but it was inevitably an example and teaching conditioned by the place and time. How do we move from the teaching and practice and vision of the Scriptures to the all too real and urgent questions of our own time? What qualification has the church as church, or the parish as parish, or the individual Christian as individual Christian to intervene in social and political affairs? Does God give us explicit rules on how to deal with substandard housing, or how to proceed on the abortion issue, or how to achieve a mutual and verifiable nuclear freeze? Clearly not. So what is our qualification as Christians?

We have to be clear that the application of the Gospel of peace to the issues of the contemporary world cannot be direct and unmediated. We need to understand the spirit and vision of the Gospel, but we also need political-technical competence to analyze contemporary issues and to see what is at stake and what can be done. Some of us have such qualifications in certain areas, some in other areas, none in all. We rely on experts. But what we do have is the vision of justice and peace against which all human institutions and decisions are to be measured. The role of the Church, then, as a body, and the role of the Christian as Christian is to view the world in the light of the Gospel and identify whatever is not as it should be. What it should be we know, for we have a vision of nation speaking peace unto nation, of people living together in truthfulness and trust, of respect for God's creation and the proper use of its resources, and all of this as a living state of submission to the rule or Kingdom of God.

Thus, the role of the Church is largely a negative one: a prophetic critique of the values and practices and institutions of the age. The Church as Church cannot offer specific solutions to problems of poverty, violence, injustice, and so forth, but it can denounce the systems and individuals responsible, and it can judge between proposed solutions, indicating one to be better than another, to the degree that it is properly informed about the situation in hand. The Church does this in the light of her past experience of living in an unjust world and in the light of the vision proclaimed by prophets and realized in Christ. Thus the Church doesn't simply apply theory to practice: she has to learn, by studying the problems of the day, what the imperative of the Gospel might be in any given set of circumstances. The problems of nuclear armaments, for example, cannot be solved simply by going to the Gospel, nor, necessarily, by simple applications of so-called just war principles which she elaborated in response to violent conflicts earlier in her history. The Church has to learn before she can teach, and the Church is a community of disciples fully in and part of the world, whose task and vocation it is to discover the will of God in the circumstances of their own life and times. This requires the Church to sponsor the study of contemporary problems by those equipped to do so. But it also requires the Church to keep alive the vision of peace and justice with which she is entrusted. In every generation, Christians have to rediscover for themselves the vision of the Gospel, the lineaments of the Kingdom of God, the order which God intends for the world. Without that constant relearning and conversion to the values of the Gospel, the Church runs the risk, and individual Christians run the risk, of unconsciously coopting the way of the world, of settling for a peace that is not shalom, or for a justice that is even less than that of the Scribes and Pharisees. Being "practical," "realistic," "defense-minded," and all the rest may well be nothing more than easy rationalizations of an actual apostasy from the Gospel to the standards of a sinful and unjust world. And this, I would suggest, is where the liturgy comes in: it is the exercise which keeps the Christian imagination and vision alive.

But how does the liturgy serve to keep the God-given vision of justice and peace alive? To some, the liturgy is an occasion for preaching about justice and peace: the result is special sermons on the topic. In one parish I know, the pastor is a deeply committed man, with a burning sense of the injustices suffered by black people in his neighborhood. He preaches on the topic incessantly, with the result that not only do the people switch off, having heard it all before, but they complained to the bishop that he, the pastor, was giving their church money away to the blacks.

To others, the liturgy is a way of expressing and celebrating the faith of the local community. They feel free therefore to depart from the lectionary and missal and to improvise with so-called theme masses, introducing various visual aids and other things to drive the point home. Once again, however, the exercise is often counter-productive: those responsible for the liturgy are making it the vehicle of their own convictions, to the alienation and anger of many.

I want to suggest that the liturgy is not a platform for addressing current issues, either by the left or by the right, and that it is more than just an occasion for preaching justice, though it may well be that also. Instead, I want to suggest that the liturgy we have inherited is an actual rehearsal of the way of life foretold in the prophets and realized in Christ: not talking about justice and peace, but a doing of justice and peace. It is a momentary realization of the peaceable kingdom of justice in a torn and savage world. How is this so? Let me give some examples to indicate what I mean by saying that the weekly celebration of the liturgy is a weekly rehearsal of the life style of the Kingdom of God, a weekly realization of God's peace and justice.

The liturgy is an action of the Church as Body of Christ. It begins therefore with the assembly or congregation of the people. People come from all over: men, women, and children; black and white and Hispanic; rich and poor; successful and unsuccessful; the educated and the uneducated. They form the Body of Christ. In the liturgical congregation, the categories and divisions which constitute secular society are transcended. In the words of the ancient baptismal hymn cited by Paul to the Galatians: "As many of you as were baptized into Christ have put on Christ. There is neither Jew nor Greek, there is neither slave nor free, there is neither male nor female; for you are all, one in Christ Jesus." The vision is realized: all the nations are flowing to the mountain of the Lord; people are saying, "Come, let us go up to the mountain of the Lord, to the house of the God of Jacob, that he may teach us his ways." As Jesus himself said, "When I am lifted up, I will draw all to myself." That is the point of the Sunday Mass obligation: to gather to become what we are—the Body of Christ—in unity and reconciliation. We confess our injustices and ask forgiveness of God and one another.

In so gathering, not only are the divisions of society overcome, but we are at one and the same time reconciled with God. We are in Christ. We are, when assembled for the liturgy, one Body in Christ, standing before the Father, animated by the same holy Spirit. Justice is done. We are reconciled with our God and one another, and the bishop presiding at the liturgy greets us as Christ greeted his disciples after the age of justice dawned: "Peace be with you." But this grace of the presence of the Kingdom in the gathered community is not given by the wave of a magic wand. Though we are members of one another in Christ, and though our differences are transcended in the unity of the one Body, we are still marked by the divisions and injustices of the society of which we are part. We have not yet become what we already are: a new creation. Hence the confession of sin, not only to God, but to one another, and the prayer for mutual forgiveness. Hence the *Kyrie*-cry for mercy. Hence the Kiss of Peace in which we turn to one another and commit ourselves to the reconciliation, justice, and peace of the Kingdom of God.

The liturgy is a rehearsal of the roles we are called to take upon ourselves throughout life. We are to become in life what we are in liturgy. The liturgy puts us into the position we are called to adopt, and week by week rehearses us in our part as members of the one Body. If we were already perfect, if we had our parts down pat, we would not need the rehearsal: the whole of life would be a celebration of Eucharist, a realization of our identity as the reconciled People of God. But rehearse we must, and each part of the liturgy is part of the vision of peace and a rehearsal of our role as peacemakers.

Let us look at the Eucharistic liturgy itself. It has four parts: the taking up of the gifts, the solemn prayer of Eucharist or Thanksgiving, the breaking and sharing of the gifts, and the act of communion.

One of the earliest and most indispensable parts of the Mass is the collection. Originally, it was a taking up of all sorts of gifts: not only bread, wine, and money, but other foodstuffs, as well as clothing, oil for lighting and cooking, and candles. These gifts were collected by the president or the deacons. Some was set aside for the immediate use of the community in the Eucharistic meal; the rest was distributed by the presider and the deacons to the sick, the imprisoned, the orphans, and the widows, that is to say, to the members of the community who could not provide for themselves. What we have here is nothing less than a redistribution of the wealth of the community. They asked themselves, not how much the poor wanted, but how much of each of them needed. What was superfluous was given back to God by being given to God's poor.

We need to reflect on that, for what is at stake here is more than charity: it is a matter of justice, not only towards the poor, but towards the natural world. The whole natural world, says St. Paul, groans for redemption. Why should nature need redemption? Surely, it is because it has been put to uses for which it was not intended by God. Justice, we saw, consists of people and things achieving the end for which they were made. Because human beings have domination over nature, nature becomes implicated in the sin and redemption of human beings. Take something like plutonium: it can be used to advance the happiness of the human race, or it can be used as a fearsome weapon of destruction. Or bread, which can be used to sustain human life, or accumulated by some at the expense of others, so that some overindulge and others starve. Thus the natural world can be used by us to advance the order willed by God or to pervert it. In the Eucharist, we rehearse the gestures of Jesus, who took bread and wine and, after acknowledging the God from whose hand these gifts come, he shared them with his disciples. The bread and wine become, not instruments of indulgence and violence, but the media through which we are joined to one another and to God. Creation reaches its fulfillment when it serves as a sacrament for the promotion of justice (God's order and God's peace) between human beings and as a sacrament of their union with God. The collection is intimately connected with the communion. Traditionally, excommunication meant that a person was barred not only from taking part in the act of communion but also from being able to offer their gifts at the altar. They had cut themselves off by serious sin from the order of justice. When they were reconciled, the act of reconciliation was called, conversely, the peace. They were readmitted to the shalom of God.

But the Kingdom of God is where justice and peace embrace, which is why we pray not only for justice but for peace. Peace is the perfection of justice. It is, we saw, wholeness, completeness, and the delight which such a state brings. The liturgy rehearses us not only in the ways of justice but in the ways of peace: that is to say, it leads us to rejoice in our relationship with God, with one another, and with the material creation. The term "eucharist" itself means acknowledgment or thanksgiving. Another term for it might be "delight." At the eucharistic rehearsal for the Kingdom, we are taught not merely to observe the proprieties of justice but to delight in our God and in the order he is establishing. The primary expression of this delight is the great prayer of thanksgiving, the blessing of God for his creation, which God has wonderfully made and more wonderfully restored. The Eucharist is not merely a brief weekly prayer: it is rather a rehearsal of the mood in which a Christian is to live in the world under God, a pervasive attitude coloring the Christian life, both personal and communal. This is clear in the other sacraments. The nuptial blessing in marriage, for example, is a blessing of God rather than of the couple, a blessing of God who has made us for love and for life in abundance. The sacrament of penance is often called confession, but the original sense of the term *confessio* referred to a confession of God, a blessing of God, a glorifying of God which was done, not only in the words of a prayer, but, more importantly, in conversion to a way of life lived in accordance with the justice of God. God is confessed, praised, and blessed in the lives of his saints. The Eucharist is not merely a ritual performance; it is a way of life, a delighted acknowledgment of God and a profound en-joy-ment of his people and his material creation.

Obviously, not everyone who attends Sunday Mass comes away filled with such convictions, otherwise the world would be a difference place, a more just place and a more peaceful place. What we need to do, it seems to me, is not to preach at people about social justice, though there is a time and a place for that. What we need to do is simply reflect together on what it is we do when we celebrate liturgy and about what it means. We need to hear what we are saying when we pray, reflect on what we do when we celebrate. The more we understand the order of the world presented and rehearsed in the liturgy, the more we fall in love with the reality of the Kingdom which the liturgy presents and rehearses, the more we shall recognize the disparity between what is and what ought to be. The liturgy does not give us principles to apply to situations of injustice. Rather, it refines our consciousness, sensitizes our intuition, stimulates our imagination, so that injustice everywhere becomes intolerable and abhorrent. Beyond that, outside the liturgy, a just and eucharistic people can put their heads together—and may even disagree—about what practical steps to take to rectify injustice and to bring about peace where there is no peace. What the liturgy will not allow us to do is to lose sight of who we are and what we are called to. It will not allow us to forget, conveniently, that the existence of eight hundred million people on this earth living at or below subsistence level while we live in unprecedented affluence is an affront to the God we claim as our own. It will not allow us to shrug off the problems of violence and war, of systemic victimization, as something that has nothing to do with us. The very actions of the Eucharist call us to justice. And not only to fight injustice but to fight ugliness and exploitation and the dehumanization of our cities and the despoliation of the earth. It will prompt us to simpler, more elegant, more frugal lifestyles. It will prompt us to treat gently and gratefully the bread on our table, the garden we care for, the countryside we enjoy. It will make us heartsick over the conditions under which people work, over the conditions under which so many, even in our own country, live. It will sensitize us not only to flagrant injustices against human beings but to the thoughtless and wanton perpetration of ugliness in our landscapes, our cities, our media, our manufacturing, and our use of language and music. These may seem trivial things to some, but justice is indivisible and shalom has to do with a wholeness and completeness of life.

Well, it might be objected, our liturgy hardly ever raises even the suspicion of these things. Our congregations come to Mass and go away as prejudiced and as unreconciled as before. Our churches are often ugly, soul-destroying places. Our liturgies are rushed through, with tatty missalettes, tasteless vestments, soulless singing, and thoughtless inattention to the meaning of the rites. Conversely, people often most concerned for justice show little understanding for or patience with the liturgy of the Church. They often dismiss beauty as a luxury that cannot be afforded. They sometimes espouse the violence of the perpetrators of injustice themselves.

So let me say this in conclusion: the proper, attentive, respectful celebration of the liturgy is itself an integral element in the Christian's vocation to be a peacemaker. We need places to gather that are places of peace, of shalom; places characterized by a frugal but elegant simplicity, a refuge from the self-indulgent consumerism and rampant individualism of a society dedicated to unregulated and unrestricted self-advancement. We need communities which take seriously their vocation to transcend the divisions of sex and race and nation, to be models of a new society, a new creation. We need celebrants and architects who are contemplatives, profoundly imbued with the vision of shalom and marked by their delight in God, their delight in their fellow human beings, and their delight in material creation; people of gentleness and respect; people with a vision of what that wholeness is that constitutes justice and engenders peace. We need a liturgy that is beautiful, that allows the beauty of word and gesture, music and song, bread and wine, stone and glass to shine forth to the glory of God and the delight of his people. Then, when there is obvious concern for authenticity of word and materials, there will be a concern too for authenticity of prayer and gesture. Then we shall begin to rehearse the Kingdom in our liturgy instead of parodying it. And when we begin to rehearse the Kingdom in our liturgy, hearing the words of the Kingdom, practicing the gestures of the Kingdom, experimenting with the lifestyle of the Kingdom, then we Christians will once again be in a position to take up our vocation to be priests and prophets and peacemakers in the society in which God has placed us.

Works Cited[1]

Adam, Adolf. *The Eucharistic Celebration: The Source and Summit of Faith.* Collegeville, MN: Liturgical Press, 1994.

Baldovin, John. *Bread of Life, Cup of Salvation: Understanding the Mass.* Lanham, MD: Rowman & Littlefield Publishers, Inc., 2003.

Bell, Catherine. *Ritual: Perspectives and Dimensions.* New York: Oxford University Press, 1997.

———. *Ritual Theory, Ritual Practice.* New York: Oxford University Press, 1992.

Bellah, Robert. *Beyond Belief: Essays on Religion in a Post-Traditional World.* New York: Harper & Row, 1970.

Bellah, Robert et al. *Habits of the Heart: Individualism and Commitment in American Life.* Berkeley: University of California Press, 1985.

Bonhoeffer, Dietrich. *Life Together: A Discussion of Christian Fellowship.* Translated by John W. Doberstein. New York: Harper & Row, 1954.

Botte, Bernard. *From Silence to Participation: An Insider's View of Liturgical Renewal.* Translated by John Sullivan. Washington, DC: Pastoral Press, 1988.

Bouyer, Louis. *Liturgical Piety.* Notre Dame, IN: University of Notre Dame Press, 1954.

Brown, Robert McAfee. "My Story and 'The Story.'" *Theology Today* 32 (1975): 166–73.

Budde, Mitzi J. "The Church's Song as Response to the Divine Mystery." *Worship* 86:3 (2012): 194–208.

Bugnini, Annibale. *The Reform of the Liturgy 1948–1975.* Translated by Matthew J. O'Connell. Collegeville, MN: Liturgical Press, 1990.

Burghardt, Walter J. *Let Justice Roll Down Like Waters.* New York: Paulist Press, 1998.

Casel, Odo. *The Mystery of Christian Worship.* New York: Herder & Herder, 1962.

Congar, Yves. *I Believe in the Holy Spirit III.* Translated by David Smith. New York: The Crossroad Publishing Company, 2001.

———. "The Structure of Christian Priesthood." In *At The Heart of Christian Worship: Liturgical Essays of Yves Congar*, 69–106. Collegeville, MN: Liturgical Press, 2010.

Crighton, J. D. "A Theology of Worship." In *The Study of Liturgy*, 3–29. Edited by Cheslyn Jones et al. New York: Oxford University Press, 1978.

Daly, Robert J. "Sacrifice Unveiled or Sacrifice Revisited: Trinitarian and Liturgical Perspectives." *Theological Studies* 64 (2003): 24–42.

---

[1] For a list of primary sources, please see appendix 1, "Mark Searle's Chronological Bibliography (1966–2006)" on pages 204–14.

―――. *Sacrifice Unveiled: The True Meaning of Christian Sacrifice*. New York: Continuum Books, 2009.

Daniel-Rops, Henri, ed. *The Liturgical Movement*. Translated by Lancelot Sheppard. New York: Hawthorn Books, 1964.

Day, Thomas. *Why Catholics Can't Sing: The Culture of Catholicism and the Triumph of Bad Taste*. New York: Crossroad Publishing Company, 1990.

Dix, Gregory. *The Shape of the Liturgy*. New York: The Seabury Press, 1982.

Dougherty, Joseph. "Silence in the Liturgy." *Worship* 69 (1995): 142–54.

Douglas, Mary. *Natural Symbols: Explorations in Cosmology*. New York: Vintage Books, 1973.

Driscoll, Jeremy. "Anamnesis, Epiclesis and Fundamental Theology." *Ecclesia Orans* 15 (1998): 211–38.

Ellard, Gerald. *Men at Work at Worship: America Joins the Liturgical Movement*. New York: Longmans, Green and Company, 1940.

Fink, Peter E. "Public and Private Moments in Christian Prayer." *Worship* 58 (1984): 482–89.

Flannery, Austin, ed. *The Basic Sixteen Documents: Vatican Council II Constitutions, Decrees, Declarations*. Northport, NY: Costello Publishing Company, Inc., 1996.

Foley, Edward. "Liturgy and *Economic Justice for All*." In *Living No Longer for Ourselves: Liturgy and Justice in the Nineties*, 116–23. Edited by Kathleen Hughes and Mark Francis. Collegeville, MN: Liturgical Press, 1991.

Fowler, James. "Perspectives on Family from the Standpoint of Faith Development Theory." *Perkins Journal* (Fall 1979): 1–19.

Francis, Mark R. "Introduction to 'Private Religion, Individualistic Society, and Common Worship.'" In *Vision: The Scholarly Contribution of Mark Searle to Liturgical Renewal*. Edited by Anne Koester and Barbara Searle, 181–84. Collegeville, MN: Liturgical Press, 2004.

Franklin, R. W. "Guéranger: A View on the Centenary of His Death." *Worship* 49 (1975): 318–28.

―――. "The Nineteenth Century Liturgical Movement." *Worship* 53 (1979): 12–39.

Freire, Paulo. *Cultural Action for Freedom*. Cambridge: *Harvard Educational Review*, Monograph Series, no. 1, 1970.

Gallagher, Patricia A. "The Communion Rite." *Worship* 63 (1989): 316–27.

Garvey, John. "Let Liturgy Be Liturgy: Stop Trying to Put a New Spin on It." *Commonweal* (December 3, 1982): 648–49.

Geldhof, Joris. "The Eucharist and the Logic of Christian Sacrifice: A Discussion with Robert J. Daly." *Worship* 87 (2013): 292–308.

Goody, Jack. "Religion and Ritual: The Definitional Problem." *British Journal of Sociology* 12 (1961): 142–64.

Greer, William R. "Susanne K. Langer, Philosopher, Is Dead at 89." *New York Times* (July 19, 1985): A12.

Grimes, Ronald. *Beginnings in Ritual Studies*, Revised Edition. Columbia: University of South Carolina Press, 1995.

———. *Ritual Criticism: Case Studies in Its Practice, Essays on Its Theory*. Columbia: University of South Carolina Press, 1990.

———. "Ritual Studies." In *The Encyclopedia of Religion*, vol. 12. Edited by Mircea Eliade, 422–25. New York: Macmillan, 1987.

Groody, Daniel. "Fruit of the Vine and Work of Human Hands: Immigration and the Eucharist." *Worship* 80 (2006): 386–402.

Groome, Thomas. "Christian Education: A Task of Present Dialectical Hermeneutics." *Living Light* 14 (1977): 408–23.

———. *Christian Religious Education: Sharing Our Story and Vision*. San Francisco: Harper and Row, 1980.

———. "The Crossroads: A Story of Christian Education by Shared Praxis." *Lumen Vitae* 32 (1977): 45–70.

Guardini, Romano. "A Letter from Romano Guardini." *Herder Correspondence* (August 1964): 237-239.

———. *The Spirit of the Liturgy*. Translated by Ada Lane. New York: Sheed and Ward, 1940.

Hall, Jerome M. *We Have the Mind of Christ: The Holy Spirit and Liturgical Memory in the Thought of Edward J. Kilmartin*. Collegeville, MN: Liturgical Press, 2001.

Hall, Max. *Harvard University Press: A History*. Cambridge, MA: Harvard University Press, 1986.

Hanson, R.P.C. *Eucharistic Offering in the Early Church*. Grove Liturgical Study No. 19. Bramcote: Grove Books, 1979.

Heschel, Abraham. *The Insecurity of Freedom*. New York: Farrar, Straus & Giroux, 1966.

Huels, John M. "The Sign Value of the Chalice: Can It Be Negated for the People?" *Worship* 85 (2012): 403–19.

International Commission on English in the Liturgy. *Documents on the Liturgy, 1963–1979, Counciliar, Papal, and Curial Texts*. Collegeville, MN: Liturgical Press, 1982.

Irwin, Kevin W. *Context and Text: Methods in Liturgical Theology*. Collegeville, MN: Liturgical Press, 1994.

———. *Liturgy, Prayer and Spirituality*. New York: Paulist Press, 1984.

———. "Models of the Eucharist." *Origins* 31 (May 31, 2001): 33, 35–44.

———. *Models of the Eucharist*. New York: Paulist Press, 2005.

———. "A Sacramental World—Sacramentality as the Primary Language for Sacraments." *Worship* 76 (2002): 197–211.

Janowiak, Paul. *Standing Together in the Community of God: Liturgical Spirituality and the Presence of Christ*. Collegeville, MN: Liturgical Press, 2011.

Johnson, Cuthbert. *Prosper Guéranger (1805–1875): A Liturgical Theologian, An Introduction to His Liturgical Writings and Work*. Rome: Pontificio Ateneo S. Anselmo, 1984.

Kavanagh, Aidan. *On Liturgical Theology*. Collegeville, MN: Liturgical Press, 1992.

Keifer, Ralph A. "Our Cluttered Vestibule: The Unreformed Entrance Rite." *Worship* 48 (1974): 270–77.

Kelleher, Margaret Mary. "Introduction to 'Images and Worship.'" In *Vision: The Scholarly Contribution of Mark Searle to Liturgical Renewal*. Edited by Anne Koester and Barbara Searle, 122–25. Collegeville, MN: Liturgical Press, 2004.

Kiesling, Christopher. "Liturgy and Social Justice." *Worship* 51 (1977): 351–61.

Kilmartin, Edward J. "The Catholic Tradition of Eucharistic Theology: Towards the Third Millennium." *Theological Studies* 55 (1994): 405–57.

———. *The Eucharist in the West: History and Theology*. Collegeville, MN: Liturgical Press, 1998.

Koernke, Theresa F. "Introduction to 'Liturgy as Metaphor.'" In *Vision: The Scholarly Contribution of Mark Searle to Liturgical Renewal*. Edited by Anne Koester and Barbara Searle, 23–26. Collegeville, MN: Liturgical Press, 2004.

Langer, Susanne K. *Feeling and Form: A Theory of Art Developed from Philosophy in a New Key*. New York: Charles Scribner's Sons, 1953.

———. *Philosophy in a New Key: A Study in the Symbolism of Reason, Rite, and Art*. Cambridge, MA: Harvard University Press, 1942.

———. "The Primary Illusions and the Great Orders of Art." *Hudson Review* 3 (1950): 219–33.

Levering, Matthew. *Sacrifice and Community: Jewish Offering and Christian Eucharist*. Malden, MA: Blackwell Publishing, 2005.

Luckmann, Thomas. *The Invisible Religion*. New York: Macmillan, 1967.

Lyon, Arabella. "Susanne K. Langer: Mother and Midwife at the Rebirth of Rhetoric." In *Reclaiming Rhetorica: Women in the Rhetorical Tradition*, 265–84. Edited by Andrea A. Lunsford, 265–84. Pittsburgh, PA: University of Pittsburgh Press, 1995.

Madden, Lawrence J. "A New Liturgical Movement." *America* 117 (September 10, 1994): 16–19.

Maldonado, Luis. "The Church's Liturgy: Present and Future." In *Toward Vatican III: The Work That Needs to Be Done*. Edited by David Tracy and Hans Küng, 221–37. New York: Seabury Press, 1978.

Mannion, M. Francis. "Liturgy and the Present Crisis of Culture." *Worship* 62 (1988): 98–123.

Marx, Paul. *Virgil Michel and the Liturgical Movement*. Collegeville, MN: Liturgical Press, 1957.

McKenna, Megan. *Rites of Justice: The Sacraments and Liturgy as Ethical Imperatives*. Maryknoll, NY: Orbis Books, 1997.

McKenna, John. "Symbol and Reality: Some Anthropological Considerations." *Worship* 65 (1991): 2–27.

McManus, Frederick R. *Liturgical Participation: An Ongoing Assessment*. Washington, DC: Pastoral Press, 1988.

Michel, Virgil. "The Liturgy, the Basis of Social Regeneration." *Orate Fratres* 9 (1935): 536–45.

———. "The Scope of the Liturgical Movement." *Orate Fratres* 10 (1936): 485–90.

Mitchell, Nathan. *Cult and Controversy: The Worship of the Eucharist outside Mass.* New York: Pueblo Publishing Company, 1987.

O'Loughlin, Thomas. "A Vernacular Liturgy Versus a Liturgy in the 'Vernacular'?" *Worship* 86 (2012): 244–55.

O'Malley, John W. *What Happened at Vatican II.* Cambridge, MA: Belknap Press of Harvard University Press, 2008.

Palmer, Parker J. *Company of Strangers: Christians and the Renewal of America's Public Life.* New York: Crossroad Publishing Company, 1983.

Pecklers, Keith F. *The Unread Vision: The Liturgical Movement in the United States of America: 1926–1955.* Collegeville, MN: Liturgical Press, 1998.

Philipart, David. *Saving Signs, Wondrous Words.* Chicago, IL: Liturgy Training Publications, 1996.

Power, David N. *The Eucharistic Mystery: Revitalizing the Tradition.* New York: Crossroad Publishing Company, 1993.

———. *The Sacrifice We Offer: The Tridentine Dogma and Its Reinterpretation.* New York: Crossroad Publishing Company, 1987.

Rahner, Karl. "Secular Life and the Sacraments: The Mass and the World." *The Tablet* 225 (March 13, 1971): 267–68.

Rousseau, Olivier. *The Progress of the Liturgy: An Historical Sketch from the Beginning of the Nineteenth Century to the Pontificate of Pius X.* Westminster, MD: Newman Press, 1951.

Rubin, Miri. *Corpus Christi: The Eucharist in Late Medieval Culture.* Cambridge, UK: Cambridge University Press, 1991.

Saliers, Don. "Pastoral Liturgy and Character Ethics: As We Worship So We Shall Be." In *Source and Summit: Commemorating Josef A. Jungmann, S.J.* Edited by Joanne M Pierce and Michael Downey, 183–94. Collegeville, MN: Liturgical Press, 1990.

Schmemann, Alexander. *For the Life of the World.* Crestwood, NY: St. Vladimir's Press, 1998.

———. *Sacraments and Orthodoxy.* New York: Herder and Herder, 1965.

———. "Sacrifice and Worship." *Parabola* 3 (Winter 1978): 60–65.

Serra, Dominic E. "The Introductory Rites: Theology of the Latin Text and Rite." In *A Commentary on the Order of Mass of* The Roman Missal. Edited by Edward Foley et al., 125-132. Collegeville, MN: Liturgical Press, 2011.

Shea, John. "The Second Naiveté: Approach to a Pastoral Problem." *Concilium* 81 (1973): 106–16.

Soltner, Louis. *Solesmes and Dom Guéranger, 1805–1875.* Translated by Joseph O'Connor. Orleans, MA: Paraclete Press, 1995.

Totah, Mary David, Ed. *The Spirit of Solesmes.* Petersham, MA: St. Bede's Publications, 1997.

Underhill, Evelyn. *Worship.* New York: Harper & Brothers, 1936.

United States Council of Catholic Bishops. *The Challenge of Peace: God's Promise and Our Response*. Washington, DC: United States Catholic Conference, 1983.

———. *Economic Justice for All*. Washington, DC: United States Catholic Conference, 1986.

———. *Fulfilled in Your Hearing: The Homily in the Sunday Assembly*. Washington, DC: United States Catholic Conference, 1982.

Vincie, Catherine. "The Introductory Rites: The Mystagogical Implications." In *A Commentary on the Order of the Mass of* The Roman Missal. Edited by Edward Foley et al., 143–50. Collegeville, MN: Liturgical Press, 2011.

———. "The Liturgy of the Word: The Mystagogical Implications." In *A Commentary on the Order of the Mass of* The Roman Missal. Edited by Edward Foley et al., 187–94. Collegeville, MN: Liturgical Press, 2011.

———. "The Preparation of the Gifts: The Mystagogical Implications." In *A Commentary on the Order of the Mass of* The Roman Missal. Edited by Edward Foley et al., 221–27. Collegeville, MN: Liturgical Press, 2011.

Vischer, Lukas. "The Epiclesis: Sign of Unity and Renewal." *Studia Liturgica* 6 (1969): 30–39.

Wainwright, Geoffrey. *Doxology: The Praise of God in Worship, Doctrine, and Life*. New York: Oxford University Press, 1980.

Westow, Theodore L. *The Variety of Catholic Attitudes*. New York: Herder & Herder, 1963.

White, James. *Introduction to Christian Worship*. Nashville, TN: Abingdon, 1980.

———. *Roman Catholic Worship: Trent to Today*. New York: Paulist Press, 1995.

Wilbricht, Stephen S. "Gesturing for an Epiphany: Renewing the Unspoken Language of Worship." *Pastoral Liturgy* 42:5 (2011): 4–8.

———. "The History, Theology, and Practice of the Prayer of the Faithful." *Pastoral Liturgy* 41:6 (2010): 4–8. (Reprinted in *The Order of Mass: A Roman Missal Study Edition and Workbook*. Edited by Michael S. Driscoll and J. Michael Joncas, 327–39. Chicago, IL: Liturgy Training Publications, 2011).

Wilson, Bryan. *Religion in Secular Society*. Baltimore, MD: Penguin, 1969.

Yzermans, Vincent A., Ed. *All Things in Christ: Encyclicals and Selected Documents of Saint Pius X*. Westminster, MD: Newman Press, 1954.

Zimmerman, Joyce Ann. "The Communion Rite: The Mystagogical Implications." In *A Commentary on the Order of the Mass of* The Roman Missal. Edited by Edward Foley et al., 615–20. Collegeville, MN: Liturgical Press, 2011.

Index

234